World Views

Modernist Literature and Culture

Kevin J. H. Dettmar & Mark Wollaeger, Series Editors

World Views

Metageographies of Modernist Fiction

Jon Hegglund

OXFORD
UNIVERSITY PRESS

OXFORD
UNIVERSITY PRESS

Oxford University Press, Inc., publishes works that further Oxford University's
objective of excellence in research, scholarship, and education.

Oxford   New York
Auckland   Cape Town   Dar es Salaam   Hong Kong   Karachi
Kuala Lumpur   Madrid   Melbourne   Mexico City   Nairobi
New Delhi   Shanghai   Taipei   Toronto

With offices in
Argentina   Austria   Brazil   Chile   Czech Republic   France Greece
Guatemala   Hungary   Italy   Japan   Poland   Portugal   Singapore
South Korea   Switzerland   Thailand   Turkey   Ukraine   Vietnam

Copyright © 2012 by Oxford University Press, Inc.

Published by Oxford University Press, Inc.
198 Madison Avenue, New York, New York 10016
www.oup.com

Oxford is a registered trademark of Oxford University Press

Library of Congress Cataloging-in-Publication Data
Hegglund, Jon.
World views : metageographies of modernist fiction / Jon Hegglund.
   p. cm.—(Modernist literature & culture)
   Includes bibliographical references and index.
   ISBN 978-0-19-979610-6 (cloth : alk. paper)
1. English fiction—20th century—History and criticism. 2. Modernism
(Literature)—English speaking countries. 3. Space in literature.
4. Geopolitics in literature. 5. Geographical perception in literature.
6. Postcolonialism in literature. 7. Cartography in literature.
8. Geography and literature. 9. Geocriticism. I. Title.
II. Title: Metageographies of modernist fiction.
PR888.M63H44 2011
823'.9109112—dc23
                                                    2011018801

Dedicated to Arline Williams
Mother and friend
1944–2010

Contents

Acknowledgments

In writing a book that makes so much of maps, it's been surprisingly easy to get lost. I've incurred an enormous debt to the many people who kindly gave me directions, rode shotgun, encouraged me to drive safely, filled me up with gas and food, or simply made losing my way that much more enjoyable. What a long, strange trip it's been.

The intellectual compass that guided this project was set during my graduate education at the University of California, Santa Barbara, where the following teachers, colleagues, and friends taught me much more than I realized at the time: Maurizia Boscagli, Enda Duffy, and Porter Abbott composed a dissertation committee that was equal parts challenging and encouraging. I give credit to them for helping me see literature in all of its complexity, nuance, and interconnectedness with the world. I was also lucky to have incredibly smart and supportive graduate colleagues as well. Special gratitude goes to Rachel Adams, Parker Douglas, Tim Wager, Jon Connolly, Madelyn Detloff, Jeanne Scheper, Kathy Lavezzo, Amy Rabbino, Simon Hunt, Jennifer Hellwarth, Patricia Ingham, and Robert Hamm. I owe considerable thanks to the late Richard Helgerson, who was more influential than he ever knew, both for introducing me to studies in critical cartography and more generally by serving as a model for humility, kindness, and clear thinking. For providing me with many years of close friendship and good advice, Roze Hentschell deserves the absolute highest degree of appreciation. At Central Connecticut State University, my first stopping point after graduate school, my dissertation was slowly transformed (out of all recognition) into the beginnings of this book. Warm thanks go to those who helped make my relatively brief time in New England pleasant and productive, especially Loftus Jestin, Stuart Barnett,

Gil Gigliotti, and Jill Weinberger. Eventually, I followed interstates, highways, and two-lane country roads to the far northwestern corner of the country, where my colleagues at Washington State University have been supportive in more ways than I can count. Among them, Debbie Lee, Peter Chilson, Alex Hammond, Will Hamlin, Michael Hanly, Carol Siegel, Leonard Orr, Pavithra Narayanan, and Lisa Guerrero deserve special thanks. In Phil Gruen, I found a kindred spirit who has inspired conversations that move quickly from Baudrillard to baseball, from Heidegger to hoops (all with a positively Joycean sense of wordplay). At WSU, support from a Lewis E. and Stella G. Buchanan Scholarship was immensely help-ful in securing time and resources to finish the first draft of the book. George Kennedy deserves a special category of gratitude all his own: he has been a model of patience, support, advocacy, and friendship: he is everything a department chair should be and more.

While the inland Northwest has proven a congenial environment for think-ing and writing, much of the work here has benefited from my getting out into the wider world. Many aspects of the book were helped immeasurably by two trips to Chicago, where I was able to work at the Smith Center for the History of Cartography at the Newberry Library: first in 2001 for the NEH Institute on "Popular Cartography and Society," and again in 2006, supported by a Newberry Short-Term Fellowship in the History of Cartography. Jim Akerman has been a most gracious host and mentor for each of these visits. The formation of the Modernist Studies Association and its annual conference could not have been better timed for the development and completion of this project, from which many sections made their public debut on MSA panels and in MSA seminars. I want to thank those who have provided helpful feedback and great conversation, especially Tom Sheehan, Jim Housefield, Jennifer Nesbitt, Kerry Johnson, Lois Cucullu, Andrew Thacker, and Peter Brooker. Eve Sorum, above all, has proven to be a remarkably adept co-organizer of panels, an always-helpful interlocutor, and—best of all—a good friend.

An early version of chapter 1 was published as "Modernism, Africa, and the Myth of Continents," in *Geographies of Modernism: Literatures, Cultures, Spaces* (Routledge). An early version of chapter 3 was published as "*Ulysses* and the Rhetoric of Cartography," in *Twentieth-Century Literature*. My thanks to the publishers for generously allowing reproduction of this work in the present volume.

Since Oxford's Modernist Literature and Culture series was inaugurated, I always hoped that *World Views* would find a place within its already-impressive list of titles. Thanks to series editors Mark Wollaeger and Kevin Dettmar for demonstrating ample patience with and commitment to this project, believing (even more than I did, at times) that the book was a good fit for the series. To the three anonymous readers who read a revised draft of the manuscript, your words were just what I needed: honest, precise, and encouraging. To the one reader who reviewed an early *and* later draft of the manuscript—you've gone well beyond the call of duty. Make yourself known at a future MSA conference, and drinks are on me. Finally, Brendan O'Neill and Molly Morrison provided invaluable editorial guidance over the last leg of the journey.

My family has always given me love and support without condition or reservation—they have always kept me grounded and oriented, even when I threatened to wander off the edge of the map. Kristie and Tod Nicosia, Karen and David Toste, Michael Hegglund, Richard and Leslie Robertson, Jim and Bev Mowrer, and Charles Williams never let me forget where I'm from while always appreciating how far I've gone. The deepest, warmest thanks go to my mother, Arline Williams. Her contemplative mind, generous spirit, and selfless love have made every word possible. This book is dedicated to her memory.

Finally, the largest share of appreciation goes to the only other person who lived every day with this book for several years: the lovely, imaginative, talented, and kind Emily Mowrer, who reminds me every day that, while viewing the world is nice, living in it is so much better.

Series Editors' Foreword

Despite growing attention to multiple temporalities and the heterogeneity of time, the reigning injunction in modernist studies is probably still "Always spatialize!" But given the insistence on (and of) the spatial turn, it is surprising that no one before Jon Hegglund has thought to bring together literary criticism and what was known as the new geography. In *World Views* Hegglund tells the story of the simultaneous emergence of literary modernism in the late nineteenth century and the articulation of geography as a distinct discipline, and he does so from a perspective informed by the latest thinking in critical geography. Far from the mythic conception of spatial form first theorized by Joseph Frank, Hegglund understands modernist fiction's experimental engagements with space as efforts to imagine alternatives to a new world order—call it territorial nationalism—that over the twentieth century increasingly became "naturalized as timeless, incontrovertible fact." Novels, in this reading, operate as ironic maps, maps, that is, that chart their distance from the abstract, totalizing vision of the world as a jigsaw puzzle of nation-states even as they acknowledge the enduring material and imaginative reality of the seemingly arbitrary geopolitical divisions that fragment the globe. What modernist novelists do differently than realists is draw on the facticity of maps to anchor texts in geopolitical reality while at the same time using the resources of fiction to question the ways in which maps represent such "reality" within a naturalized order and hierarchy

World Views thus intervenes in recent conversations about global modernisms, cosmopolitanism, and transnationality as well as in longer standing discussions of the genealogy of modernist form. Irony and defamiliarization, long understood as key tropes in modernism, are here rescued from premature consignment to the dustbin of formalism: the concept of "metageography" signaled in Hegglund's subtitle can be considered a kind of ironic geography, a way of "writing the earth" (to highlight the etymology of "geography") that defamiliarizes received modes of conceiving of the spaces in which narratives take place. In essence, beginning in the late nineteenth century, narrative modernism and the new discipline of geography came to occupy common ground in their shared efforts to mediate between a kind of literalized cosmopolitan view from nowhere—an abstract vision of the world as composed entirely of sovereign, formally equivalent nation-states—and a more particularized understanding of cartographic data as necessarily implicated in encompassing narratives of national and cultural identity. Put more boldly, Hegglund understands the modernist novel as emerging from a dialectical tension between two codes of realism, one grounded in cartography, the other in narrative: "the tension between a realist mode of narration and a more abstract, geographical representation," he argues, "constitutes a main feature of what are now commonly referred to as global modernisms." Leopold Bloom and Stephen Dedalus may walk through a 1904 Dublin that could be reconstructed, in Joyce's fantasy, from the pages of *Ulysses*, but that fictional space, which at one memorable moment disappears into the numerical coordinates of longitude and latitude, derives as well from the imperial epistemology instantiated in Britain's Ordnance Survey of Ireland.

The key term in most critical attempts to mediate between global geography and literary modernism has been empire. Fredric Jameson's seminal essay "Modernism and Imperialism" (1990) is exemplary in this respect. As Hegglund acutely points out, however, such approaches typically understand modernist texts as responses to a pre-existing geopolitical paradigm, even though "the conceptual framework of a nation-based world-system, far from being a determining context for cultures of modernism, in fact emerged *within* the same cultural matrices as literary modernism." From this perspective, modernism and political globalization come into focus as related events in a history of spatiality that play out "the same spatial drama: the interplay between totalizing universality and fragmented particularity." Acknowledging the richness of the discussions that make his own contribution possible, Hegglund reframes debates about space and the novel "by reading literature as geography by other means, and, conversely, by reading various geographical writings and productions as themselves dependent upon 'literary' qualities such as form, symbol, and dense textuality."

So what kinds of alternatives to the nation-state as universal form are posed by geographic modernism? The continent (Joseph Conrad and Graham Greene), the region (Patrick Geddes and E. M. Forster), the internal colony (the Ireland of *Ulysses*), the island (Jean Rhys and Jamaica Kincaid), and the boundary (Jawaharla Nehru and Amitav Ghosh). Hegglund's modernist archive is thus both familiar and fresh. Conrad regularly figures in treatments of the novel and empire, but not Graham Greene; Rhys has become relatively familiar in this context owing to various recent efforts to think modernism and postcoloniality together as part of an evolving global system, Kincaid less so; Joyce, of course, but Nehru and Ghosh? Forster certainly, but Geddes, the Scottish polymath and pioneer in urban planning, suggests the broad array of fresh figures in Hegglund's cultural history, from King Ibrahim Njoya of Bamun, whose map of his kingdom (now part of contemporary Cameroon) articulates indigenous concepts of community and space without erasing the imprint of imperial cultures of possession, to the altogether astonishing Halford Mackinder (1861-1947), who first bridged the gulf between physical and political geography (and thereby between natural science and humanistic study) by redefining the "writing of the earth" as "a translatable discourse rising above academic specialization to take a synthetic, global view of culture."

Indeed, Mackinder exemplifies the confluence between narrative and cartography in the new geography, writing recognizably in 1887 in the elegiac tones of late imperial romance: "The polar regions are the only large blanks on our map." Far from gloomy about the impending end of the age of exploration, however, Mackinder in effect asked, what now is Geography? The entwined, mutually illuminating answers proffered by geographers and novelists alike provide the subject matter of *World Views*, a provocative and timely contribution to the interdisciplinary study of modernism.

—Mark Wollaeger and Kevin J. H. Dettmar

List of Abbreviations

CE	Geddes, Patrick. *Cities in Evolution: An Introduction to the Town Planning Movement and to the Study of Civics*. 1915. With an introduction by Percy Johnson-Marshall. New York: Howard Fertig, 1968.
CP	Geddes, Patrick, and Victor Branford. *The Coming Polity: A Study in Reconstruction*. London: Williams and Norgate, 1917.
HD	Conrad, Joseph. *Heart of Darkness*. 1902. Edited and with an introduction by Owen Knowles. New York: Penguin, 2007.
HE	Forster, E. M. *Howards End*. 1910. New York: Vintage, 1989.
JWM	Greene, Graham. *Journeys without Maps*. 1936. New York: Penguin, 1978.
SL	Ghosh, Amitav. *The Shadow Lines*. Oxford: Oxford University Press, 1988.
SP	Kincaid, Jamaica. *A Small Place*. New York: Farrar, Straus, and Giroux, 1988.
U	Joyce, James. *Ulysses: The Corrected Text*. Edited by Hans Walter Gabler with Wolfhard Steppe and Claus Melchior. 1922. New York: Vintage, 1986.
WSS	Rhys, Jean. *Wide Sargasso Sea: A Norton Critical Edition*. Edited by Judith L. Raiskin. 1966. New York: Norton, 1999.

World Views

Introduction

The Modernist Novel as Metageography

One inmate had got so badly caught up in this India-Pakistan-Pakistan-India rigmarole that one day, while sweeping the floor, he dropped everything, climbed the nearest tree and installed himself on a branch, from which vantage point he spoke for two hours on the delicate problem of India and Pakistan. The guards asked him to get down; instead he went a branch higher, and when threatened with punishment, declared: "I wish to live neither in India nor in Pakistan. I wish to live in this tree."

—Sadaat Hassan Manto, "Toba Tek Singh"

Realism at the Boundary

Sadaat Hassan Manto's short story "Toba Tek Singh," published in 1955, is one of the more widely known and anthologized fictional works addressing the 1947 partition of India and Pakistan. The story tells of a Sikh inmate named Bishan Singh in a lunatic asylum in Lahore, unsure whether his hometown, Toba Tek Singh, has been placed into India or Pakistan as a consequence of partition. Bishan Singh (also referred to by his fellow inmates as Toba Tek Singh) is packed onto a bus as part of a swap of asylum dwellers between the two new nations. As the inmates are being exchanged at the border, Bishan/Toba Tek escapes the bus and runs to the no-man's land between the two countries, where he refuses to move and eventually collapses and dies. My epigraph, about another of Manto's asylum inmates, comments ironically on the legitimacy of partition as a means for creating new nation-states: if nations are artificial, arbitrary constructions that arise from a surveyor's pen rather than an organic cultural bond, then why choose to live in them? Why fetishize a geographical entity that seems to cause only violence and strife? Why not live in a tree instead? Manto's "insane" inmate directs us to a more profound truth about the complex twentieth-century relationships among geography, politics, and identity: that the very formation of individual subjectivity occurs within a geographical construct that both precedes and circumscribes this subjecthood. Ironic laughter is the response of a reader who understands that the cartographic abstractions that give legal existence to territorial nation-states are arbitrary, but, at the same time, knows that we are almost universally claimed by these same nation-states whether we wish it or not. As Benedict Anderson has asserted, nationality is a sociocultural "formal universal" shared by virtually every inhabitant of the globe. "In the modern world," Anderson writes, "everyone can, should, will 'have' a nationality, as he or she 'has' a gender."[1] That Manto can only challenge Anderson's claim from a madman's point of view suggests how deeply naturalized the idea of nationality had become by the middle of the twentieth century; it was a primary ontological condition from which no human subject could escape. One could conceivably live in a tree, just as one could live in a mansion, apartment block, or thatched hut, but in a much deeper and more permanent sense, one's life is only legally and "officially" claimed by one place: a sovereign, territorial nation-state. The irony that Manto exposes, therefore, is hardly liberating: the imagination that would find other possibilities, other conceptual frameworks in which to posit "life," is marginalized within the narrative as the raving of a lunatic who will eventually be forced to live not in a tree, but in a nation.

In its absurdist treatment of national boundaries and its intentional ambiguity between place and character, "Toba Tek Singh" represents a kind of twentieth-century fiction that no longer assumes that fictional worlds are anchored by stable, real-world geographies. By no means, however, is it unique. *World Views* examines many fictional examples—primarily from authors located within the cultural matrix of the British Empire—that cease to trust in the framework of geographical space as a firm ground for narrative worlds. This skepticism *about* geography manifests itself through an increased attention to the language and discourse *of* geography within literary narratives. *World Views* connects these internal textual moments of geographical reference to larger transformations in twentieth-century global geography. Specifically, I argue that such fictions can be read against the emergence of territorial nationality as the normative condition of political sovereignty in the world. As the nineteenth century turned into the twentieth, nation-states increasingly derived their primary identity from a cartographic existence that emphasized territories, boundaries, and geopolitical positions with respect to other nations. With the condition of territorial nationhood becoming more or less universal, fiction draws attention to the arbitrary, constructed existence of nations that, in the words of Eric Hobsbawm, have forged a collective cultural identity through the "invention of tradition."[2] This tension between organic, internal narratives of "traditional" nationality and the invention of nation-states through the discourses of geography and cartography becomes manifest in fiction as a structural tension between the conventions of classical narrative realism and a more abstract, spatial self-consciousness. This narrative instability yields stylistic and formal elements that comprise many features of literary modernism.

Following the expansion of modernist studies to global horizons, *World Views* understands modernism in more diverse geographical and historical contexts than Euro-American metropolitan literary works from the first half of the twentieth century. Manto's story offers an instructive example here. While "Toba Tek Singh" has frequently been classified within the specific subgenre of partition literature, it (and the work of Manto more broadly) tends to slip between the cracks of twentieth-century literary histories and geographies. Written in the Urdu language, while Manto was living in newly established Pakistan, the story frequently escapes the purview of postcolonial literature scholars, who tend to focus on works written and published in English. With the bulk of his work dating from the 1940s and 1950s, Manto also falls into a liminal literary-historical zone between high modernism, on the one hand, and postcolonial or postmodernist literature, on the other. Finally, the fabular, allegorical style of the story itself seems to fit neither with the structural and linguistic experimentation of high modernism nor with the social realism of early postcolonial fiction.[3] By reorienting the concerns of writers such as Manto within an explicitly geographical frame, *World Views* constructs a genealogy of twentieth-century fiction in which a short story like "Toba Tek Singh" has a central place.

Manto's fiction exemplifies a specific mode of modernism, not as an evolution *beyond* narrative realism, but rather as one in which two competing codes of realist space are at work: one narrative and one geographical. Narrative realism dictates that the world is a knowable, representable place predicated upon a stable social order and clear character motivations. The geography of this realist world is often made to seem a timeless, natural, stable backdrop to meaningful human action. Space is largely important as "setting," a conceptual stage upon which narratives can coherently be played out. By the turn of the nineteenth century, however, another code of realism was beginning to upset the fixed order posited by the realist novel. Through the latter part of the nineteenth century and into the twentieth, following the territorial carving of African colonies at the Berlin conference of 1885–1886, the rise of geopolitics as a new geographical "science" and the fixing

of modern European state boundaries with the 1919 Treaty of Versailles, metropolitan cultures become more saturated with the awareness of an emergent *cartographic* realism: a "real world" determined not by the thick description and shared
knowledge of place, but by the increasingly formal abstractions of geographical
space, most visibly through the widespread production and consumption of maps.
In atlases, school textbooks, newspapers, advertisements, travel narratives, and
other cultural forms, maps were widely invoked as objective indices of the world.
This map-based realism becomes allied with notions of territorial sovereignty, as
strictly demarcated boundaries establish the precise, mathematically calculated
space of governance for sovereign nation-states. "Toba Tek Singh" shows these two
ideas of realism in tension: we begin the story with the assumption that we will
follow the narrative of characters within a recognizable historical and geographical setting—1947 India and Pakistan—but ultimately Manto's use of the boundary
line as a narrative agent forces us to see his characters as mere vehicles of another,
cartographically determined reality. The imposition of partition, in this instance,
forecloses the possibility of realistic characters to "live" in a stable, coherent world.
The facts of geography cancel out the verisimilitude of fiction, and the imposed
boundary of the nation-state becomes a limit to the possibility of a classical narrative realism. "Setting" is usurped, in the last instance, by spatiality.

World Views examines the ways in which many twentieth-century writers
from Britain and its former colonies incorporate this other, geographically self-
conscious realism into their fictional worlds. Put another way, this book looks at
what happens to fiction when geography ceases to denote a naturalized place, a
world accepted as given, and instead becomes *territory*, an abstract, reified thing
that entails surveying, mapping, and precise demarcation: an explicit production
of space, to use Henri Lefebvre's term. This changing relationship between fictional and geographic space dovetails with three significant cultural movements
that were well underway by the early twentieth century. The first is the emergence
of the bounded, territorial nation-state as the normative, equivalent form of political sovereignty and self-determination in a larger global sphere. As many cultural
commentators noted around the turn of the nineteenth century, the world had
become closed to significant exploration, and terrestrial space was increasingly
seen as finite and subject to national and imperial competition. The second is the
late-nineteenth-century reinvention of geography as an academic discipline that
aimed to synthesize nature and culture in a common spatial field, an enterprise led
by figures such as Paul Vidal de la Blache in France, Friedrich Ratzel in Germany,
and Halford Mackinder in Great Britain. In particular, the "New Geography" of
Mackinder and his followers presented a world in which the relative cultural

development of different ethnic and racial groups was intimately connected to the natural environment. The third cultural movement that coincided with the reinvention of fictional space was the wider development of modernism in literature and the arts. As Stephen Kern has argued in *The Culture of Time and Space*, one of modernism's signal achievements was the increasing reliance on "positive negative space," a trope that suggested—through analytical cubism, Imagist poetry, Futurist sculpture, and many other artistic and literary forms—the materiality and centrality of space as a positive, substantive entity rather than an empty void.[4] The fiction examined in this study can be located at points of convergence between these three cultural fields: the emergence of territorial nationalism, the development of a synthetic geographical discipline, and the dissemination of cultural modernism. Placing twentieth-century Anglophone fiction in these contexts yields a genealogy of modernism that extends both its historical scope and its disciplinary frame. *World Views* examines literary representations of spatial form in literature within the contexts of the emerging disciplines of geography, geopolitics, and international relations, positing that modernism's experimental engagements with space intended to—if at times obliquely—imagine alternatives to a new world order that was, over the course of the twentieth century, becoming naturalized as timeless, incontrovertible fact.

As my title suggests, *World Views* is intended to contribute to the robust critical conversations about transnational, or "global," modernisms. Certainly, the opening up of modernist literature and culture to locations, movements, and networks that stretch far beyond the Euro-American metropolitan axis has been a welcome development in the field. Perhaps because of its affinities and ongoing conversations with postcolonial studies, the study of global modernisms has tended to privilege geographical and cultural particularity over a more systemic, totalizing view. Susan Stanford Friedman, for example, calls on modernist studies to consider "the possibility for polycentric modernities and modernisms at different points of time and in different locations."[5] In the introduction to their collection, *Geomodernisms*, Laura Doyle and Laura Winkiel similarly advocate a critical approach that "reveals diverse modernisms formed against and through each other, proximate or distant, and constituted by their locations in the world."[6] Arguably, no development in the previous generation of modernist studies has been more influential than its encounter with postcolonial theory and criticism, a methodological shift that has exposed a previously insular Euro-American tradition to diverse and disjunctive geographies. In this laudable desire to open up modernism to transnational approaches, however, critics of modernism have at times idealized the "trans-" without fully considering the implications of the "national." Without discounting the importance of geographical and historical specificity, I hope to complement the attention to the particularity of global modernist studies by look-ing at the "world" into which these locations, routes, and networks are inscribed. Even as early twentieth-century culture was becoming more mobile, the world system through which such cultural artifacts moved was coalescing into a totaliz-ing conceptual structure. Throughout most of the twentieth century, the world was primarily represented and understood as a serial collection of nation-states, each existing with a formal equivalency to one another. Even as many territories were formally administered as colonies well into the 1960s, the normative form for a cultural being-in-the-world was a national one. As a literary mode that came into a full flowering as a primarily national genre in the nineteenth century, fiction does not simply transcend this national attachment in the twentieth. Instead, the works under consideration here continually mediate the scale of the national—which is typically associated with the space of realism—and a perspective "outside" of the national, which yields the textual features of abstraction, defamiliarization, and self-consciousness frequently identified with narrative modernism.

I hesitate, therefore, to follow recent precedent and call this externalized per-spective "global," or even "transnational." These terms imply a point of view at another geographical scale, one that simply moves beyond the nation toward a wider, encompassing realm. What I am interested in, however, is not so much another geographical scale that encircles and contains the nation, but rather an enunciative space within literary discourse that ironizes the notion of geographi-cal space itself. Following the work of the geographers Martin Lewis and Kären Wigen, I refer to this position as "metageographical." Lewis and Wigen define metageography as "the set of spatial structures through which people order their knowledge of the world; the often unconscious frameworks that organize studies of history, sociology, anthropology, economics, political science, or even natural history."[7] Metageography, in other words, is the conceptual framework that presents the condition of possibility for geography, the architecture within which various geographies are housed. Although the etymology of the word "geography" implies a totalizing mode of representation ("the description of the earth's surface"), the word has come to mean something quite different in modern parlance. Geography, in its contemporary usage, denotes the spatial arrangement of phenomena in the world—the particularities of place—without explicit reference to the totality of that world. Metageography, by contrast, defines the very orders and categories of space that we use to plot locations, itineraries, and distances in the world. Rather than posit another spatial scale that simply outflanks the nation-state, then, I examine how the turn to fictional metageography implies both identification with a "national" position while at the same time offering a perspective internal to the literary text that denaturalizes the perceived organicism and "givenness" of the nation. Irony, then, becomes the literary mode best suited to metageographical fiction; metageography, in other words, might be thought of as "ironic" geography. As Clare Colebrook has written, irony permits us to "discern the meaning or sense of a context without participating in, or being committed to, that context."[8] If the context of realist fiction is a stable geographical environment anchored in a given knowledge of the world, then metageography distances us from participation in and commitment to this world. In "Toba Tek Singh," our awareness of the boundary as a spatial construct determining the limits of "life" leads us to treat the story as an ironic fable or allegory of partition rather than a character-driven narrative prompting our empathetic identification. Yet this ironic detachment is not completely stable either. The man in the tree, functioning as an ironic commentary on partition, eventually descends: "When he was finally persuaded to come down, he began embracing his Sikh and Hindu friends, tears running down his cheeks, fully convinced that they were about to leave him and go to India."[9] Metageographical fiction ironizes its "participation in and commitment to" a national community, but it also acknowledges that such communal attachments can and do remain strong and compelling reasons for the persistence of the nation-state—most of us, eventually, descend from the tree, lest we lose our own sense of community and cultural identity. To better understand how this unstable irony works, I want to look more closely at the relationship between the two codes of realism at play in twentieth-century fictions of metageography: the narrative and the cartographic.

Imagination Becoming Geographic

As the narrator of E. M. Forster's *Howards End* describes the southern English landscape from the high promontory of the Purbeck Hills, he meditates on a view that moves from the direct visual apprehension of local places and landscapes ("the valley of the Frome... the Stour, sliding out of fat fields, to marry the Avon beneath the tower of Christchurch") to a more abstract form of perception (*HE* 142). As the description—improbably, unrealistically—expands to encompass the totality of the nation, the narrator celebrates an "imagination" that "swells, spreads and deepens, until it becomes geographic and encircles England" (*HE* 143). "Imagination becoming geographic" suggests an intertwining of sensibilities that aren't often associated with each other. Imagination, the stuff of literature and art, connotes a creative faculty unfettered by the hard materiality of the world. Geography, on the other hand, implies that very worldliness, the realm of clear, knowable facts: everything in its right place. Forster, however, suggests that the "imagination becoming geographic" is not a fall from airy dreams to hard earth, but rather a kind of transformative expansion, one that opens up a world much larger than the situated view from the hilltops of southern England. *World Views* looks at a number of twentieth-century novels from Anglophone writers to explore the literary and political implications of this geographical imagination. I argue that the tension between a realist mode of narration and a more abstract, geographical representation constitutes a main feature of "global" modernism in literature. Each chapter explores what it means for the novelist's imagination to "become geographic," to suspend the limits of a spatial realism by combining the face-to-face, local scale of fictional narrative with a broader, detached perception of cartographic distance. In a sense, *World Views* examines novels that work like maps. They pull back from the local, particular, and immediate, often in disorienting or self-conscious ways, to a cartographic overview that places the narrative scene in a new, disjunctive context. In the example of *Howards End*, a realistic, local scene—several characters on a hilltop overlooking the landscapes of southern Dorset—is quickly transformed into an overview that "encircles England," as one could literally do with a pencil or finger upon a map.

I want to pause briefly to explain a central distinction between the meanings of geography and cartography, which is important to my argument. Cartography refers to the specific discourse of maps, particularly the institutions of their production and the codes of their representation. Its relationship to geography, however, is often less clear. I use cartography in this specific, artifactual sense to refer to maps and their related concepts. I use the term "geography" in two ways throughout the book, and I trust that context will clarify which meaning I intend at any given point. The first sense is the broadest: "geography" simply refers to any element of place as considered within the wider horizon of a world totality. This definition calls upon its Greek roots: geography as "world writing." Even as the modern meaning of geography has changed to accommodate scales of space smaller than the terrestrial, the word still implies a uniform, systematized global space of which various sections or parts may be described and studied. In this sense, every representation of "real-world" space, be it artistic, cinematic, literary, or scientific, implies a geography. Such representations are situated (whether implicitly or explicitly) within a relational structure of other places, the sum total of which makes up the world.[10] The second sense has to do with the understanding of geography as a specific disciplinary mode of knowledge institutionalized in Europe and America in the late nineteenth century, which took as its goal the description of the relationship between humans and their environments in all of their complexity and causal relationships. By making this distinction, I do not mean to imply that geography and cartography are categorically different. In fiction, references to cartography often stand as shorthand for the "geographic imagination" by drawing attention to space as an inscription and abstraction, a text whose meanings are not intrinsic or self-evident.

By saying that novels can signify "like" maps, I mean to highlight differences as well as similarities between these two forms of representation. Where maps have generally become accepted, in the post-Enlightenment era of scientific cartography, as indices to an actually existing world, fiction establishes a looser relationship with geography. In many pre-twentieth-century novels (including some from the twentieth century as well), maps have often appeared in frontispieces or as appendices, intended to serve as reference guides to the events that unfold within the narrative. Many authors and texts have inspired considerable efforts by fans and professional critics alike to produce and market maps and atlases that plot events of the narrative onto a real-world cartography. Such maps allow the reader to create a mental image that organizes the spatial relationships between narrative events or the progress of a character on a journey, frequently toward a place that serves as both a destination and a narrative climax. As Franco Moretti describes this process, "maps bring to light the *internal* logic of narrative: the semiotic domain around which plot coalesces and self-organizes."[11] Eric Bulson echoes this idea, pointing out a complementary relationship between map and novel: "Literary maps give readers something that novels do not: an image, a structure, a way to visualize form and narrative design."[12] Whether internal or external to a particular novel, the "map-as-guide" serves a secondary, supportive function to the novel; the map functions as a fixed, inert background that provides a frame and stage for the events that unfold within the narrative. This is not to say that maps cannot "speak back" to a text; in fact, Moretti's work uses the indexical function of maps to open up new insights into the social spaces of the nineteenth-century realist novel. One could even go so far as to define classical literary realism as narratives that can be literally mapped onto an existing geography in the world.

After the turn of the nineteenth century, however, maps begin to take on a different role within fiction. The self-conscious incorporation of maps as artifacts *within* narratives constituted a significant aesthetic and formal current of fictional modernism. For reasons explored below, many authors cease to include maps in the front matter while at the same time maintaining, and often increasing, the amount of topographic detail within their narratives. This overload of geographical particularity had the effect, ironically, of *de*naturalizing the "background" spaces of fiction. As Bulson writes of modernist authors, this spatial precision instead highlighted the *un*reality of fiction, prompting a feeling of "oriented disorientation," making readers "feel like they are at home in the world when they are not."[13] Moreover, maps increasingly migrate from their background, referential function as a visual overview toward a narrative description *within* a text. Textually described maps function much differently than their visual counterparts. Once inserted into the narrative flow of a text, maps acquire symbolic and thematic resonance, no longer functioning as mere guides for the location of story events. In *Howards End*, for example, when Margaret Schlegel looks upon a map of West Africa in Henry Wilcox's waiting room, it is presented as literary symbol rather than geographic index. We note the simile that Margaret uses to describe it ("like a whale marked out for blubber"), which inserts the map into the textual economy of Margaret's hesitations about Henry's materialist outlook on the world and Forster's own ambivalence about the morality of economic imperialism and its connections to the livelihood of England's genteel classes. This is but one of many examples that I discuss at length, but it serves to point out that narrated maps do not simply allow the reader to attain an overview of narrative events; rather, they occasion meditations on the very nature of geography itself. Does space connect, or separate? How can the simultaneity of distant spaces be accounted for? What, in our mental mapping of the world, is foregrounded or emphasized, and what is repressed or forgotten? All of these geographical elements—the scale-bending perspective, the inclusion of dense topographical detail, and the literary textualization of maps—have the effect of defamiliarizing an existing world.

"Becoming geographic," however, does not necessarily entail a step *beyond* narrative realism. To the contrary, this geographic turn enters into a dialectical relationship with classical narrative realism. Even at the height of modernism's most radical experiments with narrative—think of *Ulysses*, or *The Waves*—virtually all works of fiction still embody a kind of mimetic contract: a promise that no matter how abstract or formally self-conscious, its words refer to a simulacrum of a world like our own, populated by people, things, and places that are understood "as if" actually existing.[14] The development of a modernist narrative aesthetic might have drawn more attention to the nature of the signifier, but by no means did it abandon its real-world referents. Stephen and Bloom still walk the streets of Dublin, just as a chorus of voices in *The Waves* still implies interpersonal human relationships between Woolf's characters. Novelists did, however, become more self-conscious about the possibilities and limitations of mimesis in a world that seemed increasingly mobile, interconnected, and subject to constant spatial transformations. Novels could still give reference points in the real world, yet that real world was no longer to be construed as a stable, unchanging background from which character-based plots could be easily separated. Rather, as many critics of the new modernist studies have recognized, space, landscape, and location become agents *within* the narrative economy of modernist fiction. As Laura Doyle and Laura Winkiel assert (with a conscious echo of William Carlos Williams), for modernist writers at large, "so much depends…on place, proximity, position."[15] The geographic modernism that I discuss here is not identical with, but is very much a part of, this foregrounding of space as an active narrative agent rather than as a naturally given "setting." Herein lies the distinction between geography and metageography, then, as they relate to fictional narrative: geography speaks to the particularities of place, proximity, and position, while metageography interrogates a broader system that makes the particularities of place and position possible. The reader's attention, in other words, is drawn to the production of geographical space.

What purpose, then, was served by the introduction of this geographical self-consciousness into literature? Significantly, in the novels I look at, the process of becoming geographic is almost always a move outward, away from the local, human-centered scale of character-driven actions and plots toward a more detached overview of a wider global space. Forster's language in the earlier passage is instructive here: the geographic imagination "encircles" the nation, taking on this distant, external view. Although Forster does not literally invoke cartography in this scene, the narrator's perspective assumes a position from which the entire "English" nation could be viewed, as if looking down upon a map. This exterior view calls to mind a literalization of the cosmopolitan viewpoint, in which the viewing subject rises above the place-bound attachments of the nation-state to take the measure of the world as a wider totality. Increasingly, maps provided the portal for such overviews, and, after cartography's late-eighteenth- and early-nineteenth-century scientific turn, the form of the map itself implied a coherent, quantitatively knowable totality. Influenced by the projects of the European Enlightenment, mapping began to acquire a rhetoric of totality and scientific accuracy. As Matthew Edney points out, "the map was thus the conceptual unifier of geographical knowledge: as Burke, and Diderot, and d'Alembert all signaled, a means to and metaphor for global ordering."[16] Maps, then, came to imply a totality of which the pictured view was merely a part or section. While offering a powerful form for the spatialization of knowledge, maps remained marginalized within the discipline of geography itself. Maps were often seen as mere instruments, visual devices to serve as shorthand for more profound observations about space. In fact, the "new geography" of the late nineteenth century was much more concerned with narrative than with cartography. Cartography was an instrumental necessity for "proper" geography, but the focus of the new discipline was less about yielding accurate maps than placing such cartographic data within larger narratives of national and cultural identity. In this respect, literature and the new discipline of geography began to occupy common ground.

Geographical Modernism

Geography, before the late nineteenth century, was largely understood less as a coherent academic discipline than a heterogeneous collection of genres: explorers' narratives, botanists' notebooks, surveyors' observations, and catalogs of place names, to list a few. These artifacts and practices were largely centered in professional organizations like the Royal Geographical Society (RGS) in London. Many, however, wanted the discipline to have a well-defined area of inquiry and a common methodology. Halford Mackinder led the movement that became known as the "new geography" in Great Britain, which aimed, ambitiously, to reinvent the discipline as a means of linking nature and culture within the common field of space. To do so, Mackinder wished to find a relevant place for geography within a larger cultural narrative of Great Britain and Europe. Geography and literature, then, both converged on common questions of spatiality and culture, each attempting to negotiate between the distinctiveness of cultural identity on the one hand and the possibility of a uniform, systematized global space on the other.

Geography began to confront its own disciplinary definition explicitly, largely through Mackinder's efforts. On January 31, 1887, Mackinder began his address to the members of the RGS by confronting the question of geography's identity.[17] This was occasioned not simply by an institutional imperative toward disciplinary coherence, but more broadly by a need for geography to find its proper narrative within the world-historical moment. This moment, argued Mackinder, was one no longer characterized by exploration of the blank spaces on the map. "We are now near the end of the roll of great discoveries," he explained. "The polar regions are the only large blanks on our maps. A Stanley can never again reveal a Congo to the delighted world."[18] Without such compelling tales of conquest in the name of civilization and knowledge, Mackinder feared that geography would find itself relegated to the mere collection of data without any overarching story to tell. "As tales of adventure grow fewer and fewer," Mackinder laments, "as their place is more and more taken by the details of Ordnance Surveys, even Fellows of Geographical Societies will despondently ask, 'What is Geography?'"[19] Recognizing that geography can no longer reside in the dying art of the travel and exploration narrative,

Mackinder issued a challenge to its practitioners to find a new narrative, a new framework in which spatial knowledge could be rendered meaningful. Mackinder in fact makes an appeal that is less about empirical data and more about narrative form: if the standard narrative of knowledge, civilization, and light beating back ignorance, savagery, and darkness can no longer obtain, then what kind of narrative can be written for a geographical condition characterized by "the details of Ordnance Surveys"? What sort of story would this knowledge reveal? Ultimately, Mackinder would find such a narrative in his famed 1904 paper "The Geographical Pivot of History," which argued for the necessity of defending the coastal realms of the world from the Eurasian "heartland." Mackinder's thesis, which formed one of the main wellsprings of the new discipline of geopolitics, drew upon the scientific rhetoric of geography to justify the continued maintenance of the British Empire, particularly its maritime supremacy (just as Karl Haushofer would use Mackinder's ideas to argue for German expansionism toward coastal realms).[20]

Mackinder, however, posed these problems in 1887, in a moment of genuine concern about the role geography might play both within institutions of academic knowledge and, more broadly, in the shaping of cultural narratives about space. As Stephen Kern and others have detailed, the 1880s witnessed the emergence of cultural anxieties, particularly in metropolitan Europe, about the impending end to the "age of exploration." Only three years before, leaders from around the world agreed that Greenwich, England, would become the prime meridian, thus inaugurating an epoch of unified, interwoven global space. Only a year prior to Mackinder's address, imperial leaders met in Berlin to map out their claims on sub-Saharan Africa, effectively exerting territorial control over the last "dark space" in the world. In light of this epistemic change, geography, which had grown up largely as a result of global exploration, now had to consolidate a new authority over how citizens should cognitively map their relationships with community, nation, and the world. For Mackinder, "the details of Ordnance Surveys" suggest a metonymic representation of what he dismissively refers to as "descriptive geography." Descriptive geography, according to Mackinder, is simply the compilation of topographical facts about the world without any attempt to trace causality between humanity and its environments, "a body of isolated data to be committed to memory."[21] Mackinder fears that without an adequate narrative, a scheme into which geographical data can be placed, geography's importance as an academic discipline and mode of cultural knowledge would diminish into insignificance. While Mackinder aims in his address to sketch out a methodological way forward for geographers, the value of this methodology relied upon on the coherence of an overarching narrative of cultural centrality.

Two elements of Mackinder's geographical method seem especially relevant to the emergent literary aesthetic of modernist fiction: spatial self-consciousness and imaginative projection. Spatial self-consciousness speaks to the desire for a theoretical framework of space that can integrate and synthesize specialized disciplinary knowledges—a kind of epistemological Rosetta Stone able to translate between scientific and humanistic discourses. The chief disciplinary division that needed bridging, according to Mackinder, was that between "physical" and "political" geography. The former had been most closely aligned to the scientific discipline of geology, while the latter had strong kinship ties to history. Physical geography, in other words, concerned itself with nature, while political geography lay within the realm of culture. In an attempt to bridge these heretofore opposed areas of disciplinary inquiry, Mackinder proposed a new definition of geography: "the science whose function is to trace the interaction of man in society and so much of his environment as varies locally."[22] Not only would geography have the unique role of uniting nature and culture, science and humanism, it must do so in order to rejuvenate an enervated, fragmented national culture. "One of the greatest of all gaps," Mackinder writes, "lies between the natural sciences and the study of humanity. It is the duty of the geographer to build one bridge over an abyss which is in the opinion of many upsetting the equilibrium of our culture."[23] Mackinder argues that geography must be a translatable discourse rising above academic specialization to take a synthetic, global view of culture. This totalizing view, however, served specific political interests, as he imagined the history of geography as a justification for and explanation of British cultural superiority.

Where Mackinder explicitly imagines geography from a metadisciplinary epistemological position, literary narratives likewise begin to grapple with questions of perspective. Space in particular becomes denaturalized in literary and artistic representations. Modernist literature adopts a self-consciousness about the space in which narratives take place, with this denaturalized perspective occasionally standing outside of conventional modes of description and narration. As Moretti argues in *Atlas of the European Novel, 1800–1900*, the nineteenth-century "realist" novel was a genre peculiarly fitted to the politico-cultural form of the nation-state. On the one hand, its multilocational omniscience could speak beyond the immediately local, but, on the other, its genial, "natural" voice addressed an imagined community that, as Raymond Williams has posited, was still "knowable." Of Jane Austen's narratives, for example, Moretti writes that they "take the strange, harsh novelty of the modern state—and turn it into a large, exquisite home."[24] With multiple perspectives of experience and knowledge accumulating toward the end of the nineteenth century, most notably through the practice of colonization and the culture of imperialism, the interior, homely, natural space of the realist nation-novel was no longer tenable. And just as Mackinder posits geography's need to both outflank and absorb different disciplines, modernist narrative likewise struggles to account for the irreconcilable spaces outside of the national home. Thus evolves a self-reflexiveness about space, about the comfortable certainty of telling stories *within* a common, objectively "real" matrix. Conrad's Marlow provides one of the earliest examples of this emergent self-consciousness: the tale of navigation up the Congo River in *Heart of Darkness* is constantly mediated though anxieties about its translatability; that is, the space of Marlow's African experience is seen to be qualitatively, even ontologically, different than the familiar space of the crew resting on the iconic English waterway of the Thames.

Perhaps the most concentrated moments of spatial self-consciousness occur in narrative instances that I will call *metatopographia*. If the trope of topographia designates any description of a place, then metatopographia would be the narrative instance of what is clearly marked as a *representation* of place—a description of a description. Examples of metatopographia therefore include narrative descriptions or citations of photographs, landscape painting, travel narratives, geographical studies, guidebooks, or other mediations on place and space. Perhaps the most conspicuously modern instance of metatopographia is the narrative incorporation and description of maps.[25] As nearly ubiquitous documents of the popular culture of imperialism in the late nineteenth and early twentieth centuries, maps acquired deeply symbolic associations within metropolitan European cultures, most notably in Britain. Authors writing within the matrix of British imperialism—including virtually every author discussed at length in this study—frequently introduce maps as objects of narrative reflection and contemplation. In *Heart of Darkness*, the young Marlow gazes dreamily upon maps of Africa, maps that will come to represent possessive imperial rivalries in his adult years. Forster's Margaret Schlegel, as we have seen, compares the cartographic image of Africa to an endangered whale (*HE* 167). Similarly, James Joyce's Leopold Bloom, Jean Rhys's Antoinette Cosway, and Amitav Ghosh's unnamed narrator in *The Shadow Lines* gaze upon maps in order to derive some symbolic, affective meaning beyond the simple utilitarian function of wayfinding. Maps themselves become symbolic, speaking to cultural identification, imperial expansion, social injustice, or geopolitical destinies. These literary reflections on representations of space often draw attention to the *constructed* nature of space and place, thus denaturalizing a static, hierarchical geographical order. In these map-conscious moments, readers are frequently invited to view with skepticism the discursive authority of cartography, photography, and other forms of spatial representation.

In their thrust toward metadiscursivity, literary geographies also begin to address the tensions between various scales of space, frequently presenting examples of what Neil Smith has called "scale-bending."[26] Where Mackinder presents a world in which scales nest neatly into one another, however, literary geographies begin to exploit the tensions between various scales of space in moments of poetic and narrative experimentation. This phenomenon becomes manifest in moments when the normative scale of realist fiction—the "organic" national (if not state) geography described by Moretti in *Atlas of the European Novel*—ceases to be isomorphic with the scope of narrative representation (Moretti's study, tellingly, leaves off at the cusp of the twentieth century). Scale-bending can occur in narrative instances such as Graham Greene's layering the "image of Africa" onto a woman in a Leicester Square bar, the (previously discussed) imaginative visual "realization" of England through the narrator's view from the Purbeck Hills in *Howards End*, or the use of numerical coordinates of latitude and longitude to describe the bedroom of Leopold and Molly Bloom in the "Ithaca" chapter of *Ulysses*. Literary scale-bending, by juxtaposing spaces that shouldn't "fit" together, prompts readers to question the assumptions that attend a hierarchical, concentric organization of geographical knowledge. During a historical moment when the nation-state is becoming the scale with the tightest grip on individual and cultural identity, literary representations of spatial scale as an arbitrary construction prompt readers to treat with skepticism the idea that any one scale is more "natural" than another.

In addition to its metadiscursive self-consciousness, another significant element of the "new" geographical method as formulated by Mackinder is the employment of imaginative description and projection in the representation of space. As R. Mayhew puts it, Mackinder required a more "readable" form for geography: "Contrary to the structured paragraphing of gazetteers, geography books should be written in 'ordinary literary form,' that is, as continuous prose, preferably with a strong narrative line, engaging the reader."[27] The discipline should adhere to certain principles of aesthetic form: narrative coherence, concrete imagery, and figurative language were needed to present its insights fully and persuasively. In other words, as much as geography was to be given the imprimatur of science, it also needed to filter the apprehension of space through the active faculty of personal imagination. Mackinder's methodology, grounded in a commitment to the teaching of geography, appealed primarily to the imaginative sensibilities of his listener or reader. In contrast to the "lists" that Mackinder imputed to a purely physical geography, Mackinder's aim was to bring to life the natural and cultural history of a place in the minds of his listeners and readers. "Imagine thrown over the land like a white tablecloth over a table, a great sheet of chalk," Mackinder begins his analysis of the geography of southern England. "Let the sheet be creased by a few simple folds, like a tablecloth laid by a careless hand."[28] For a practitioner of a discipline trying to acquire the cultural legitimacy of science, Mackinder's style and exposition are decidedly literary, relying upon colorful description and figurative language. Space could not be a dead, inert realm exterior to the senses. In order to maintain and enhance its cultural relevance, geographical discourse had to intertwine the objective rhetoric of empirical fact and rational argumentation with the aesthetic appeal of the literary and visual arts. Geography was not simply an external realm of static data; it was the lived experience and imaginative transformation of space. To paraphrase Joseph Conrad, a writer who also dabbled in geography, the geographer's job was not entirely different from the novelist's: "before all, to make you see."

The intertwining of interior, subjective apprehensions of space with a concrete, objective "reality" was likewise at the heart of modernist experiments with narrative perspective. Many modernist works transpose the observer with his or her environment, creating instability between inner and outer representations of space. Conrad's work is perhaps the earliest signal example of this blurring between phenomenological and physical geographies. In *Heart of Darkness*, Marlow tries to describe a trip up the Congo River in Africa to a group of listeners on board a boat at anchor in the River Thames. The dreamlike descriptions and meditations by Marlow throw a scrim over what would have previously been a "factual" tale of exploration. Marlow also comments upon this ineluctable interiority, remarking to his listeners that "we live as we dream—alone" (*HD* 33). Where Marlow seems to lament the interiorized phenomenology of spatial experience, other writers approach this blurring of subjective and objective space with an attitude of conscious experimentation and play. In the "Proteus" chapter of James Joyce's *Ulysses*, for example, Stephen Dedalus muses upon the blurring of physical and metaphysical geographies, wondering, "Am I walking into eternity along Sandymount Strand?" (*U* 31). Stephen in fact draws upon his interior experience of space to reimagine Ireland's position within global history, emphasizing the island's engagement with the world through maritime travel, trade, and conflict rather than its nominal dependence as a colony of Great Britain. While much has been made of the modernist narrative's use of an interiorized stream-of-consciousness narration, such narrative modes do not so much withdraw from the exterior world as blend a subjective, psychologized perception with the hard, physical "reality" of exterior space, in the process unsettling both epistemological perspectives.

While these two elements—discursive self-consciousness and imaginative, subjective observation—are common to both the new geography and new forms of modernist narrative, the former moves toward the explicitly political agenda of geopolitics while the latter tends to pose rather than resolve questions of spatial knowledge. Mackinder approaches the uncertainty of culture's relationship with a new epoch of spatiality with definite ends. His methodology, which promised a systematized archive for future geographical knowledge, was oriented toward a coherent narrative: the justification for Britain's global dominance in spite of its increasingly marginalized and threatened geopolitical position. Literature, however, would come to more varied conclusions about the new global spatiality. The early-twentieth-century transformation of world geography from ground to figure, "reality" to text, dovetails with the representation of narrative space in literary modernism. Recent literary and cultural criticism has articulated the relationship between literary modernism and global geography through the history of European acquisitive imperialism. Modernism, in these historicist accounts, is typically understood as the aesthetic, affective representation of the radically new condition of global imperialism. Because modernism attempts to grasp a condition outside the possibilities of conventional "realistic" representation, it reinvents form in its efforts to accommodate the unrepresentable. Literary critics, including Fredric Jameson, Edward Said, Enda Duffy, and Ian Baucom, have made persuasive and insightful connections between European modernism and the more widespread cultural, political, and economic contexts of imperialism.[29] Typically, for these critics and others, the formal traits of literary and cultural modernism are seen as a kind of response to an existing geopolitical condition: whether as a project to represent an unknowable economic totality of globalized capital (Jameson), to systematize in literature the disjunctions and contradictions of nonwhite, non-European racial and cultural otherness (Said), to find an appropriate aesthetic form for the situation of emergent anticolonial revolution (Duffy), or to negotiate the contradictions of an inwardly focused national identity with an expansionist imperial outlook (Baucom). In each case, modernist texts are largely understood as cultural responses to and reworkings of preexisting geopolitical conditions. *World Views* proposes that the conceptual framework of a nation-based world system, far from being a determining context for cultures of modernism, in fact emerged within the same cultural matrices as literary modernism.

Rather than looking at modernism's spaces within a particular geography of imperialism and globalization, I examine modernism and political globalization as related events in a history of spatiality. In many ways, modernism and globalization play out the same spatial dynamic: the interplay between totalizing universality and fragmented particularity. In *The Production of Space*, Henri Lefebvre suggests, through a reading of Picasso's cubism, a way of perceiving space that accounts for both aesthetic form and geographical context. Lefebvre describes the viewer's perception of Pablo Picasso's analytical cubism as "a paradoxical process whereby the third dimension (depth) was at once *reduced* to the painted surface and *restored* by virtue of the simultaneity of multiple aspects of the thing depicted."[30] Picasso, argues Lefebvre, articulates a space that replaces realist perspective with something quite different, "a space at once *homogeneous* and *broken*."[31] Lefebvre argues that the space of cubism does not so much respond to preexisting cultural and historical circumstances as express a certain spatial condition that had heretofore escaped representation. Picasso's artistic deployment of cubism emerged "in parallel with imperialism—and with the Great War, which was the first sign that a world market was at last becoming established, and the earliest figure of the 'world.' "[32] The representation of the interconnected world, as a new geographical condition, was articulated through a similarly modernist dialectic of homogeneous and broken space. The geography of the world after World War I shares this fragmented yet seamless quality: the world-image depends upon a totalizing unbroken sphere, yet the constituent parts of that sphere exist in a state of irreconcilable difference and disjunction.

Understanding modernism and globalization through the lens of spatiality likewise allows us to trace a fundamental connection between the age of modernism and the post–World War II era of decolonization. Because the world-image only comes into being through the articulated political space of the nation-state, any anticolonial discourses of liberation must necessarily engage with the problem of geography not only by reclaiming place and social practice locally, but also by working within the mapped and administered territorializations that authorize sovereignty in the worldwide political sphere. While postcolonial theory has largely been concerned with advocating self-determination and sovereignty through *cultural* politics, it also must interrogate the institutionalized forms of space that ground any possibility of political autonomy. These spaces are, in their very nature, premised on the idea that geography can yoke together the qualitative, affective realm of organic culture and the quantitative, administrative territory of the bureaucratic state. The tensions of national legitimacy and sovereignty that continue to play out in postcolonial nation-states represent an uneasy and, at times, unstable compromise between the situated cultural perspective of Romantic nationalism and the objective, ordered, universal knowledge of Enlightenment scientific inquiry. *World Views* argues that fiction often sets these two versions of global geography against each other so that their contradictions can be brought to light.

Ironic Nationality

I have discussed the geographical consciousness of modernist fiction in terms of its formal relationship to cartography and its aesthetic similarities to disciplinary geography. I want now to consider the more political dimensions of the invocation of geography within fiction. Just as narrative realism is not simply superseded by a modernist aesthetic, so too is fiction's sense of national attachment maintained even into an age of twentieth-century cultural globalization. Rather than look-ing at the turn toward geographical imagination as an escape from nationhood, then, I understand the turn toward metageographical fiction as an ironic position *within* a national identity. Certainly, my title suggests the expansiveness of a fic-tion attempting to represent scales beyond the nation; however, I also intend the sense of "worldview" as *weltanschauung*, a specific, located point of view on the world. In other words, the recourse to geography as a totalizing, objective mode is always mediated by a situated perspectivalism. Here, I follow recent critics of the new cosmopolitan studies, including Bruce Robbins, Kwame Anthony Appiah, and Rebecca Walkowitz, in understanding "globalized" cultural production not in terms of a transcendence of national identities, but as a dialectical relationship between a particularized place of identification and a detached space of enuncia-tion from which one can put that national identity in a larger, extranational con-text. This is not an either/or position. The provisional removal of perspective to a place of overview need not nullify an affective attachment to the more grounded locations of human attachment. As Robbins puts it, "cosmopolitanism or inter-nationalism does not take its primary meaning or desirability from an absolute and intrinsic opposition to nationalism."[33] Appiah advocates a similar attitude, phrased in more explicitly ethical terms: he advocates a "partial cosmopolitan-ism," which "take[s] sides neither with the nationalist who abandons all foreigners nor with the hard-core cosmopolitan who regards her friends and fellow citizens with an icy impartiality."[34] Following this line of thinking, *World Views* exam-ines the ironic use of geography as a way of mediating cosmopolitan desires and national attachments, a stance that permits the writers in this study to step outside a national homeland without sundering a meaningful, felt attachment to an imag-ined national community.

Reading the dynamics of globalization alongside the emergence of national form in the twentieth century requires something of a binocular gaze. While the turn to spatial studies has proven helpful in understanding modernism's routes, networks, and movements (which obviously go well beyond the nation-state), such globalizing moves often ignore a crucial historical fact: the twentieth century saw the universalization of the territorial nation-state as the primary form of collective sovereignty and self-determination. Cornelia Navari highlights this dramatic historical development, pointing out that a "cultural and political map of the world drawn as late as 1870 would have revealed a bewildering variety of social and political forms. A similar map drawn in 1970 would reveal common conceptions of citizenship, much more similar forms of political and social organization, and many shared social and political objectives."[35] Mapping modernism onto this large-scale political history demands a revision of a narrative that seemed to become dominant in the 1990s. Responding to the first wave of postcolonial theory, modernist studies justifiably explored the conjunctural relationships between early-twentieth-century modernism and the latter stages of (typically British) imperialism. With the early exceptions of Ireland and, later, India and Pakistan, the modernism of the early twentieth century eventually died out amid a waning of metropolitan energies, and the widespread decolonization of Africa and the Caribbean in turn yielded a growing corpus of "postcolonial" literature in the 1950s and 1960s. David Ayers, however, gives us another way of thinking about the political forms of sovereignty in the long twentieth century, positing instead a history of "de-imperialization" that begins in earnest around the end of World War I, with the dismantling of the Russian, Ottoman, and Austro-Hungarian empires, continuing into the breakup of the Western European empires later in the century.[36] Out of these empires came nation-states, virtually all of which, following the Versailles treaties of 1919, adhered to the same principles of territory-based sovereignty and self-determination. In the chapters that follow, I explore how this emergent, increasingly universal form retained a central imaginative significance to writers of fiction.

As Sonita Sarker helpfully reminds us, "In the last turn-of-the-century's battle of modernities, the nation-state was the universal model under dispute among socialist, anarchist, and capitalist philosophies for colonial as well as anticolonial subjecthood, as it is at this turn into the twenty-first century."[37] Sarker extends this observation to the political aesthetic of modernist writers, pointing out that "while modernist authors supersede national boundaries, they believe in the cultural uniqueness of their respective nations."[38] As I will argue, the literary mode best suited to the expression of this tension is a particularly geographical irony. Let me cite a specific modernist example to illustrate how the fictional citation of geography can be used to represent an ironic nationalism that is neither identical to, nor exclusive of, a "partial cosmopolitanism." Early in James Joyce's *A Portrait of the Artist as a Young Man*, the young protagonist Stephen Dedalus sits in the middle of a geography lesson pondering the ever-widening circles in which he locates himself.

Drawing from the systematized, "factual" knowledge presented in his geography book, Stephen understands his relationship to space in terms of a neatly ordered hierarchy in which each geographical scale is enfolded within another, larger scale: "Stephen Dedalus/Class of Elements/Clongowes Wood College/Sallins/County Kildare/Ireland/Europe/The World/The Universe."[39] Stephen's list of scales seems almost comically comprehensive. Beginning with the boundaries of his body and moving next to the small community of students in the classroom, Stephen follows each scale until his musings reach the blurry area between physical and metaphysical geographies. The ordered series of concentric circles that takes Stephen from the self to the universe bespeaks a post-Enlightenment hierarchical arrangement of knowledge, with every scale of space fitting neatly into the next. We might even suppose that such an episode has formed Stephen's cosmopolitan sensibilities, as it is precisely such a view of space that would allow the young artist to think that he could "fly by the nets" of national attachment. With "Ireland" simply listed as one scale among others, a cosmopolitan "escape" would simply mean canceling out "Ireland" with "Europe" or "the World." The geography book's nested hierarchy of space gives the scale of the nation no singular or exceptional role as anything more than an inert, reified geographical signifier.[40]

Joyce, of course, complicates matters. As if to counter the unexceptional position of the nation within a nested hierarchy of scales, Joyce includes a piece of doggerel written by Stephen's classmate Fleming: "Stephen Dedalus is my name,/Ireland is my nation./Clongowes is my dwellingplace/And heaven my expectation."[41] These recto and verso images of Stephen's relationship to the different scales of geographical identity typify the tensions between the implied objectivity of post-Enlightenment cartography and the primary attachment demanded by the nation-state.[42] The jigsaw-puzzle world of sovereign nation-states obscures the fact that the nation is but one geographical scale among many that press their claims to shape individual and cultural identities. Within the neatly enfolded hierarchy of geographical scales—world, continent, nation, region, city, neighborhood, home—the nation both fits into and stands above other scales. While the movement of the spatial scale from the microcosm of Stephen's own embodied identity to the largest of conceivable macro-scales—the universe—satisfies the post-Enlightenment requirement for ordered, classifiable knowledges, it has no way of singling out the geographical realm to which Stephen should be most intimately attached: why "Ireland" over "County Kildare," "Europe," or even "The World," for that matter? The piece of verse on the facing page functions as a supplement, however, to render Ireland with an affective quality that the other scales lack: the poem moves from embodied self, to nation, to dwelling place, finally fixing on the final *telos* of Stephen's identity, which binds all of Stephen's temporal identifications within the eternal. Even in this "childish" piece of verse, the nation is portrayed as the geographical space that mediates between the human scale of the body and its surroundings and the ultimate horizon of spiritual-religious destiny. The arbitrary geographical signifier of "Ireland," itself apparently no more exceptional than other arbitrary designations, requires, in Anderson's words, "the magic of nationalism to turn chance into destiny."[43] The "destiny" that was a self-evident narrative *telos* throughout the history of the realist novel is now self-consciously cited as a geographical artifact, one that is not immediately or naturally preferable to other, "objective" registers of spatial identification.

As much as Stephen (and Joyce) will seek out the "silence, exile, and cunning" of the cosmopolitan artist, it is still the "uncreated conscience" of Ireland that Stephen (and, presumably, Joyce) takes as the primary subject matter of art.[44] Ireland is at once a purely arbitrary spatial signifier, as the abstract space of post-Enlightenment cartography would have it, but it also retains the "specialness" of an imagined national community. This sense of providential nationality is derived from a romantic, organicist tradition that Pheng Cheah describes in his book, *Spectral Nationality*. Drawing on the early-nineteenth-century writings of Johann Gottlieb Fichte, Cheah describes how the metaphysics of nationalism are able to subsume the necessarily geographical construction of the modern nation-state. In this metaphysic, "the nation's borders are internal, spiritual borders more powerful than any physicoempirical territorial borders, which are simply their external retracings."[45] Cheah here points out that the myth of the modern nation requires an internally driven demarcation of space for which geography is simply an external, secondary representation. The nation, in other words, is not *primarily* a geographical artifact. Rather, it derives its existence from an organic fusion of land and culture. This organicist nationalism devalues the imposition of borders as a merely mechanical, state-driven project necessary to ensure a relative stability within an international order. As Anderson has pointed out, however, the rise of a cartographic culture led to the practice of detaching the outline of the nation and projecting that outline itself as a "logo" that could be "wholly detached from its geographic context," thus encouraging the jigsaw-puzzle view of nationality discussed earlier.[46] What we see, then, is not simply a continuation of Fichtean romantic nationalism into the twentieth century, but rather a reformatting of the nation as an entity whose existence is increasingly derived *from* its bordered, territorial inscription. With this territorialized nation comes both a form of attachment to the nation as a unit opposed to a larger "world," and, simultaneously, an awareness of the nation-within-the-world, which threatens to diminish its providential, "unique" identity. *World Views* therefore tries to capture the unstable irony of a dynamic that approximates Wittgenstein's famous duck-rabbit image. Seen one way, the nation stands out as a positive, substantive entity whose borders separate it from the negative space of its exterior. Seen another way, however, the nation is simply part of a gridded, abstract field whose unity is to be found in the spherical entity of global geography rather than the arbitrary marking off of national boundaries. This tension operates not simply as a thematic, but also a structural dynamic in each of the literary texts under consideration.

Geography by Other Means

This study is geographical in the broadest sense possible; it is, in other words, concerned with how, where, and why "writing the earth" has shaped and continues to shape the natural and built environments in which we live. Although the academic discipline of geography in Europe and North America has largely developed in accordance with national and imperial interests, I follow recent critical historians of geography by viewing it as a more open-ended, contextual mode of representation. At the turn of the nineteenth century, the discipline encompassed a variety of practices and areas of inquiry: exploration and travel writing, cartography, biology, geology, meteorology, political and military sciences, to name just a few.[47] The idea that geography now referred to a discrete discipline rooted in scientific observation and empirical fact was by no means taken for granted. The discipline itself was being constructed and defined as the "New Geography" in Great Britain (and in similar though by no means identical ways as the *Nouvelle Geographie* in France) by a number of thinkers, most notably the aforementioned Halford Mackinder. Mackinder's synthesis, in its ideal forms, would weave together humanistic fields such as history, art, and literature with more scientific areas such as geology, meteorology, and biology. Many writers and intellectuals who were influential in the development of late-nineteenth-century and early-twentieth-century geography worked outside of conventional disciplinary boundaries: Elisée Reclus, for example, who interwove art, folk history, and regional description into his multivolume work *Les Hommes et le Terre*; Patrick Geddes, the tireless Scottish reformer and educator who portrayed the scale of the region as a rich cross-disciplinary text; and even the novelist Joseph Conrad, who in addition to deploying geography, travel, and empire as major themes in many of his fictional works, wrote several non-fiction essays about the history of geography and global exploration. Eventually, geography carved out an institutional home with some subdisciplines in the social and some in the physical sciences. What is striking, however, is that, until very recently, both European and American geography banished the literary, the artful, and the aesthetic from its "proper" disciplinary purview. Interdisciplinary or extradisciplinary thinkers such as Reclus, Geddes, and Conrad were not widely seen as having meaningful roles in the history of academic geography.

At the risk of oversimplification, I hope to redress such disciplinary narrowness by reading literature as geography by other means, and, conversely, by reading various geographical writings and productions as themselves dependent upon "literary" qualities such as form, symbol, and dense textuality. This particular intersection between critical geography and literary criticism has been called for by geographers as well as by literary critics. Marc Brosseau, for example, suggests that geographers look to literature as a way to understand how points of view are constructed and how "geography's rational discursivity" can be persuasively critiqued.[48] Literature and geography are significant contributors to the frames through which we organize, understand, and act within the world. Their interpenetration speaks to a fundamental ambiguity and complexity in matters of geography and politics, qualities that are rarely allowed to exist in the sphere of nation-based international relations. Each chapter of *World Views* expands upon a geographical space or scale that in some way questions, complicates, or denies the originary primacy of the nation-state as a fundamental, essential category of geographical knowledge. Whether the continent, the region, the internal colony, the ocean, or the boundary line, each of these alternative geographical spaces has occasioned a thoroughgoing inquiry into the nature and necessity of the nation-state as the proper political form for the securing of human freedoms. Each of these alternative geographies forces us to view the world through a different lens and, in so doing, constitutes acts that are no less creative than they are fundamentally political.

Chapters 1 and 2 read early-twentieth-century geographical texts alongside British modernist narratives for their staging of metageographical crises—that is, crises of how to conceive of the world's fundamental spatial divisions. Each of these two chapters moves between fiction and "literary" forms of geography, such as the travel narrative and regional description. The literary works I examine introduce other foundational scales of space to question the primacy and efficacy of a world order in which territorial nation-states are both the only legitimate protagonists in the drama of international relations and the primary space through which individual subjects mediate any notion of personal and collective identity. These various imaginations of world order are limited, though, precisely because they accept an order of space built on both Enlightenment models of hierarchical knowledge and histories of European territorial imperialism. Chapter 1 explores the macroscale of the continent as an alternative to a world system of nation-states. I read texts by Joseph Conrad and Graham Greene, each of which imagines the continent as a countermyth to the territorial nation-state. In *Heart of Darkness*, Conrad understands the African continent through the lens of geographical determinism, the belief that the geographical facts of topography and climate played a decisive role in the formation of both individual and cultural identities. Going against the prevailing wisdom of the day, however, *Heart of Darkness* shows Africa as a more powerful continent than Europe in its ability to undo centuries of European acculturation through its primeval landscapes and hostile climate. Greene gives Africa no such intrinsic power but maintains a continental view by portraying Africa as a mere receptacle for the export of European mass culture. In *Journeys Without Maps*, Greene imagines Africa as a dystopian symptom of a European modernity gone global. For Greene, the sovereignty of Liberia—the only sub-Saharan state governed by a nonwhite population at the time of Greene's writing—points not toward future decolonization and indigenous self-determination but rather toward a debased, failed imitation of the national idea. In contrast to these mournful European visions, I read a series of documents authored by King Njoya of Bamum (in modern-day Cameroon), including an early-twentieth-century map of his kingdom, which offers a different metageography than a continental vision based upon a fundamental homogeneity. Njoya's map understands space not in terms of the political interests of the nation-state or the imaginary blankness of the continent, but in terms of an imaginative compromise between Western notions of territoriality and indigenous spatial practices based upon the historical lineage of tribal community. Njoya's history also gives insight into a more particularized, complicated history of Africa that contradicts its portrayal as a uniform, homogeneous space.

While chapter 1 explores the idea of a continental metageography in a world system composed of colonial extensions of the territorial nation-state, chapter 2 examines the articulation of the region as another metageographical response to the form of the nation. Here, I focus on the writings of the geographer and urbanist Patrick Geddes, particularly in his 1915 volume, *Cities in Evolution*, and on the novels of E. M. Forster, particularly *Howards End* (1910). Where Conrad's and Greene's continentalism relied upon the opposition of civilization and primitiveness, regionalism appealed to visual, tactile, and lived experience as another countermyth to the nation-state. Patrick Geddes advances a vision of region that attempts to synthesize natural and built environments, along with a consideration of how space embodies a simultaneity of past, present, and future. Geddes' vision of place expresses ideas about urban, suburban, and rural space through a hybrid form of inquiry that combines ethnography, biology, landscape painting, and literature. What unifies the diverse modes of knowledge in Geddes' methodology is the importance of both embodied vision and human scale. I draw distinctions between an abstract "God's-eye" view of the world operative in imperial geopolitics and Geddes' reliance on a subject-centered, perspectival vision of place. Where Geddes approaches the problem of the region in the context of modernity, however, he is less concerned with how individual subjects might imaginatively grasp their environments and cognitively map their relationships to regional spaces. In *Howards End*, Forster attempts to reconcile the individual to both region and nation, though his characters are never "at home" in any communal place and can thus only view regionalism from an exterior, dis-placed position. Even as the situated eye suggests a more immediate, embodied relationship to place, it ultimately occludes any kind of isomorphism between the local region and the imagined community of the nation.

The final three chapters explore metageographical literary texts that are more self-consciously positioned against the normative form of the territorial nation-state. Each of these chapters explores how the reinvention of narrative form serves as a way to question and complicate both the static hierarchy of spatial scale and the necessary mediation of the territorial nation-state in articulating individual and communal forms of identity. These three chapters also explore what Partha Chatterjee has called the "derivative discourse" of postcolonial nationalism, arguing that literature can escape the opposition of "authentic" and "false" nationalisms by refusing the primacy of the very form of the nation as a foundation for individual and collective rights and freedoms. Chapter 3 examines Joyce's encyclopedic text as an object generated out of imperial cartographies of the internal colony of Ireland. Beginning with an examination of the nineteenth-century Ordnance Survey of Ireland undertaken by the British military, the first comprehensive cartographic survey of a colonial territory, I inquire into the rhetorical and aesthetic dimensions implicit in the idea of *survey*. Drawing on the tensions between the Enlightenment models of detached scientific observation and the necessary aesthetic and formal choices involved in creating a survey, I contend that the imperative to codify the existence of the colony always betrays a fuzzy, complicated relationship between the subject-nation and the object-colony. Joyce's novel, famously plotted with precision onto a map of Dublin (derived from the original Ordnance Survey maps), uses the imperial map of a bounded, objectified colony to emphasize the tensions between the map as a tool indicating imperial possession and the map as a canvas for the creation of an emergent communal identity that refuses to fall into the tried-and-true form of the territorial nation-state. Ultimately, I claim that Joyce creates a world that is *anti*topographical, subverting the mimeticism of the novel's early chapters with a formalism that denies the possibility of his novel having any kind of stable spatial ground. Such antirepresentational formalism, I argue, extends to the political vision of the novel, which is not necessary nationalist (as some recent critics have argued) but radically *antinational* in its suspicion of any static spatial representation of culture.

The theme of resignifying an imperial metageography is continued in chapter 4. This chapter begins with Mackinder's famous pronouncement in his essay "The Geographical Pivot of History" that the world's landmass is best thought of as a large island on which the nation that controls the "Heartland" would possess the balance of geopolitical power. While a radical formulation of metageography, Mackinder's observation is used primarily to serve the ends of an imperialist geography, elsewhere expressed in Mackinder's geography textbook, *Britain and the British Seas* (1902). In contrast to the supercontinental "world-island," I consider literary metageographies based upon the much smaller islands of the Caribbean treated in Jean Rhys's *Wide Sargasso Sea* and Jamaica Kincaid's *A Small Place*. The titles of each text suggest an ironic ambivalence about the national aspirations of the island realms of Jamaica, Dominica, and Antigua. Rhys's narrative, which exists within the unspoken gaps of Charlotte Brontë's *Jane Eyre*, creates gaps of its own, particularly the geographical gap between England and the Caribbean, represented by the Sargasso Sea, or North Atlantic. I argue that the novel is in fact structured through unrepresentable gaps, which gives oceanic space a curious centrality to a narrative about a cross-cultural marriage, highlighting the inadequacy of a worldview that sees oceans as empty extensions of imperial territory. Kincaid's essay, located more firmly in the postcolonial moment, similarly imagines the centrality of oceanic space as an unbridgeable gap between neocolonial geographies that designate certain nations as zones of tourism. Kincaid ironically rewrites spatial history so that the "small place" of Antigua becomes a territory written over and over again by intrusions from across the sea. Her account of Antigua suggests a view of the ocean-island relationship as the fundamental metageography of colonial and neocolonial identity.

The wide "space between" of the ocean is distilled into the terrestrial boundary line in chapter 5. This chapter explicitly treats the idea of the boundary line, a fundamental yet strangely ephemeral component of the territorial nation-state. I first examine the debates surrounding the proposed partition of the Indian subcontinent that was to follow British decolonization. In writings and speeches by intellectuals, including Jawaharlal Nehru, Mohammed Jinnah, Mulk Raj Anand, and A. M. Ambedkar, the discourses of geography and cartography are used to naturalize either pro- or antipartition arguments. Partition is, in a sense, the final stage in the metageography of the nation-state, implying that cultural differences can be prescribed by the drawing of boundary lines. In response to what would prove to be the tragically violent process of partition, Amitav Ghosh's novel, *The Shadow Lines*, presents a critical and ironic treatment of the fetish of the boundary line in the partition of India and Pakistan. Through a narrator who attempts to make sense of partition decades later, the line is rescued from its image as a border, a space of cultural and metaphysical difference in the politics of partition, and reimagined as a space of connection, able to link histories and geographies arbitrarily sundered through the metageography of national form.

This book aims to reconcile conventional geographical and literary perspectives, and in so doing to complicate and trouble both disciplinary points of view. It begins to seek answers to questions that might trouble geographers and literary critics alike. What if geographical knowledge did not repress its artfulness with its scientific rhetoric, its fancy in the face of hard fact? What if students who studied geographical information systems read the philosophical meditations on boundary lines in Amitav Ghosh's *The Shadow Lines*? What if land surveyors read about the ambivalent engagement with Ordnance Survey maps in *Ulysses*? In fact, literature has remained an important discourse for critical geographers and historians of cartography. As Marc Brosseau argues, the discipline of geography has had a long engagement with literature, one that has been renewed with the emergence of critical and "oppositional" geographical studies in the 1960s and 1970s. Rather than signal a new development in humanistic geography, I would argue that the reemergence of literature as a legitimate area of concern for geographers constitutes something of a return of the repressed. Perhaps we can, in fact, look at the "scientific" rhetoric of geography not as geography's normative mode but rather as a deviation from a history deeply intertwined with narrative, figuration, and imagination. Yet, if geography as a discipline has shown a reengagement with the "softer" discourses of literature, art, and imaginative representation, much still remains unquestioned about the fundamental metageographies that organize and code the terrestrial surface of Earth. It is thus with no small sense of irony that *World Views* claims one of the most "formalist" concepts of modernism as its most radically political: what Victor Shklovsky called *ostranenie*, or defamiliarization.[49] By holding up *meta*geography—not mimetically represented space but the organization of spatial concepts—geographical modernism invites us to interrogate spaces that were long accepted as natural and "given." We can find nothing more familiar, everyday, and unquestioned than the quite literal ground of terrestrial space upon which we base so much knowledge and signification. As the old Irish schoolmaster Hugh remarks in Brian Friel's 1981 play, *Translations*, "it can happen that a civilization can be imprisoned in a linguistic contour which no longer matches the landscape of...fact."[50] Within British imperial cultures of the last several hundred years, it has been the business of geography to fuse such linguistic contours to the landscapes of fact. *World Views* argues that it has been—and continues to be—the work of fiction to pry them apart.

1. Continent
Modernism, Geographical Determinism, and the Image of Africa

"Firing into a Continent"

Sailing down the west coast of Africa en route to the mouth of the Congo River, Joseph Conrad's steamer captain, Marlow, comments on a French gunboat lying just off the coast, lobbing shells into the coastal interior. As Marlow recounts, the French refer to this action as a "war" with native "enemies." He concludes wryly: "In the empty immensity of earth, sky, and water, there she was, incomprehensible, firing into a continent" (*HD* 16). Marlow finds the scenario bizarrely incongruous, implying both the misguided interpretation of resistant native tribes as "enemies" and the uselessness of blindly firing into the jungle as an act of war. Wars, Marlow implies, are between the standing armies of nation-states. What Marlow sees, by contrast, is an "incomprehensible" act; by "firing into a continent," the French have got it all wrong. In this phrase, Marlow suggests that the futility of this particular endeavor lies less in its almost certain strategic failure—the indigenous tribes can easily move down the coast or retreat inland, out of the range of the gunboat's fire—than its categorical misjudgment. Continents are of an entirely different geographical order than nations; they do not presume a political-cultural identity and, in many cases, a clearly marked border. Typically, continents have not commanded the kind of affective, sentimental attachment that nations are meant to inspire. And while continents might be seen as the mediating scale between nation-states and the globe in a hierarchical vision of geographical knowledge, they have historically been associated with qualitatively different geographical concepts. By the late nineteenth century, as nation-states established their borders and claims over the landforms of the world, continents were seen as the timeless, geological bedrock upon which the shifting dynamics of history took place. As Martin Lewis and Kären Wigen write, the categories of the "continental system" were "increasingly naturalized, coming to be regarded, not as products of a fallible human imagination, but as real geographical entities that had been 'discovered' through empirical inquiry."[1] To "fire into a continent," in other words, is not only an error of scale but also an error of category. Like a modern-day Canute mistaking his cultural authority for the ability to control the oceanic tides, the French gunboat uses the means of warfare, based upon military encounters between organized national armies, to "attack" what Marlow sees as an undifferentiated, primeval, precultural entity.

Even if Marlow aims his irony squarely at one of the "civilized" European empires, his view of the continent as an undifferentiated, primeval space partakes in one of the most pervasive (and still lingering) myths of geography: that of environmental, or geographical, determinism. In the late nineteenth century, most theories of geography were based on some determinist foundation, looking to space and environment for causal explanations of human physiology, behavior, and cultural organization. David N. Livingstone points to Jean-Baptiste Lamarck's theories of the inheritance of acquired traits and Charles Darwin's evolutionary paradigm as "ample justification for shaping the newly professionalizing discipline on an environmentalist template."[2] As Lewis and Wigen point out, continents became key concepts in describing the relationships between environment and culture. "Proponents of geographical determinism," they write, "have often construed the intensity of environmental influence as varying according to continental location.... Europe has been depicted as the arena of environmental *possibilism*. Asia and Africa, by contrast, have been often viewed as continents of climactic rigor and physiographic uniformity, whose people have been subject to a corresponding set of 'iron physical laws.'"[3] Although Conrad's sympathies might, in this instance, seem aligned with the "continent" of Africa rather than with the imperial states of Europe, he effectively subordinates any indigenous human activity or social organization to the brute fact of Africa's topographical immensity. Conrad's irony is aimed at the categorical error of the French that "enemies" exist to be attacked at all. Not only are these adversaries incomparable to a national military force—which would be seen as the only legitimate opponent in a war—they aren't even properly human, instead reduced to a feature of Africa's topographical surface.

Conrad's view, however, is more complicated than a mere naturalization of Africa as a land stuck in primeval, prehistoric time. In much the same way as Halford Mackinder's geographical writings, *Heart of Darkness* also explores the causal relationships between physical environments and human culture. Within the discipline of geography, Mackinder and others largely gave causative priority to environments—"Man and not nature initiates, but nature in large measure controls," as Mackinder once put it.[4] In *Heart of Darkness*, Conrad likewise comes down on the side of the physical environment as a determining factor in the development of culture. Where Conrad differs from Mackinder, however, is in his recognition of a contradiction at the heart of an environmentally deterministic theory of geography: although it claims to be a theory that can apply equally across different areas of the earth, it in fact operates differently with respect to Europe than other parts of the world. Europe's environments, according to such theories, are conducive to the development of a *techne* that allows, paradoxically, for the *overcoming* of geographically induced constraints—a determinism that eventually yields a "possibilism." Yet, if environment is, in the last instance, the determining cause of human culture, then the formative power of environmentally deterministic places such as Africa (or Asia or South America) would seem to trump the European environments that gave rise to the technologies, institutions, and cultures of modernity, among them the inclination and ability to travel around the world and subjugate the populations found in distant locales. This dilemma was not only at the heart of the new geography; it was also a crux that modernism continually addressed in one form or another: do Europeans have the ability to master the difficult environments of the colonial world?

This chapter explores two authors that draw on a continental comparison between Europe and Africa as a way of arriving at a vision of a global geography that exists outside of a nation-based world system. I first look at Joseph Conrad's *Heart of Darkness* in dialogue with Conrad's later essay, "Geography and Some Explorers." The continental schema of global geography allows Conrad to contrast a geographical determinism with a national mythology of England as a providential nation-state empire. Tied more closely to human nature, continents determine cultures far more thoroughly than ethnically or linguistically derived national identities, providing a layer of character formation beneath the superstructural "falsity" of culture. Conrad encounters difficulties, however, when the pan-European Kurtz spends enough time in Africa to have his identity *re*-determined. If human character and social organization are ultimately formed by large-scale environmental surroundings, then it stands to reason that Europeans, as members of a "weaker" continent further removed from nature, will be re-formed by the more powerful, primeval environments of Africa. Conrad therefore presents a kind of dystopian version of Mackinder's environmental determinism: in *Heart of Darkness*, European possibilism is a weakness rather than a strength. This doubled connection of Europe and Africa is reproduced in the form of the novel, as Marlow's experience with Kurtz leads to an ontological confusion between Europe and Africa. The geographies of nation-based imperialism are discredited in the novel, yet Conrad's alternative is an even more arbitrary gap between Europe and Africa, a forced separation that manifests itself in the structural irony of the novel, which is finally unable to unify the world of Marlow's tale on the Congo and the world of its telling, in the Thames estuary, on the deck of the *Nellie*.

Graham Greene, writing almost forty years later, reproduces elements of Conrad's continental metageography in his travel narrative to Liberia, *Journeys without Maps*. In many ways, Greene's narrative is a self-conscious update of *Heart of Darkness*, as he begins his narrative in the Liberian Consul, arranging a visit not through the offices of a trading company but through the bureaucratic channels of international travel from one sovereign nation-state to another. Through the course of the narrative, however, it becomes clear that Greene's imagined destination is not the sovereign nation-state of Liberia but the mythic, precultural, continental idea of Africa. Unlike Conrad, Greene ascribes little deterministic power to the environment of Africa; rather, its undifferentiated "continental" blankness has only rendered it as a screen upon which images of European modernity are projected. Even as Greene painstakingly narrates the quotidian international experience of visiting consulates, securing visas, undergoing border checks, and paying duties, this nationalized African modernity is still largely readable only as an externalization of an imported mass European consciousness. The natural power of continents, therefore, mocks the arbitrary division of nations. As with Conrad, however, this worldview finds it difficult to work through the confusion between the determinism of a prehistoric nature and the possibilism of a place that fosters purposive human endeavor, the *telos* of which is the transformation and subjugation of the power of brute environments to shape human identity and culture.

As Europeans whose sensibilities were formed during an era of sustained imperial attention to Africa, both Conrad and Greene view the continent largely as a cartographic construct: a landmass that is both longitudinally proximate to Europe yet still (until well into the twentieth century) considered a blankness unmarked by the cultural differentiation that characterizes European modernity. By conflating historical development with a nation-based geography, Africa is *by definition* excluded from modernity, as its natural continental existence forms a substratum of truth upon which cultural "development" can only appear as an artificial mimicry of European culture. To challenge this view, I conclude the chapter by examining the work of King Ibrahim Njoya of Bamum (a former kingdom in contemporary Cameroon). Njoya, who commissioned a map of his kingdom to be presented to King George V of Great Britain in 1916, had authored a possible geography of Africa that preserves indigenous conceptions of space and community while at the same time acknowledging modern imperial cultures of territorial possession. While Njoya's map never achieved its aims—to have his territory administered by the British, which he viewed as the most benevolent of imperial nations in West Africa—it reflects a lost pathway toward an indigenous African modernity that escapes both a continental and a nation-based view of the world.

Continental Determinism in *Heart of Darkness*

By merely thinking of the continent as a foundational geographical unit, Conrad implicitly subverts an emergent world order based upon the universal form of the territorial nation-state. Yet, in the late nineteenth century, Africa remained "stuck" in the continental scale largely because of the lack of differentiation shown in existing cartographies. Under the paradigm of post-Enlightenment geographical knowledge, cartography was wrested from the province of imaginative art and given over to the strict demands of a scientifically governed empiricism. According to these new imperatives, maps should only reflect data that were achieved through carefully monitored observation and should be presented in a sober style that eliminated all unnecessary traces of fanciful artistry. For maps of Africa, this meant that speculative or fantastic elements suddenly disappeared, now replaced with the white space of unexplored territory.[5] As one late-nineteenth-century historian of cartography noted, the purging of African maps seemed to indicate a regression in knowledge. Within a few decades, "lakes and mountains disappeared" from African maps, and, paradoxically, "maps of the seventeenth century often appear to display more knowledge of the interior of Africa than those of the beginning of the nineteenth."[6] Of course, it was not that nineteenth-century maps reflected less knowledge than their predecessors; rather it was that what counted as knowledge had changed. In a matter of several decades, from approximately 1740 to 1820, maps of Africa that had seemed to show a plentitude—of villages, tribes, and topographical features—were transformed into austere documents with immense empty spaces save for the longitudinal and latitudinal lines of the map's graticule.

With little cartographic differentiation, African maps reflected a continent devoid of recognizable cultures and distinct places. For many nineteenth-century observers such as the young Marlow (and his author), Africa was only knowable as "the biggest, the most blank" of the world's remaining unmapped spaces (*HD* 11). In fact, this is the first of three maps of Africa on which Marlow gazes in *Heart of Darkness*. From this white blankness of an unwritten page in his boyhood world atlas, the adult Marlow notes that, prior to his taking the commission to retrieve Kurtz, it had "got filled since my boyhood with rivers and lakes and names" (*HD* 11–12). Marlow's observation reflects the exploration of Africa in terms of its physical geography, and, tellingly, it is the cartographic representation (rather than travel narratives or pictorial images) of the river Congo that awakens his impulse to travel to Africa. This map, in contrast to the multicolored map of colonial possessions that Marlow will see in the offices of the trading company, shows Africa as a primarily natural entity, whose topographical features are the first elements of the continent to be charted and named. Africa's existence as a precultural, fully "natural" space thus takes narrative precedence over its territorial possession in the name of European nation-states. The "rivers and lakes and names" represent the work of the eighteenth- and nineteenth-century Geography Militant, an epoch that Conrad describes in his later essay, "Geography and Some Explorers." For explorers of this era, "geography is a science of facts, and they devoted themselves to the discovery of facts in the configuration and features of the main continents."[7] Africa, of course, in the late nineteenth century was the only main continent left that had not yet been carved up (for the most part) into nation-states or colonial possessions. As such, it offered a contrast of an undifferentiated, "natural" landmass to the map of the rest of the world, which was, by 1900, increasingly differentiated into bordered territorial nation-states.

As Conrad sees it, Geography Militant, with its rhetoric of neutrality and scientific factualization, gave way in the late nineteenth century to Geography Triumphant, an era in which geography was made to serve social, political, and economic interests. These interests are in part reflected by the map that Marlow looks upon in the offices of the trading company, which shows Africa as a parody of a nationalized Europe: "There was a vast amount of red—good to see at any time, because one knows that some real work is done in there, a deuce of a lot of blue, a little green, smears of orange, and on the East Coast, a purple patch, to show where the jolly pioneers of progress drink the jolly lager-beer. However...I was going into the yellow" (*HD* 13). This map portrays an entirely different continent, one that no longer reflects the natural truth of "rivers and lakes and names" but now is only legible through the color-coding of European imperial nation-states.

Conrad means for us to see this map, a product of Geography Triumphant, as false or inauthentic, with mere colors substituting for the proper names of colonizing nations (in spite of his half-hearted endorsement of the English "red," about which more later in this chapter). This Europeanized map does not reflect the "true" Africa, Conrad implies, for Africa-as-continent cannot be made to conform to the nationally motivated territorial carvings of its colonizers. Africa's truth lies in its continental nature, but paradoxically, *as* nature, the continent is categorically prohibited from becoming a more "developed" geography of culturally differentiated and distinct places.

For late-nineteenth-century geographers such as Mackinder and Ratzel, however, Europe remains an apparent exception to the determinist rule of continents. As Lewis and Wigen put it, "proponents of geographical determinism have often construed the intensity of environmental influence as varying according to continental location—opening the way for exempting Europeans from the strict rule of nature."[8] Mackinder illustrates this logic in the first chapter of his 1902 textbook, *Britain and the British Seas.* In his introductory chapter, Mackinder begins his analysis from the standpoint of a purely physical geography, noting that Europe's cultural fates have been determined by having "the five historic parts of the world...accessible from its waters," lending "inevitably a maritime aspect to European civilization."[9] Although Mackinder's primary aim is to justify the specifically British exception to brute determinism, he deduces from this "maritime aspect" a providential history in which natural facts almost imperceptibly become cultural features. Writing of the European influence on the character of English peoples and institutions, Mackinder asserts that "two distinct streams of ethical and artistic influence converged upon [Britain] from the Rhine delta and from the estuary of the Seine."[10] Essentially, Mackinder argues that the geography of Europe determined the predominance of maritime travel and exploration, which led to a continent that could "develop" through the expropriation of resources and the assimilation and synthesis of other cultural traditions. While all of this, in Mackinder's narrative, leads inevitably to British superiority, the cultural pinnacle of the British Empire is merely part of a longer narrative of European continental exceptionalism. In short, as Lewis and Wigen summarize, "the bonds of geographical concordance, especially those linking human developments with physiographic features," are much more powerful in continents such as Asia and Africa than in Europe.[11] Geographical circumstance, therefore, is what *enables* Europe to become "Europe" but also constrains Africa to its essential "Africanness."

In *Heart of Darkness*, Conrad sets up the distinction between Europe and Africa as a more profound opposition than the merely epiphenomenal difference between nation-states, though with much more ironic detachment than Mackinder or other environmental determinists. Although Marlow's own identity is putatively English, his role in the novel is not attached to a specific geography: as the initial narrator notes, Marlow is the only man on board the *Nellie* "who still 'followed the sea'" (*HD* 9). Marlow emerges as a kind of maritime cosmopolitan, a citizen of the world by virtue of his time away from any particular homeland. His narration sets the terms for our understanding of the novel's geography, which seems to become less national and more continental as he travels upriver in the Congo. European men lose their specific national identities, becoming part of a broader category. The brickmaker at the Central Station is given no national origin of his own but "alluded constantly to Europe," according to Marlow (*HD* 27). The sham Mephistopheles speaks of Kurtz as an avatar of a continental *mission civilisatrice*, "the cause intrusted to us by Europe, so to speak, higher intelligence, wide sympathies, a singleness of purpose" (*HD* 28). While it might be tempting to dismiss the brickmaker's European perspective as yet another example of Conrad's ironic distance, Marlow himself seems to adopt this outlook in his encounter with Kurtz. Even though Conrad traces Kurtz's lineage to two specific nations ("his mother was half-English, his father was half-French), he conveniently leaves the other half of Kurtz's cultural DNA unspoken. This omission permits Marlow to attribute Kurtz's identity to a continent rather than a nation: "All Europe contributed to the making of Kurtz" (*HD* 50). Transcending the venal interests of imperial nation-states— merely concerned with marking their colors on a map—Kurtz moves beyond the limited politics of national identity to a symbolic register more metaphysical than political. Kurtz's lack of specific national origin would have been conspicuous to readers in a turn-of-the-century cultural climate in which personal traits were often seen a function of national character. As Christopher GoGwilt rightly points out, Kurtz's European identity is modified by his particular connection to England—in addition to his half-English mother, Kurtz "was partly educated in England and...his sympathies were in the right place" (*HD* 50). GoGwilt comments on the ambivalence of Kurtz's European identity: while Conrad takes pains to remove Kurtz from a specific national origin, it is "dubious...in the sense that [Kurtz] needs to state his sympathies."[12] Conrad bends the "rules" of identity in this instance to create Kurtz as a symbol removed from the limitations of a specific national character while also taking great pains to create a pan-European Kurtz in order to set Europe and Africa in a dialectical relationship. Simply put, Kurtz represents the problem of "Europe" in Africa. Because characters in realist fiction tend to be described in terms of their places of origin and can thus be attached to particular cultural traits, "placeless" characters such as Kurtz (or Heathcliff, or

Jay Gatsby) are particularly freighted with symbolic importance. Kurtz, therefore, becomes as much a geographical abstraction as a realistic, psychologically complex portrait, embodying the traits and values that subsume petty national antagonisms into a broader continental framework.

In his creation of the pan-European Kurtz, Conrad presents a test case for theories of environmental determinism based upon continental categories. Typically, deterministic theories were invoked as a way of instantiating racial difference, as geography gave late-nineteenth-century social science a material explanation for racial classifications. Coming out of a combination of Darwinistic theories of natural selection and a neo-Lamarckist emphasis on inherited traits, geography could posit physical and character features as an accumulation of environmental influences. Much of this discourse centered on ideas of climate, which the geographical historian David Livingstone refers to as a "diagnostic language of ethnic judgment."[13] Large-scale climactic zones, roughly contiguous with continents or world regions, began to demarcate racial characteristics, particularly coalescing in an opposition between a "cold" North (i.e., Europe) and "tropical" South (i.e., Africa, South Asia, South America, and the South Pacific). James Hunt, a Victorian ethnologist, boiled down the essence of these climactically determined traits: southern, tropical climates produce "a low state of morality" with " essentially sensual" inhabitants while the frigid North yields peoples with "increased activity of the brain."[14] While this schema justified a European racial superiority and therefore could underwrite colonial enterprises with a moral authority putatively based upon science, the problem with climatological theories was this: if white Europeans were to venture southward to colonize the more tropical regions of the world, what would the climate do to *them*? A good deal of geographical, anthropological, and medical debate ensued about whether or not white Europeans *could* become used to tropical climates, or whether those climates had the power to transform Europeans into something completely, categorically different. If racial makeup was largely determined by environmental factors, it was unclear whether or not white Europeans would lose some distinct racial identity by spending too much time in the tropics. As an immediate, environmental influence, climate therefore presented something of a conundrum for late-nineteenth-century deterministic geography.

In writing the fate of Kurtz, Conrad adopts much of the logic of geographical determinism, yet the problem of climate suggests that Kurtz, and by extension Europe, cannot remain unchanged by an encounter with Africa. In keeping with contemporaneous theories of continental determinism, Kurtz's European identity is largely expressed through the domain of culture. Prior to his journey to the Congo, Kurtz embodies the stereotype of the "Renaissance man" and thus the pinnacle of European achievement: he is at once explorer, philosopher, musician, artist, and poet, all traits that reflect the "increased activity of the brain" ascribed to inhabitants of the North. Yet, contrary to the guiding ideas of the *mission civilisatrice*, he does not enlighten the benighted tribes of Africa with the progress of European civilization (as his famous verdict of brutal extermination suggests); rather, it is the *nature* of Africa—frequently phrased in terms of climate—that changes him. We are first introduced to the problem of the African climate when Marlow meets the Belgian doctor after accepting his commission in the Congo. The doctor, wanting to believe that the transformative effects of the continent can be measured through such physiological features as cranial size, ultimately concedes that "the changes take place inside" (*HD* 15). As Marlow leaves, the doctor sends him off with a final warning: "In the tropics one must before everything keep calm.... *Du calme, du calme. Adieu*" (*HD* 15). The tropical climate of Africa, it seems, is especially dangerous to those who cannot maintain their cool European demeanor. In light of the doctor's warning, we can understand Kurtz as one of those Europeans who cannot keep calm and is therefore prey to the dangers of the African climate. When Marlow first encounters Kurtz, the ivory trader is gravely ill, presumably from some "tropical" disease that has attacked his weak European constitution. Indeed, as the uncle of the Central Station manager morbidly remarks to his nephew about the "problem" of Kurtz, "the climate may do away with this difficulty for you" (*HD* 33). Yet in spite of this vague medical explanation for Kurtz's illness and subsequent death, the narrative blends his physical decline with a metaphysical corruption, so it becomes difficult to ascertain whether the changes in Kurtz have taken place "inside" or "outside," as it were. We are thus left with the disturbing possibility that Africa can change Europe in ways that go beyond the merely physical. As the quintessential European, Kurtz provides an argument in favor of environmental determinism, but not in the way that Mackinder and other geographers would support. Kurtz disproves the European exception to the iron law of environments: as an undifferentiated continent still fused to its natural environment, Africa seems to easily overcome the weaker bonds between geography and environment characterized by Europeans. "All Europe" may have made the "original" Kurtz, but Africa remakes him utterly.

The English Exception

By taking the logic of environmental determinism to its ends, Conrad levels a serious critique at the geographical myth of European exceptionalism. If Africa is "environment" par excellence, then Europeans who venture to Africa risk being changed both physically and psychologically to the point where they can no longer claim a distinct racial or biological identity from indigenous Africans themselves. Conrad, however, preserves an ambivalent rhetorical separation from compromised Europeans such as Kurtz. Even as Marlow is primarily one who "follows the sea," like Kurtz his sympathies are in the right place. Great Britain remains a place apart from continental Europe, as its geographical detachment ensures that it remains culturally distinct from the "all Europe" that created Kurtz. Here, Conrad follows Mackinder's confident proclamation that Britain is "*of* Europe, yet not *in* Europe."[15] Conrad appears to echo this exceptionalist sentiment by portraying Marlow with lingering, if ambivalent, affinities with England and Englishness. Inside the "red" territories of the British Empire, Marlow insists, some "good work" is being accomplished, while, by implication, other imperial states are less orderly and productive. Reading Conrad at face value here suggests his investment both in a nationalized worldview and in notions of historical progress—that is, some nation-states are better than others at advancing the cause of civilization. Even as the rainbow map supersedes the romantic image of "white space" that Marlow links to his boyhood dreaming, the adult Marlow acknowledges a moral contrast between the different cultures that have since filled in these spaces. In short, extrapolating from a distinction made elsewhere in the novel, the British are proper "colonists" who accomplish their civilizing mission with "efficiency," while others, namely the Belgians under whom Marlow serves during his voyage up the Congo, are mere "conquerors" using "brute force" to secure their dominance of territory and resources (*HD* 10). Underscoring the argument for the relative benevolence of British imperial conquest, Conrad makes his distinction clear to both Marlow's auditors and the novel's readers. Describing the company in whose service Marlow enters, he insists: "You understand it was a Continental concern, that Trading Society" (*HD* 9). Such a nationalist vision accords with the turn-of-the-century sense that Africa was no more than an empty space upon which imperial rivalries were to be played out, with some empires clearly more able to take up the white man's burden than others.

Marlow's case for British exceptionalism comes to seem rather dubious, however, in light of another geographical argument established within the very structure of the novel itself. Over and against a global map carved up into discrete territorial nation-states, Marlow imagines a precultural world that resists the kind of subjugation and abstraction identified with the rainbow map. What is striking, however, is not that Marlow locates this ungovernable primitive nature in Africa (which, along with many late Victorian contemporaries, he does). But rather than simply project Africa in a static opposition to European civilization, Marlow imaginatively compares "primitive" Africa with the very center of "civilization." Recall that the novel begins—and never really leaves—the Thames estuary just east of London. The initial narration, by an unnamed narrator, celebrates the Thames as an icon of imperial triumph, invoking "the memories of men and ships it had borne to the rest of home or to the battles of the sea" (*HD* 4). The river assumes a central role in a cultural mythology of the island nation, built into an empire on the masculine heroism of those sailors who issued forth from its shores. Immediately following the narrator's encomium upon British maritime greatness, Marlow begins his own narration, *in medias res*, with a comment that immediately and devastatingly undercuts the celebratory tones of the narrator: " 'And this also,' said Marlow suddenly, 'has been one of the dark places of the earth' "(*HD* 5). It is the river itself that occasions Marlow's transposition of late Victorian England to early Roman Britannia: "I was thinking of very old times, when the Romans first came here, nineteen hundred years ago—the other day . . . darkness was here yesterday" (*HD* 6). Marlow's meditation on the "natural" Thames rather than the nationally mythologized version of the previous narrator leads to a kind of imaginative temporal compression through which his nineteen centuries can be rendered as a matter of days. This use of the space of the river to short-circuit historical time is strategic, because it allows Marlow to relativize the fundamental opposition of civilization and savagery that undergirds the imperial project. Imagining the experience of a Roman sailor sent out to the far edges of the earth, Marlow muses: "Land in a swamp, march through the woods, and in some inland post feel the savagery, the utter savagery, had closed round him—all that mysterious life of the wilderness that stirs in the forests, in the jungles, in the hearts of wild men" (*HD* 7). While this de-civilizing of the Thames does not reverse the hegemonic binary that casts Africa as the "dark continent"—make no mistake, Conrad never grants civilization to indigenous Africans—it does set up a vertiginous echo between the primitiveness of both the Congo and the Thames, using topographical *similarity* rather than temporal difference to give ontological priority to a "natural" world that precedes—and will inevitably supersede—the territorialized map of Africa inscribed by the imperial states of Europe.

For Marlow, the river is the isomorphically similar feature that connects the "natural," precultural continent of Africa to the "civilized," historical nation of England; it is the means of transference whereby Marlow can imagine a world prior to the one defined by territorial imperialism. Indeed, Conrad borrows the methodology of the "new geography" to establish the causative priority of rivers and their basins in the establishment of cultures. As we have seen, the "naturalist" emphasis of the new geography could lead very easily to an environmental deter-minism—England has become a dominant maritime empire, Mackinder argues, because of its peculiar geographical situation. One of the features of Britain's geog-raphy was the orientation of its rivers, which, according to Mackinder, provided a unique condition for the development of both civilization and a maritime empire. In this passage from a 1909 essay, "Geographical Conditions Affecting the British Empire," Mackinder argues that England—particularly the placement of its river basins and estuaries—exists both within European civilization and set apart from it by an even more providentially placed topography:

> Picture a great plain, low-lying, fertile, free from long winter frost, free from long summer drought, agricultural, densely populated, and traversed by slow navigable rivers which are entered by the tides. A shallow channel, tide-swept, extends through the centre of that plain, so that one section of it, the plain of southern England, is superficially detached from the re-mainder, namely, the plain of Northern France, the Netherlands, and North Germany. But in all its parts it presents the same characteristics and condi-tions for the development of human societies, saving only the insularity of Britain.[16]

By contrast, while cultural superiority could seem naturalized through reference to physical geography, physical geography could also be used as a critique of an existing political and cultural order. Conrad ultimately suggests that the territorial map of Africa—and, by extension, the territorial map of Europe—is merely a veil hiding an ungovernable nature resistant to any kind of political possession. The continental landforms and their respective rivers, mountains, and coastlines can be seen, in this view, as a far more permanent and powerful force than the mere explorers, soldiers, and administrators that march over and stake out these lands in the name of one flag or another. With the filling in of the map lamented by Marlow, only the imaginative return of geography to its prenational origins—for Europe as well as Africa—offers Conrad a suitable means to critique the territorial imperial-ism that was rapidly laying claim to every parcel of space on the map.

　　While the novel's pairing of the "cultural" river of the Thames with the "natural" river of the Congo effects a critique of acquisitive imperialism and its associated geographies, we shouldn't forget that such a comparison also relegates Africa and its inhabitants to a primeval, prehistoric state of nature. The most forceful argu-ment against Conrad's naturalization of Africa remains Chinua Achebe's blistering critique, "An Image of Africa." Achebe rightly notes that "*Heart of Darkness* proj-ects the image of Africa as 'the other world.'"[17] Achebe points out the structural pairing of the two rivers, the Thames and the Congo, arguing that the novel endorses the Thames as the civilized, nationalized waterway and the Congo as its primitive, untamed "antithesis."[18] Achebe fails to observe, however, that the novel's encomium on the Thames is voiced by a narrator whose worldview is ironically undercut by Marlow's narration. This is not to suggest that Marlow grants anything "civilized" to the Congo—Achebe is right when he says that "it is not the differentness that worries Conrad but the lurking hint of kinship."[19] But it is important to note that the novel most certainly wants us to see the Thames as part of an ungovernable, unknowable nature, not a tamed and disciplined culture. To the geographically minded Conrad, the aim is to shift the terms of debate from imperial rivalries between nations to a more fundamental and unresolvable tension between an imperial metageography of territorial acquisitiveness and the timeless brutish facticity of physical geography, of nature, of continents. That he neglects the cultural and geographical specificity of Africa for its role as a mirror on the desires of Western imperialism shows us the inherent limits of such a metageographical, "continental" critique.[20]

The Portable Continent: Greene's *Journey*

In Conrad's view, Africa becomes a continent that is a supplement to the order of nations. It exists as a place blocked from modernity, unable to be partitioned from its undifferentiated form. Furthermore, the prohibition of African modernity exposes the impossibility of a global order based on a formal equality of nation-states: these political forms only exist as colors on a map, patches as ineffectual and makeshift as those composing the threadbare coat of Kurtz's Russian protégé. The idea that Africa was both a paradigmatic *and* an exceptional continent is further elaborated in Graham Greene's 1936 autobiographical travel narrative, *Journeys without Maps*. Greene's narrative forms a useful point of comparison to Conrad's if for no other reason than its self-conscious rewriting of its literary predecessor. In his book, Greene recounts his travels to the west African nation of Liberia in search of…what? Greene himself seems not to have a satisfactory answer to this question. "It is not the fully conscious mind," Greene reveals about his choice of destination, "which chooses West Africa to Switzerland" (*JWM* 20). By locating his motives for travel behind the inaccessible screen of the unconscious, Greene implicitly acknowledges that his travels are more about his own desires than any objective, autonomous Africa that he might seek to find. Yet Greene's rhetoric of nonfictional self-disclosure leads him to record the (often) mundane, quotidian facts of his journey. This tension, between a descriptive realism and an impression-istic self-consciousness, often manifests itself in a shifting view of Africa as both an undifferentiated abstraction seemingly outside of history and a place made utterly banal by the thorough permeation of European mass culture. This dual perspective presents a different spin on the idea of a continental Africa: where Conrad relegated the continent to the primeval authenticity of an ungoverned nature, Greene simply presents a space written over by the "seedy" commodifica-tion of an imported mass culture. Ultimately, for all of their contrasts, the passage from Conrad to Greene reveals Africa as a space whose continental nature both contradicts a modern world order of states but, in doing so, is consigned to being an abstraction, a vehicle for critique rather than a realm of cultural diversity and differentiation.

In choosing Liberia as his destination, Greene visits one of only two nations in 1930s sub-Saharan Africa (Ethiopia was the other) with a sovereign state not controlled by a major colonial power.[21] On the face of it, Greene's travels are not into an uncivilized *terra incognita* but rather to a modern, independent nation-state governed by international laws and institutions. The narrative begins with a scene analogous to Marlow's visit to the trading company in Brussels (albeit with little of Conrad's sense of foreboding): Greene goes to the Liberian Consulate in London to seek information about traveling to the West African nation. The very act of visiting a consulate to obtain a visa for travel suggests a significant difference in the political landscape of Africa in the nearly forty years between Marlow's and Greene's travels. Where Marlow traveled under the auspices of a private company to a place frequently described as an uncivilized, undifferentiated nature, Greene seeks to enter Africa through the bureaucratic channels afforded to sovereign nation-states. It seems, however, that Greene has not chosen Liberia for its political advancement but rather as a parody of African sovereignty and self-determination. Commenting on Liberia's founding by freed American slaves, Greene notes with irony that "the Republic was founded as an example to all Africa of a Christian and self-governing state" (*JWM* 18). Of the nation's motto, Greene acidly writes: "'The love of liberty brought us here,' but one can hardly blame these first half-caste settlers when they found that love of their own liberty was not consistent with the liberty of the native tribes" (*JWM* 18). Ultimately, Greene concludes that the difference between Liberia and the colonial territories that surround it are of little consequence, concluding that "the history of the Republic was very little dif-ferent from the history of neighboring white colonies" (*JWM* 18). As with Conrad, Greene makes a nominal differentiation of Africa into the colors on a colonial map, but its underlying geography consists of an unrelenting sameness.

Unlike Conrad's naturalization of Africa, Greene's vision of an indistinct continent does not fuse it to nature but rather makes it into a portable concept, a trope that can be exported to entirely different geographical contexts. Early in his text, Greene interrupts his account of the voyage from Liverpool to the West African coast with a brief section called "The Shape of Africa." In the travel narrative proper, Greene has just arrived in Dakar, Senegal, his point of embarkation on the continent. This narrative interlude, however, is filled with strangely disconnected impressions that have no explicit connection to Africa. Greene begins by recounting a memory of a distraught, lonely woman in a Leicester Square bar. The next memory-fragment details Greene's recollection of looking down at the lights of Berlin from a landing airplane. The third fragment recounts an episode from Paris: Greene arrives by train at the Gare St. Lazare, checks into a hotel, attends a meeting of the Communist Party in a Paris slum, and witnesses a man and a woman copulating under a streetlamp. The next paragraph takes us back to Greene's childhood and his memory of a dead dog in an English country crossing. Finally, we return to the woman in the Leicester Square bar.

> I watched from the other end of the bar; she wept and didn't care a damn; she embarrassed everybody; they cleared a space as if a fight was on and she sat there drinking gin and tonic and crying with empty chairs on either side; the barman kept on serving drinks at the other end. I thought for some reason even then of Africa, not a particular place, but a shape, a strangeness, a wanting to know. The unconscious mind is often sentimental; I have written "a shape," and the shape, of course, is roughly that of the human heart.
>
> (JWM 37)

The disconnected fragments of memory presented without explicit transition or interpretation seem of a piece with modernist narrative technique; any reader familiar with *The Waste Land* would surely not be put off by Greene's disjunctive narrative style. What is surprising, however, is that, under the title "The Shape of Africa," Greene includes impressions drawn exclusively from scenes of European modernity. Aside from the title of the section and its enigmatic reference to Africa in the final paragraph, the only other suggestion of Africa is in the first sentence: "A reminder of darkness: a girl at the Queen's Bar" (JWM 35). Greene implies that, following Conrad, one instinctively associates Africa with the concept of darkness, so that any "reminder of darkness" can in effect be a metaphorical equivalent to "Africa." What is this interlude doing in a travel narrative of Africa? How are we to connect these disjointed memories of urban modernity to the narrative present of his journey? One way to read Greene's memory-fragments is through a characteristically modernist trope: the disenchantment of the world brought about by the comprehensive exploration of its unknown spaces. As Andrew Thacker puts it, overlaying Europe on top of Africa recreates the "mapped" Africa anew, "giv[ing] the literary traveler the right to contest the scientific discourse of cartography with a more artistic or exotic discourse."[22] Because Africa is now known, the argument goes, the twentieth-century traveler has to empty the continent of its mapped spaces, thereby recreating it as a symbolic *terra incognita*.

Yet, initially at least, Greene does not remap the continent with stock scenes from the archive of African images. The episodes that Greene recalls suggest another one of Greene's keywords frequently associated with Africa throughout the narrative: "seediness." The darkness that Greene sees in the signifier "Africa" is not the primeval chthonic darkness of Conrad's novella but rather the darkness of the city, of modern sexuality, of evanescent mass culture. Greene is repeatedly disappointed by what he sees as the contamination of "authentic" Africa by the detritus of colonial institutions and modern consumerism. When he arrives in Freetown, Sierra Leone, a British colonial capital, Greene remarks of the British, "They had planted their seedy civilization and then escaped from it as far as they could. Everything ugly in Freetown was European" (*JWM* 38). Later, in the Liberian village of Kpangblamai, Greene is invited to the home of a chieftain's son, hearing that it is a " 'plenty plenty fine house' covered with pictures." Apparently expecting to see "native" artifacts, Greene is surprised by the following scene:

> The walls were papered thickly with old advertisements and photographs out of illustrated papers, most of them German or American. Over a chair made out of an old packing-case was an article by General Pershing on Youth; beautiful women showed their teeth brushed with Chlorodone, handsome men displayed their ready-made suitings, somebody wondered why she wasn't a social success, and a man in uniform denounced a clause of the Treaty of Versailles.
>
> (*JWM* 111)

In the heart of "darkest Africa," Greene finds that the alterity of the continent has already been papered over—literally—with the banality of mass-produced consumer culture. This contamination has in fact framed the entire expedition; returning to the coast from his journey into the interior, Greene comments pointedly, "The journey had begun and ended in a lorry in the stink of petrol" (*JWM* 223). Greene never seems to locate the Africa for which he searches. Perhaps this is both because the Africa he encounters is less an image than a screen, and what he finds projected onto this screen are nothing more nor less than the landscapes of European urbanized, mass-produced modernity, precisely that from which he was fleeing in his voyage. In addition to discovering such outward scenes of banality, Greene also finds a more inward, psychological projection: "But what had astonished me about Africa was that it had never been really strange....The 'heart of darkness' was common to us both. Freud has made us conscious as we have never been before of those ancestral threads which still exist in our unconscious mind to lead us back" (*JWM* 248).

Greene frankly admits that Africa is not a "place," but a "shape, a strangeness, a wanting to know." Africa represents desire itself, reflecting its enigmatic meaning back onto Greene's own consciousness and memory. The specificity of Africa is also lost in the interpretation of its "shape" as that of the universally "human heart." As the interlude suggests, the continent functions as a blankness that can accommodate any number of highly arbitrary representations. Because Africa means nothing specific, it can mean anything at all. Greene's projection of images of modernity onto the "shape of Africa" seems to be merely a variation on the conventional Victorian representation of Africa as the "dark continent." Yet alongside his projection of modernity onto the blank signifier of "Africa," Greene reveals a more particular sense of African geography than is suggested in the "Shape of Africa" episode. While discussing his motives for travel to Liberia, Greene comments on the difference between specific *places* within Africa and the space of the continent itself. "Africa" does not symbolize a particular image to Greene, but the concept of the image itself. "And when I say that to me Africa has always seemed an important image," writes Greene, "I suppose that is what I mean, that it has represented more than I could say" (*JWM* 20). Greene, however, acknowledges particular associations with places within the continent: "To the words 'South Africa' my reaction, I find, is immediate: Rhodes and the British Empire and an ugly building in Oxford and Trafalgar Square. After 'Kenya' there is no hesitation: 'gentleman farmers, aristocracy in exile and the gossip columns.' 'Rhodesia' produces: 'failure, Empire Tobacco,' and 'failure' again (*JWM* 20). Certainly, Greene's perception of specific places is narrowly confined to a British colonial epistemology, but these places are anchored to specific historical and political circumstances. Two Africas therefore emerge in Greene's discussion: an Africa of specific places—Rhodesia, Kenya, South Africa—located within late colonial modernity and, by contrast, a purely symbolic, homogeneous "Africa" that can be yoked to any meaning Greene sees fit to designate. Africa's specific geographical locales are modern but essentially European; Africa as a continental signifier, however, remains irredeemably unknowable in itself.

Greene embodies the peculiar doubleness with which many early-twentieth-century writers and intellectuals viewed Africa. On the one hand, the continent was a compendium of colonial territories, each of which emerged as an object of study and knowledge for explorers and colonists, therefore fulfilling the Enlightenment geographical imperative to move ever closer to a comprehensive knowledge of the world. On the other hand, once the continent was viewed in its totality, "Africa" was a transcendent "image" cut loose from any specific place, culture, or history, and thus free to reflect back visions of everyday life in the modern metropolis. Although an apparent contradiction, this separation of places-within-Africa from Africa itself typifies one common modernist response to Africa. Modernist writers record visions of Africa as a symbolically weighted place, but in making the imaginative journey to Africa, modernism tends to cut the continent loose from an actually existing geography, projecting any number of symbols onto the blank screen of the continent.

Hybrid Cartography: King Njoya's Map of Bamum

In many ways, Africa held a special place in the early-twentieth-century discourse of emergent globalization, as it was seen to stand in stark contrast to a more rapidly developing world. This worldview did not admit a specifically African modernity. Africa was "primitive," and any traces of modernity on the continent were attributed to either the inexorable advance of Western civilization, or, for less optimistic voices such as Greene's, the contamination of a primeval, pure world with the soiled artifacts of modern commodity culture. From the point of view of both aesthetic modernism and the cultural criticism of modernity, then, Africa functions as a hazy signifier reflecting back a negative image of the modern world. What is missing from these irreconcilable views of Africa are, of course, representations of space that come from cultures indigenous to the continent itself. With Picasso's masklike figures of *Demoiselles d'Avignon* as a signal example, African cultural artifacts only seem to find admission into the hallowed halls of modernist achievement through the side door of primitivism. As Colin Rhodes makes clear, "Primitivism describes a Western event and does not imply any direct dialogue between the West and its 'Others.' "[23] Recent criticism has been especially skeptical of the "African" influence on modernist writers and artists. Simon Gikandi identifies a persistent "puzzle" for critics of modernist art: "whether Africa has to be considered a categorical imperative in the theory and practice of modern artists or just a passing fad in the ideology of modernism."[24] Gikandi's question is a provocative one, yet its phrasing tilts the playing field unfairly: any consideration of Africa within the ideology of artistic or literary modernism will inevitably find its influence to be negative; modernism authored a version of itself that was defined in opposition to African otherness. Looking at modernism within the wider, more complex cultural processes of modernity and modernization, however, allows us to find a less one-sided argument.

If we abandon the "continental vision" of Africa as a homogeneous, purely symbolic space, we can see more clearly the specific histories and geographies of interactions between Western and African cultures, admitting the possibility of an African modernity that cannot be neatly collapsed into the process of Eurocentric globalization. These interactions are particularly—though by no means uniquely—complex in the former west African kingdom of Bamum, located in what is now north-central Cameroon. The kingdom had existed for nearly four hundred years by the time German explorers arrived in 1902. In the preceding decade, the king of Bamum, Ibrahim Njoya, had invented an Arabic-inspired alphabet for the Bamum language, and he subsequently authored a history of the kingdom.[25] A cultural reformer and sophisticated politician well before the arrival of German colonists, Njoya set about to preserve his own tribe's territorial and cultural autonomy in the face of the European scramble for African colonies. Njoya, writes Christraud Geary, "never lost sight of his goal: to maintain and consolidate the Bamum kingdom in face of external changes, turmoil, even intervention."[26] Geary acknowledges a central point about precontact indigenous societies: they were seldom unified and "whole" prior to European arrival. Njoya's kingdom did not simply fall from a prelapsarian state with the arrival of the Germans; his kingdom was already very much imbricated within a complex history, and his attempts to consolidate diverse communities through the invention of a language and the authoring of a tribal history can be seen as analogous to the formation of "imagined communities" that Benedict Anderson identifies with Western and "Creole" nationalisms.

Understanding the extent of European colonial power, Njoya initially followed a policy of accommodation and diplomacy with the German colonial administration. He was able to maintain some measure of autonomy even as the Germans undertook to establish rule in all parts of Cameroon.[27] At the outset of World War I, however, Germany began to recall many of its colonial bureaucrats and soldiers from Africa, and by 1915, the few remaining German residents in Bamum had left the kingdom.[28] In 1916, British troops temporarily occupied the area, which lay close to the demarcation between French and British colonial spheres of influence. In the face of such geopolitical uncertainty, Njoya appealed to King George V of Great Britain, sending the monarch a letter and map in order that Great Britain might recognize Bamum's autonomy and protect it from French conquest. In an introductory letter, Major-General C. W. Dobell assures its London recipients that the letter is "entirely spontaneous, the idea of it and its phraseology are [Njoya's] own" and that the accompanying map is "the handiwork of Njoya himself."[29] The letter to King George shows Njoya as a skilled diplomat, flattering the English while subtly asserting his own legitimacy and authority as ruler of Bamum.[30] He begins by thanking the English, who have "delivered me from the hands of the German [sic] who are men of darkness, who have no belongings, who are liars, who trouble the people continually."[31] He puts himself at the mercy of the British king, but does so by offering a symbolic gift of his own monarchical power: his ancestral throne and the two largest elephant tusks in the kingdom. The letter is signed "NJOYA. The 16th King of Bamum," legitimizing his rule by identifying the long, continuous history of its lineage.[32] The petition can certainly be read as a willing acquiescence to the least possible evil among the invading colonial powers. Yet it also shows an indigenous African ruler both savvy and courageous enough to engage in a diplomatic dialogue using the power of the written word.

Just as Njoya's petition to King George combines an insistence on cultural autonomy with an acknowledgment of Bamum's place in a larger geopolitical sphere, the production of his *lewa ngu*, or map of the kingdom, likewise merges elements of indigenous Bamum culture with European scientific methods of cartography. The map uses the Bamum alphabet and iconography, but it was produced using borrowed Western methods of survey. Before the German occupation of Bamum, Njoya had undertaken various mapmaking projects in order to consolidate his rule over the territory. As the historian Thomas J. Bassett speculates, however, the map sent to King George shows evidence that Njoya adopted methods learned from a German cartographer, Max Möisel.[33] Njoya's map of Bamum represents the kingdom as an empirically verifiable place on the earth, yet it in no way implies that the space is merely a small unit within the totality of a homogeneous global space. Western maps after the eighteenth century implicitly acknowledged the unitary and homogeneous quality of cartographic space by plotting each representation on a graticule of longitude and latitude. With this information, each map, at whatever scale, could be integrated with others to produce a scientifically verifiable and therefore accurate version of the world. Njoya's map, however, makes no claims to mimetic accuracy, instead organizing its space with more explicitly rhetorical purposes in mind. As Bassett notes, the map "is the product of a political transition in which Njoya used his mapmaking skills to safeguard the territorial claims of Bamum and to preserve his role as its traditional sovereign."[34] Although the survey was carefully monitored according to Western conventions, the production of the map itself did not need to reflect the discursive imperative of "scientific" accuracy.

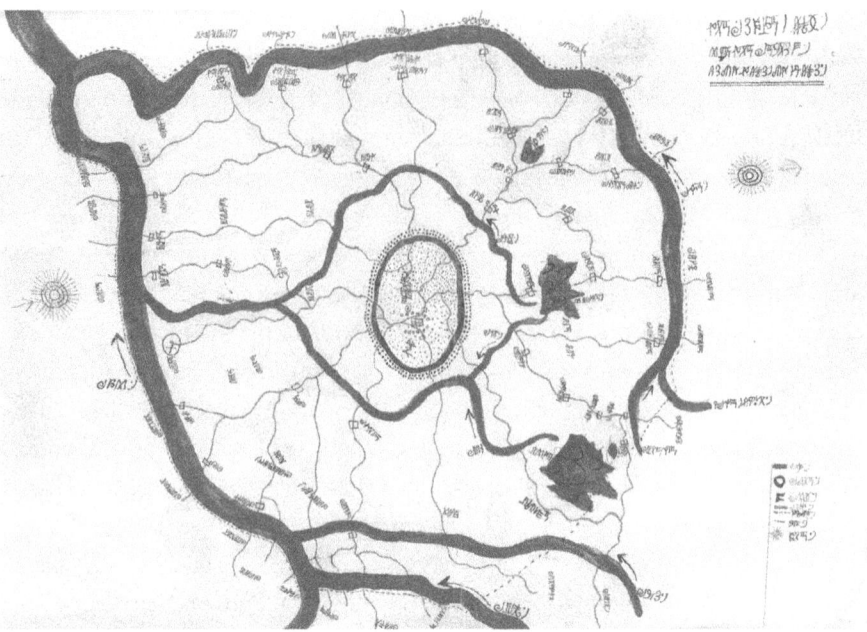

Figure 1.1. King Njoya's map of Bamum (London: Public Record Office: CO/649/7).
Courtesy of the National Archives, United Kingdom.

Njoya's map does not refer to the global space of latitude and longitude, yet the map itself presumes a systematic view of space. At a first glance, the map seems to embody Thongchai Winichakul's description of premodern indigenous cartographies of Siam (now Thailand): "In a premodern map, there was no inference that a spatial unit depicted was part of a spatial wholeness. There was no indication of the position of that unit on the earth's surface."[35] The concentric river systems, and the radial extension of the roads leading out of Fumban, suggest an ordering of space into an aesthetically coherent whole. Furthermore, the iconographic representations of the rising and setting sun place the local topography of Bamum into a broader cosmology. The map literally turns the Western understanding of space upside-down: the map is oriented to the south rather than the north, with the motion of the sun going leftward from east to west across the page. Though its production is rooted in the discourse of Western imperial cartography, the map itself makes no reference whatsoever to a colonial presence in the kingdom, implicitly dismissing the claims of European imperial powers. In an age when all credible maps became part of a global space through their plotting on a graticule of latitude and longitude, Njoya's map recognizes no such convention. Yet his map is an aesthetically coherent space. It represents the kingdom as a totality in itself, not simply a part of a larger global space. To layer the map of Bamum onto a map of the world would involve changing its space out of all recognition until the place represented on the map would cease to exist entirely. In effect, this is what eventually happened in Bamum after 1916: its political and territorial autonomy was not preserved by the French administration, and the kingdom eventually became an administrative district within the French colony of Cameroon. Njoya was exiled to Morocco, where he died in 1937, and his map was consigned to the dustbin of colonial history as a curious artifact, a museum piece.

Although the political disempowerment of Njoya—along with any number of indigenous elites in Africa and elsewhere—was certainly a complex and overdetermined process, we cannot underestimate the discursive power of Western representations of space in the legitimation of colonial rule. Because post-Enlightenment cartography had carved out a niche for itself as a scientifically produced, factually reliable form, its maps could be used to discredit whatever content was found in indigenous maps. "Modern geography," Winichakul writes, "had the potential to drive itself to usurp those properties of the indigenous knowledge, asserting itself as a new channel of message transmission. It . . . took advantage of the overlapping domains to make the indigenous language unstable, or ambiguous, and then proposed itself as a new way of signifying those terms."[36] Even as Njoya incorporates aspects of Western cartographic technique into the production and iconography of his map, its "indigenous" features relegate it to the status of a primitive artifact. The very elements that proclaim the cultural autonomy and identity of the kingdom of Bamum also ensure that the map will not be taken seriously by colonial authorities as a legitimate territorial claim. One senses this in the comment of a Colonial Office diplomat who treats Njoya as more of a curiosity than a sovereign ruler. Although his "remarkable invention of an alphabet" and his "skill as a mapmaker" are noted, he ultimately comments of Njoya's appeal to the king, "It would probably be best not to answer it."[37] The British can only recognize the claims of another Western power—in this case, France—to the territory of Bamum. Fearing a diplomatic row with an imperial rival, the Colonial Office ignored Njoya's appeal.

The dispute that Njoya asks King George to adjudicate is not so much a contest between European empires as a conflict between two paradigms of sovereignty and territory. Njoya's map is presented through a rhetoric of community and historical lineage rather than the internationally sanctioned discourse of professional survey and recognized boundary commissions. The territorial discourse that executes the "law" of colonial possession has no way of recognizing the autonomy of indigenous communities, and once again "legitimate" geography can only see Africa as a blank space, a continental void. This speaks to larger issues than imperial rivalries. Geography, according to Gearóid Ó Tuathail, "is not just a battle of cartographic technologies and regimes of truth; it is also a contest between different ways of envisioning the world."[38] King Njoya may have been on the losing side of this particular contest, but his attempt to translate a map of his kingdom into territorial, political, and cultural autonomy helps us to better understand how twentieth-century Africa could still be imaginatively excluded from globalized modernity. Politically, the Enlightenment geographical conception of Africa as a space of truth to be unveiled, mapped, and archived has enabled the kind of territorial control that inevitably extends political control to those who make the most precise maps. This Western view of space as static, inert, and finite has led to any number of border disputes in postcolonial Africa and around the world.[39] By contrast, the symbolic view of an undifferentiated, ahistorical continent carried to us through the "image-bites" of mass media throws up a scrim between Western eyes and the complex political, cultural, and historical conditions in twentieth- and twenty-first-century Africa. If nothing else, Njoya's example teaches us to be wary of totalizing pronouncements of globalization as a historically necessary end to a progressive evolution of geography. Too often, such assertions only reproduce attenuated, imprecise versions of the world's political geographies at scales far too small to offer any productive transcultural understandings.

Njoya's cartography of Bamum, when looked at as a primitive artifact, simply reinforces the power of post-Enlightenment cartography to claim epistemological priority on the totality of the earth's surface. Absent the rhetorical conventions of scientific mapping, Njoya's project seems to retain a tenuous claim on geographical truth. Thinking about Njoya's map as an artifact of a specifically African modernity, however, opens up a space of critique in which Western representations of the continent appear limited, at best. Amidst the totalizing project of post-Enlightenment cartography—which would bring Africa into a global order, by any means necessary—Njoya projects a qualitatively different space. This representation, while drawing from Western cartographical method, projects a place not so easily assimilated into a Eurocentric worldview. Moreover, Njoya's map and accompanying letter force us to rethink the reductive flattening of Africa into an undifferentiated continent. Instead of the impenetrable sameness of Marlow's "prehistoric earth" (*HD* 37), we are reminded that Africa not only has a history, it has innumerable histories. And these have unfolded not within the blankness of continental space but within the plentitude and immanence of local and regional *places*.

2. Region
Geddes, Forster, and the Situated Eye

<hr />

Modernist Chorography

This chapter explores a question confronted by both geography and fiction in the early twentieth century: if the decades-long fascination with empire and its global cartographies remade the world in the abstract, territorial image of the map, then what happens when this map-influenced consciousness returns to a more local scale? This question, I argue, is worked out largely through a new articulation of the region in both geography and fiction. One of the key challenges faced by the two figures I examine here, Patrick Geddes and E. M. Forster, is the desire to keep the region from being merely folded into a territorial nationalism that had become part and parcel of the drive for imperial conquest. If a subnational region could indeed be part of a larger global space, it would need to mediate between a scale of knowable human perception and the abstraction of cartographic overview. Both Geddes and Forster find possibilities for such perception through what I call a "situated eye," a perspective distant enough to survey a valley, town, or coastline, but still attached to a material, embodied human identity. For Geddes, particularly in his 1915 work, *Cities in Evolution*, this perspective proves to be a compromise between a disembodied Cartesian detachment and a participatory citizenship. In *Howards End*, Forster's 1910 novel, the narrative incorporation of a surveying view offers a structural device to fuse more abstract notions of space and spatiality with a conventionally realist narrative space. Both Geddes and Forster advocate a cartographic overview of space not as a consolidation of territory, however, but as a way to connect human perception to scales of community beyond the local. While Geddes is more explicitly antinational than Forster, their works point toward a reassertion of the region as a way to reconstruct the world as something other than a system of exclusive nation-states.

In the first decades of the twentieth century, both geography and literature were confronting the same problem that King Njoya addressed in his cartography of Bamum: how to represent a finite, knowable place in qualitative terms without reducing it to a set of coordinates on a map or a pawn in a geopolitical game of chess. This is difficult to do, as geography in its very definition ("earth-writing" or "earth-description") implies a global totality. Places, in this schema, become little more than fragments of a larger whole. This totality is often suggested through the use of various conventions: the cartographic inscription of latitude and longitude, for example, or the discursive reference to a larger, totalizing geographical field or system.[1] Njoya's map, by contrast, is more properly described as a *chorographical* document, a more tactile, localized, less "scientific" representation. Matthew Edney characterizes the distinction Ptolemy and other classical thinkers made between geography (earth-description) and chorography (region-description):

> Geography entailed the study of the world as a whole and of mapmaking (general or mathematical geography) and the listing of all of the world's constitutive regions, described by their broad physical, demographic, and economic attributes (descriptive or special geography). Chorography was the description of a particular region and its inhabitants without reference to the rest of the world and placed a great deal of emphasis on history (genealogy, chronology), antiquities, and topography; for very small areas, local folklore was used to distinguish one region from otherwise similar neighbors.[2]

Rather than define his kingdom quantitatively as a circumscribed territory within a homogeneous spatial field, Njoya's map evokes a deep, qualitative sense of place radiating outward from an organic social and political center. This chorographical document, moreover, combines a mode of representation with a particular scale of space. Bamum, in Njoya's map, adheres to the traditional definition of region: "a large tract of land; a country; a more or less defined portion of the earth's surface" (*OED*). A region, in this sense, is, above all, a *knowable* space: one that has an organic coherence and identity distinct from places exterior to it. It is a space more expansive than a settlement or town, but its totality can be subjectively known and experienced.

Njoya's map of Bamum is no traditional chorography, however. Even as the map itself employs a visual rhetoric of self-sufficiency and autonomy, Njoya's letter to King George acknowledges precisely the opposite: that the kingdom is in fact subordinate to a Western territorial order of space. Understanding that Bamum's only chance for survival is to find its way into a "proper" cartography of one or another imperial power, Njoya realizes that maintaining the sovereignty of his kingdom is likely a futile project. As much as he wishes to project Bamum as an immanent, self-present place in his map, the context of its production—a struggle between two empires over territorial boundaries—forces two apparently incompatible views of the world together. While Njoya represents Bamum as a rooted, sovereign, self-sustaining region independent of any global totality, it is precisely the existence of this totality—the earth as a finite territory—that forces Njoya's mapmaking in the first place. (In this respect, Njoya's regionalism isn't far off from European and American literary and artistic conceptions of regionalism in the early twentieth century.) The problem of a modernist chorography, then, is this: how can place be represented in all of its tactile, rooted placeness without fictitiously or naïvely repressing the larger, abstract spaces against which the region is necessarily defined? Far from being a sphere of immanent self-identity, regional representation is necessarily formed in response to a perceived "world." Speaking of literary regionalism, Tom Lutz argues that regional representation is by definition characterized by its "cosmopolitan investments," its themes of "the relation of different groups to ongoing technological, economic, and social change, or, in other words, the relation of the region to the rest of the world."[3] By this definition, regionalism could not exist before the advent of widespread networks of technology, information, and commodity exchange, those features that characterize the interconnectedness of the modern world system. Regionalism, in other words, always implies the question: a region of what? After the late-nineteenth-century establishment of a closed world, local chorographies would always and necessarily be figures upon a wider *geo*graphical ground.

This chapter takes up two imaginative projects that represent the localized, embodied region within the abstract totality of the world: the work of the Scottish polymath intellectual Patrick Geddes, particularly in his volume *Cities in Evolution* (1915), and the novel *Howards End* (1910) by the English writer E. M. Forster. Though Geddes and Forster worked in very different intellectual realms, both might be said to address the question: how can lived human experience be both modern and located? That is, how can humans be a part of an interconnected

social world while still retaining an organic bond with specific places? Both thinkers view the region—Geddes explicitly, Forster implicitly, as I will argue—as the
largest possible scale of space that can accommodate both visions. Significantly,
both maintained a skepticism toward the territorial nation-state as the primary
institution of cultural and political identification. Geddes' conception of the
region was designed to introduce a structural similarity between cultures that
bridged what he saw as artificial divisions and rivalries—for him, the ideal world
system would effectively be a series of free regional municipalities, centered on a
dynamic city centers with self-sustaining relationships to surrounding towns and
rural districts. Forster, on the other hand, did aim to recover a kind of English
national feeling, but it was one that was directly opposed to a more expansive,
imperial model of Britishness. Forster's regionalism tries to become a nationalism but fails precisely because the localized *Gemeineschaft* of the region cannot
be stretched far enough to encompass the more expansive territory of the nation-
state.

What Geddes and Forster both offer, however, is an imaginative frame for the
thinking of the world and its constituent parts. These metageographies, based
upon the idea of the region, attempt to reconcile the existence of a global totality with knowable spaces of community. In an age when imperial competition
between European nation-states began to fuse territorial demarcation with cultural difference—particularly in the run-up to World War I and its aftermath at
Paris and Versailles in 1919—Geddes and Forster remake the image of the world
precisely by focusing on its landscapes in all of their immediacy and immanence.
As if to combat a world too often represented from a detached, God's-eye perspective, both Geddes and Forster invest a central role in what I call the "situated
eye": a view from above that is both detached and embodied. Most notably, both
writers foreground places of height—for Geddes, an urban tower, and for Forster,
a hilltop—from which a literal survey may be made of a surrounding region. The
immediacy of the visible region can become a catalyst for an imaginative projection of larger scales. As one of the first textbooks of regional survey described this
methodology:

> If we can stand upon an eminence and say "Athens is straight over there" or
> "Cape Town is precisely in that direction" these places with all their associa-
> tions immediately become real to us. We gain a vivid impression of the fact
> that they do exist on this same earth and have a geographical relationship
> to the intimate details of our own town or village as depicted on the centre
> of the chart.[4]

The resonances between the situated perspectives of Geddes and Forster and the methodology of regional survey geography highlight the constituent role of the imagination within the process of visual observation. Seeing, in other words, was not simply a Cartesian disembodiment pressed into the service of a utilitarian empiricism. Rather, looking at what was close by could lead to the imaginative perception of *in*visible (or perhaps more accurately, *extra*visible) places. The region could give a located image of place, but rather than dissolve into an abstract space at its horizonal edges, regional perception instead prompted the imagining of *other* places. Moreover, the further one's eye moved from the immediacy of the local, the more uncertain and hazy observation would become. In that marginal haze where empirical observation turns more self-consciously into aestheticized imagination, we can find a particularly fertile zone of geographical modernism.

Reconciling Regionalisms

At one point in the middle of *Howards End*, Margaret Schlegel gazes upon two maps of Africa in the office of her fiancé, Henry Wilcox. After gaining entry into the inner sanctum of his offices at the Imperial and West African Rubber Company, Margaret stares up at the source of Henry's mysterious business endeavors, hoping to make some sense of "the formlessness and vagueness that one associates with Africa" (*HE* 167). Yet, what Margaret discovers ultimately fails to illuminate, revealing, in addition to more "formlessness and vagueness," a fundamental homogeneity associated with the spaces of commercial imperialism:

> She found only the ordinary table and Turkey carpet, and though the map did depict a helping of West Africa, it was a very ordinary map. Another map hung opposite, on which the whole continent appeared, looking like a whale marked out for blubber.... She might have been at the Porphyrion, or Dempster's Bank, or her own wine-merchant's. Everything seems just alike these days.
>
> (*HE* 167)

The cartographic space upon which Margaret gazes is merely an abstraction without any aura of particularity, made even more banal by its appearance among the quotidian objects in Henry's office. Later in the same chapter, after returning from London to Howards End, she reflects on the maps she had seen in the office: "She remembered again that ten square miles are not ten times as wonderful as one square mile, that a thousand square miles are not practically the same as heaven" (*HE* 172). Margaret's response to the maps of Africa is also Forster's rejoinder to an imperial sensibility that measures national well-being through a tabulation of the square miles under the rule of the Union Jack or the comforting glance at the wide swaths of pink that dominate a global map. The map may measure the extent of Britain, but it misses the truth: space may be tallied and commodified, but through this process, it becomes eviscerated, deadened, a "whale marked out for blubber." Margaret yearns for a proper scaling of space, a space recovered from the flattened abstractions of cartography to be perceived on a decidedly more human, sensory scale.

While apparently very different at first glance, literary and geographical regionalism both answer to Margaret's desire for a re-scaling of space. Literary regionalism was, in the nineteenth and early twentieth centuries, associated with places, landscapes, and dialects that, if not explicitly rural, are certainly seen in some opposition to or distinction from metropolitan urban centers. We are more likely to see regionalism in Cather's Great Plains or Hardy's Wessex than in Dos Passos's Manhattan or Woolf's London, though particularities of place and location are arguably no less important for the latter two metropolitan writers. Literary regionalism, however, typically involves its mediation by an urban or cosmopolitan observer-translator. As Donna Campbell describes of American regional fiction, "The narrator is typically an educated observer from the world beyond who learns something from the characters while preserving a some-times sympathetic, sometimes ironic distance from them. The narrator serves as mediator between the rural folk of the tale and the urban audience to whom the tale is directed."[5] Regionalism thus identifies an ethnographic space often confirmed in its difference, according to Tom Lutz, by the common trope of "the visitor who frames, interrupts, and/or invades the scene."[6] The visitor from the city who enters into the locales of regional fiction is generally portrayed as being alienated in some form (though frequently unaware of this alienation), and the particularity and authenticity of the regional "place" is held to have some transformative, meliorating power. Regional fiction, furthermore, could merge ethnographic observation with armchair tourism. Writing of nineteenth-cen-tury British regional fiction, K. D. M. Snell notes that regional writing became a vehicle for the "internal tourism" of the British Isles. "By the mid-nineteenth century," Snell writes, "at the same time as a proliferation of 'hand books for travelers,' regional fiction was becoming one of the most important means by which regional landscapes were distinguished from a generalized countryside."[7] Literary and artistic regionalism, then, can be seen as thoroughly modern genres whose internal structures and external circumstances of readership can both be linked inextricably to the rise of the metropolitan *Gesellschaft* and its crowds of consumers (one of whom might very well be Margaret Schlegel), seeking a nostalgic authenticity outside of the abstracted, homogenized space of mass-produced, urbanized modernity.

Different, yet related coordinates of regionalism emerge in British geographical discourse of the early twentieth century as the movement toward the methodology of regional survey took hold in the academy. As H. C. Darby remembers of his days at Cambridge in the 1920s, many believed that "the 'core of geography' lay in 'regional synthesis,' in which the facts of geology, climate, agriculture, industry and so on could, by some artistry, be fused into the delineation of 'the personality of a region.'"[8] The regional survey movement in early-twentieth-century geography unequivocally makes claims toward the qualitative representation of place. Certainly, descriptions of places that centered upon the region had been a feature of many travel narratives from the seventeenth century onward, but to keep with the need for geography to establish its credibility as a legitimate disciplinary field, such localized descriptions would need to be integrated into a rigorous, systematic methodology. In Britain, this was largely done through the transformation of "description" into "survey." British regionalists adapted the French enterprise of *géographie humaine* as practiced by Paul Vidal de la Blache, who sought through geography "a more synthetic knowledge of the physical laws governing our earth and...the physical beings which inhabit it."[9] The British regional survey movement worked toward a similar kind of synthesis between nature and culture, its methodology rooted in empirical perception and observation of topography.[10] The importance of a topographic overview was paramount to regional geography's emphasis on the interrelationships between local knowledge and national (and international) citizenship. While the regional survey movement was unquestionably interested in the systematized description of topography, the logical end of regional geography's interest in the nature-culture relationship was to focus on centers of human settlement. The Scotsman Patrick Geddes addressed these issues explicitly in his 1915 treatise, *Cities in Evolution*. In this text, Geddes applied the biologistic sense of evolution to bridge the gulf between nature and culture. Cities were the evolutionary product, Geddes claimed, of the human interaction with the land. Geddes thus imagined geographical regionalism as "the study of town in country, and of country in town, and these through past and present alike," an approach that would, he hoped, "end...the ancient feud, the artificial separation of town and country" (*CE* 343). Geddes' insights led to the development of the regional planning movement, which moved beyond the merely academic to determine much of the policy of local governance in Britain from the 1920s onward.

At a glance, then, literary and geographical regionalisms, broadly speaking, seem to differ in this sense: literary regionalism tends to be positioned with an ambivalence toward the urban, metropolitan sphere, while geographical region-alism increasingly incorporates the city into its conception of regional identity. Geographical regionalism, however, could be put to different ideological uses. David Matless distinguishes between "planner-preservationist" and "organicist" regionalisms. Planner-preservationist regionalism, ascendant during the inter-war period, advocated the sensible use of governmental planning to avoid the unplanned sprawl located in both the Victorian city and twentieth-century subur-bia. As Matless explains, "Preservationists argued that in the nineteenth century an attitude of laissez-faire had destroyed the town, and the twentieth century was destroying the country."[11] Organicist regionalism, on the other hand, rejects the bureaucratized modernity of the planner-preservationist, but does so from the scientific perspective of physical geography and geology. "Organicists," Matless writes, "build up the region from geology and topography as a counter-modern unit."[12] Rather than look down upon the landscape from the point of view of dis-embodied Cartesian mastery, organicists saw themselves as proceeding from the very soil upward. A whiff of environmental determinism can be detected here, as nature is seen to be the prime mover for the life and character of a particular region, including its cultural, social, and economic structures. While these two notions of regionalism seem superficially opposed, both in fact share a modern, rationalist epistemology with respect to problems of culture, tradition, and land-scape: planner-preservationist regionalism with its faith in the political structures of democratic governance, and organicist regionalism with its "natural" founda-tion in the physical sciences. Like literary and artistic regionalisms, then, regional-ism in geographical discourse cannot be easily squared with an insular, localist, antimodern ideology. Rather, both types of regionalism stage the region as a scale at odds with (if sometimes claiming to speak for) the nation-state. Regionalism argues for a more immediate form of subjectivity, embodiment, and citizenship located within a knowable, culturally self-contained geographical scale.

According to Matless, the distinction between planner-preservationist and organicist outlooks takes hold from the 1920s onward, eventually becoming central to both cultural and policy debates during the post–World War II era of national reconstruction in Britain. Thinking retrospectively of various early-twentieth-century regionalisms on the planner-preservationist/organicist continuum, however, helps us to see representations of regional identity decid-edly within the matrix of modernity. Planner-preservationist regionalism speaks to the potential for regional representation to veer toward picturesque tourism, while also acknowledging the impulse to provide governmental regulation of green space and undeveloped "nature." As Matless puts it, planner-preservationist regionalism "saw the region as a unit of modern planning."[13] Organicist regionalism, by contrast, grants a certain political and cultural autonomy to the region in explicit opposition to the bureaucratic state. It would be wrong to suggest that organicism was a wholly antimodern point of view, however. The argument for a self-sustaining regional identity often derived its authority from modern advancements in the physical sciences, particularly geology, horticulture, and agriculture. One argument for a geological regionalism makes a direct connection between natural and cultural particularity, asserting that "the rocks of England speak a different language among one another, just as did the men."[14] As Matless described it, organicist regionalism used science as a way to argue for a particularity that could in fact lead to the re-enchantment of nature. In this sense, organicist regionalism shares much in common with contemporary bioregionalist movements, which, according to Greg Garrard, "promote decentralization of the economy, in the form of regional diversification and self-sufficiency."[15] Organicist regionalism likewise celebrated local biological and cultural particularity, but in a way that engaged directly with modern political and social institutions.

An overview of Geddes' work in *Cities in Evolution* would suggest that he could safely be classed a planner-preservationist—after all, his volume is subtitled *An Introduction to the Town Planning Movement*—while Forster's romanticization of the agrarian folkways of Hertfordshire in *Howards End* would seem to brand him as a precursor to organicist regionalism. Looking closely at both, however, this distinction appears less certain. First of all, the planner Geddes appears decidedly organicist in his foundational reliance upon both biology and geology, both of which provide the raw materials out of which cultural regions grow and evolve. Forster, on the other hand, appeals to the planner-preservationist desire to arrest the unchecked growth of "Suburbia" while at the same time providing the urbanized lower middle-classes (what John Carey metonymically identifies as the "clerks") with the opportunity to gain access to unspoiled patches of nature.[16] Seen this way, Geddes' geography and Forster's fiction are part of the same cultural debates about the fate of locality and particularity in an abstract global space. Both offer tentative answers to Margaret Schlegel's antipathy toward the gridded, quantified space of imperial cartography and cultural homogenization. Moreover, Geddes and Forster, while understanding the region in a thoroughly modern context, resist the urge to transpose regionalism with nationalism. Their peculiar blends of planner-preservationism and organicism avoid the elevation of a particular region as a site for an authentic national identity. Each offers a way to think about the world less as a jigsaw puzzle of national territories on a two-dimensional cartographic surface but instead as a series of localities that retain a three-dimensional, sensate immanence.

Synthetic/Synoptic

In a retrospective essay recounting the development of geography in Britain between the wars, H. C. Darby recalls that "the adjective 'synthetic' became a common one in geographical writing."[17] Within the subdiscipline of regional geography, "synthesis" denoted a quasi-holistic view of a knowable space, wherein different modes of inquiry could meet and combine, including geology, agricultural sciences, climatology, sociology, and history. The early-twentieth-century geographical method of "regional synthesis" owed much to Geddes (who was described by the regionalist C. C. Fagg in 1928 as "the main spring of our river").[18] The idea of synthesis (from the Greek "putting with" or "placing with") is very closely related to a term that Geddes uses early in *Cities in Evolution*. Citing Aristotle as the "founder of civic studies," Geddes recalls Aristotle's insistence upon "seeing our city with our own eyes. He urged that our view be truly *synoptic*...a seeing of the city, and this as a whole; like Athens from its Acropolis, like city and Acropolis together—the real Athens—from Lycabettos and from Piraeus, from hilltop and from sea. Large views in the abstract...depend upon large views in the concrete" (*CE* 13–15, author's italics). If "synthetic" is "placed together," then "synoptic" is, of course, "seen together."[19] The prefix "syn-" carries a meaning of simultaneity, "at-onceness" but it also suggests the experiential and situated rather than the abstract and disembodied. Synoptic vision, for Geddes, was a way to literally open one's eyes to the world without the prejudices and filters of theories, systems, or narrow disciplinary perspectives. Geddes' synoptics also suggest an epistemological standpoint that is at once ocularcentric but also anti-Cartesian. Certainly, Geddes unquestionably privileges vision as the most efficacious of the senses. This vision, however, is attached not to a disembodied God's-eye perspective but to an embodied citizen-subject in a particular location.[20]

The perspective of this situated eye was best employed from some height—usually from a hilltop, promontory, or tower. From this elevated point of view, the seeing subject could, ideally, take stock of her surroundings: the history of a town as illustrated by the diverse architectural styles and street plans, the organization of industry through the locations of factories and ports, the connections to other locales through rail and road networks, and the surrounding countryside with its particular topography and land uses. This, to Geddes, was the essence of regional synthesis: to see all of this at once in its concrete and particular immediacy. This fundamental scene—seeing one's surroundings from a point of height—tells us much about Geddes' conception of the region. For Geddes, the region is less a clearly demarcated geographical space than a transdisciplinary, transhistorical mode of knowing. Geddes imagines a regionalism in a distinctly material and historical context, more interested in the interrelationships of nature and society than in a retreat from society into nature. Geddes' regionalism was also an out-ward-looking philosophy in this sense: if regions, in all of their particularity, represent different evolutionary adaptations to their surroundings, they nonetheless share the same structural features—a kind of common genetic ancestry. In an age when cultural difference was literally inscribed onto the map, Geddes proposed an entirely different view of the world: one in which regions shared an isomorphic sameness across national, cultural, and linguistic boundaries. Ultimately, Geddes' structuralist regionalism regarded an active civic consciousness more highly than a predetermined subjection to one's nation-state. Particularly in the wake of World War I, Geddes saw the nation-state as an obstacle, rather than a path, to a rational, humane modernity.

In lieu of a comprehensive treatment of Geddes' many intellectual projects, I will discuss two particular icons important to Geddes' conceptions of the region: the Outlook Tower in Edinburgh and his template document of regional inquiry, the diagram of the valley section. The most widely acknowledged and immediately visible legacy of Geddes' thought is the Outlook Tower in Edinburgh. In 1892, Geddes converted a disused five-story tower into what he called a "Civic Observatory and Laboratory," a public building designed to educate its visitors in the different realms of social and geographical space to which they belonged. Inspired by his earlier work at the Paris Exposition of 1889, Geddes envisioned the Outlook Tower as a kind of permanent exhibition for the public, an interdisciplinary museum treating issues in "meteorology, history, geography, anthropology, geology, physics, chemistry, astronomy, and economics."[21] Geddes preferred visitors to begin at the top of the tower and move downward through the tower's five stories, each of which contained a separate exhibit oriented toward a distinct spatial scale. At its apex, the tower had a domed camera obscura through which visitors could see projected views of the surrounding landscape on a wide table. Beneath the camera obscura was a parapet offering a 360-degree prospect of Edinburgh and the surrounding region. Descending the tower, the visitor would see exhibits on Edinburgh, Scotland, English-language cultures, Europe, and the World. The Outlook Tower maps the participating subject in concentric geographical scales,

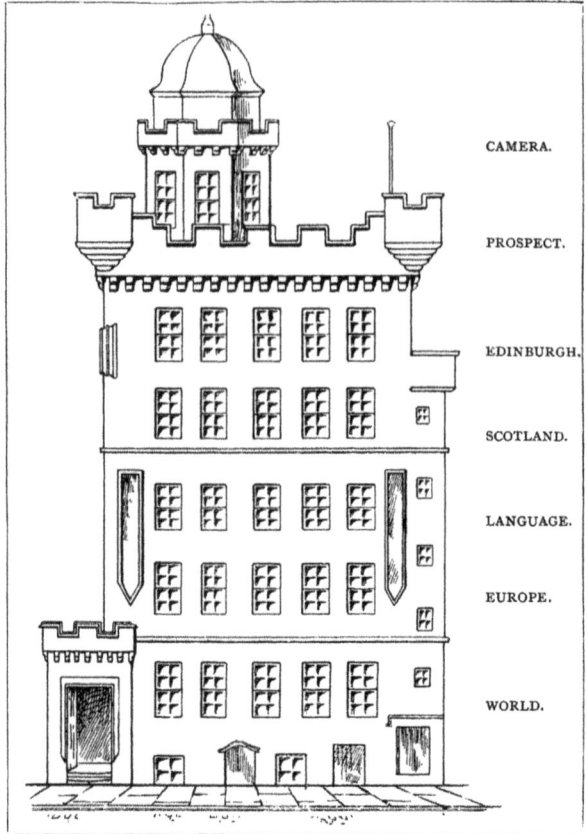

CAMERA.

PROSPECT.

EDINBURGH.

SCOTLAND.

LANGUAGE.

EUROPE.

WORLD.

Figure 2.1. Geddes' diagram of the Outlook Tower, from *Cities in Evolution* (1915).

moving from the immediate visual apprehension of one's urban and regional environment through widening spatial realms before emerging into the Edinburgh
street with, Geddes hoped, a newfound sense of one's local *and* global citizenship. As he wrote in his volume on urban planning and design, *Cities in Evolution*,
Geddes wished to impress upon visitors "the primacy of the civic and social outlook, intensified into local details with all the scientific outlooks of a complete
survey; yet all in contacts with the larger world, and these successively in enlarging
social zones, from that of the prospect outwards" (*CE* 325).

Geddes' assumption that regional citizenship begins with the "prospect" and
moves outward into more abstract social zones suggests the primary importance
of the visual apprehension of landscape, one of the most common contexts for
the representation of the pastoral. For Geddes, however, the landscape view is less
an ethnographic gaze of the disembodied tourist than an initial mapping of the

viewing subject within society. At its apex, a camera obscura projects an image of the surrounding landscape on a large table, which Geddes could then use in his lectures to visitors. By abstracting a "frame" from the landscape and display- ing its image on a flat surface, Geddes indeed turned the urban environment into an object of aesthetic reflection. As Geddes suggests, the view from the camera obscura "harmonizes the striking landscape, near and far, and this with no small element of the characteristic qualities of the best modern painting" (*CE* 321). The view through the camera obscura was, first and foremost, an aesthetic and emotional experience that more easily rendered the world "visual and concrete" (*CE* 321). Yet the experience of apprehending scenes from the region as objects of beauty was a necessary precursor to the desire for participation in the urban and regional *civitas*. Geddes ultimately wishes the viewer to descend the tower and apply her knowledge to the particular problems of the city-region. This use of landscape is quite different than the disembodied ruling gaze that W. J. T. Mitchell ascribes to "imperial landscapes" or that Mary Louise Pratt associates with "see- ing man."[22] With the movable camera obscura intended for pedagogical as well as aesthetic purposes, the landscape from the Outlook Tower is intended to be a dynamic view that is subject to continual reframings. Moreover, aesthetic appre- ciation is not the sole end of one's gaze on the landscape; rather, it is the *first* step toward a more participatory citizenship.[23] Literal sight is only a precursor to a con- ceptual and historical survey that layers broader spaces onto the local and regional as the visitor descended through the successive floors of the tower. As Geddes puts it, the true citizen-reformer would need to transcend the limited perspectives of the disciplines and instead "recognize and utilize all points of view" with an epis- temological approach that "must include at once the scientific and, as far as may be, the artistic presentment of the city's life: it must base upon these an interpreta- tion of the city's course of evolution in the present: it must increasingly forecast its future possibilities; and thus it may arouse and educate citizenship" (*CE* 320–321). The prospect of a city and its surrounding region was not to be solely indulged in for picturesque pleasure; rather, the visceral, direct apprehension of landscape was meant to provide the viewer with a cognitive visual map onto which subsequent inquiries and practices must necessarily return.[24]

In this constant re-visioning of the image of the city and its surrounding region, Geddes saw a dynamic that was, as the title of his volume indicates, evolutionary. The notion of regions as evolutionary organisms was fundamental in Geddes' phi- losophy, though not in a strictly Darwinian sense. As David Matless has pointed out, Geddes blended Darwinian natural selection with Lamarckian environmental determinism into a dialectical philosophy that "insist[ed] on an active adaptation of organism to environment."[25] Geddes' idea of evolution, continues Matless, was "a spiral, moving ever upward but, with a consistent meander, ever renewing the same pattern, the old recurring in ever new forms."[26] In the opening chapter of his *Cities in Evolution*, Geddes uses the metaphor of the weaver's loom to suggest a tangled complexity to the process of urban evolution: "The patterns here seem simple, there intricate, often mazy beyond our unraveling, and all well-nigh are changing…these very webs are themselves anew caught up to serve as threads again, within new and vaster combinations" (*CE* 4–5). But this is no detached science; citizens are both implicated within this weave and possess the power to modify and transform it: "Yet within this labyrinthine civicomplex there are no mere spectators. Blind or seeing, inventive or unthinking, joyous or unwilling—each has still to weave in, ill or well, and for worse if not for better, the whole thread of his life" (*CE* 5). In his belief in the evolutionary development of cities and their constituent regions, Geddes imagines urbanization itself as an organic, natural process rather than as something conceptually opposed to the idyllic, unspoiled "nature" of the countryside. Geddes' view on the nature of regions and on the role that nature plays within regions can be seen with reference to one of his favorite heuristic tools, the valley section.

In *The Coming Polity*, a 1917 volume that he coauthored with Victor Branford, Geddes identifies adjoining river valleys as a fundamental structure in the organization of regions. The authors advise would-be regional surveyors to begin by making a longitudinal section of a pair of adjoining river valleys. "We have here," write Geddes and Branford, "one of the most characteristic pieces of earth structure" (*CP* 81). Existing river valleys serve as a multilayered text allowing the regionalist to interpret historical development through the dispersal of human activity and occupation among the descending sections of the valley. The forested summits of the hills or mountains give rise to mining and hunting; beneath these, shepherds and their flocks dot the "pastoral hillsides"; beneath these are the "scattered arable crofts" and the "sparsely dotted hamlets" leading to the "small upland village" (*CP* 88). Downward, the surveyor reaches a prosperous foothill village containing a railway terminus, then onward to broad expanses of agricultural land, the market town, and the "larger country-town at the tidal limit of a…navigable river" (*CP* 88). Finally, as Geddes and Branford conclude, the valley opens out to a river estuary "where rises the smoke of a great manufacturing city, a world-market in its own way" (*CP* 88–89). While the authors acknowledge the existence of "wide departures" from this scheme, they emphasize the "considerable conformity" in this pattern throughout the world. The landscape is both synchronic and diachronic: we see both the relationship between communities in the present day and are given intimations of the long sweep of historical and cultural development. As we descend through Geddes' valley section, we are led forward through history on a local geographical scale, almost as if we were experiencing Marlow's voyage up the Congo in reverse.

The valley section was to be used to gain a synoptic and historical understanding of one's region, which would ideally promote a citizenship oriented toward both heightened consciousness and practical reform. Geddes wished to infuse this newfound sensibility into the material, cultural, and spiritual life of a region, where it could be put to use in contexts ranging from the management of water supply to the planning of civic festivals. Certainly, Geddes wishes to recapture the metaphysical importance of the urban center of a region in a way that the cathedral cities of the premodern age functioned. At times, this comes close to yet another variation of nostalgia so common in modernity's valuation of the pastoral as a "lost" age, as in the following criticism of a society of contracts and self-interest: "And must not the rustic, the vital, the ethical—in short, the regional outlook, as we use that term—increasingly supplement the recent and present too purely urban outlook with its mechanical, venal, and legalistic point of view, which is, and so long has been, alone predominant in our politics, in our education, and even in our science?" (CP 247). Geddes, however, does not wish to escape to the rustic simplicity of the countryside, or reverse the flow of history. As suggested by his own tireless efforts in suggesting schemes, plans, and reforms, Geddes' regionalism was of considerable practical value. The nostalgic contemplation of nature, for Geddes, was only useful if it led to a plan for better living in the here and now.

The pastoral values of Geddes also differ significantly from many early-twentieth-century representations in their refusal to be co-opted toward the ideological aims of ethnic and cultural nationalism. Geddes' regional epistemology is, at best, ambivalent toward nationalism and decidedly opposed to statism—there is a floor of the Outlook Tower devoted to Scotland, and a floor devoted to the Anglophone world, but there is no mention of Great Britain or the United Kingdom. In fact, the pastoral sense that Geddes wishes to promote in the idea of the region is explicitly opposed to the usurpation of cities by the nation-state. "The modern State," Geddes and Branford write, "has taken over and absorbed into itself as much as it could grasp of the heritage that properly belongs to its constituent cities" (CP 150). Geddes insisted on looking at imperial capitals such as London as both world cities and regional centers. Imaginatively approaching London as the port city of the Thames valley certainly helps explain why it became the imperial capital of Great Britain but it also links it historically and geographically to the Cotswolds, Oxford, Reading, and other smaller, more *heimlich* regional locales. By approaching the metropolis regionally, "we are prepared to understand and appreciate the legend of the imperial capital, the manner of its growth and the vogue of its being, without letting it overpower us" (*CP* 169).

Murdo Macdonald refers to Geddes' guiding political philosophy as a "practical internationalism."[27] It might seem odd to refer to someone who thought of his field of action in terms of the knowable, viewable spaces of city and region as an "internationalist." What Macdonald suggests, however, is that Geddes saw regions as isomorphic geographical and cultural spaces whose general laws could apply to Edinburgh as well as to London, to Montpellier, France as well as to Madras, India (all cities in which Geddes worked). The recognition of a deep structure in Geddes' regionalism supersedes a competitive imperial nationalism based upon ideas of cultural and racial difference, a political condition that Geddes saw as *un*sustainable. The reconstruction of Europe along regionalist principles, Geddes hoped, would discourage future wars between nation-states. As he writes during World War I, regionalism presents "a very different view of Europe and its politics from that of the warring empires—its seven Romes instead of one. Deep in the hearts of those who are responsible for the policies of these seven Romes there must needs be doubt whether this is a state which can possibly be stable. Can seven such centres of empire co-exist permanently?"[28] Cultural identities based upon difference, Geddes suggests, lead inexorably to war. A sustainable peace, by contrast, could only be brought about by seeing fundamental structural similarities beneath differences of language and custom. If our first inclination might be to dismiss Geddes' idea of the "evolutionary" region as quaintly anachronistic in its quasi-mystical organicism and its unrelenting structuralism, we would do well to put his ideas back in their early-twentieth-century European context. Geddes' philosophy, both regionalist and internationalist, remains an underexplored model of citizenship within the frame of industrialized modernity and without the exclusions of territorial nationalism.

For all of its "artistry" (to borrow H. C. Darby's somewhat dismissive description), Geddesian regional synthesis had more difficulty imagining an embodied consciousness behind its ocular perspective. While rejecting a completely detached Cartesian view, Geddes' synoptic approach does not particularly concern itself with the affective terms through which individual subjects, in their gendered, raced, classed, and nationalized particularity, experienced place and space. Geddes' philosophy of change presumed that individuals and, consequently, groups would act in rational self-interest based upon the evidence of the eyes, relinquishing parochial or naïve attachments to ethnocultural nationalisms. And while Geddes' ethic of rational regional planning found its way into much post–World War II policy, both in Britain and around the world, the appeal of territorial nationalism remained a central force in world politics. Rather than dismissing nationalism as an atavistic, irrational political fetish, could a regional view instead transform the nation into a more humane and just community? Returning to Margaret Schlegel's encounter with the map of Africa, could a modernist regional chorography reconstitute an anti-imperial England in danger of being flattened by its own two-dimensional perceptions of the world?

House/Region/Nation

In his incisive reading of *Howards End*, Andrew Thacker sees a similarly synthetic view of geographical locality, though one not so easily separated from national identity. Forster's representation of idyllic rural spaces such as the Dorset hills, the wych-elm at Howards End, or the area around Oniton in Shropshire "has a dual function: first, as a resistance to the flux of modernity symbolized by the city; second, as a synecdoche for the national space of England itself."[29] In this formulation, Forster might seem to be in line with a more conventional pastoral regionalism, which locates the true heart of the nation in a particular local landscape. "However," Thacker notes, "neither of these aspects can avoid the movements of modernity, for both concern not just enclosed spaces but the borderlands around them."[30] Villages are overrun by motorcars, forests give way to suburbs, and fields are riven by paved roads and streetlamps. As Thacker recognizes, Forster's pastoral England has been irrevocably compromised by the homogenizing spatial imperatives of what Forster simply calls "flux," which appears in various guises as acquisitive imperialism, commercial capitalism, new modes of transportation, and unchecked urban and suburban development. By yoking these various components of modernity under a common signifier, Forster invites us to see spatial resonances between them, many of which are concentrated in the Wilcox family. Henry's mercenary view of land leads to both a dispassionate, commercial valuation of Howards End as well as an objectified view of Africa as nothing more than a store for natural resources. The very motor cars that Henry fetishizes are of a piece with the accelerating expansion of London's suburban ring. Henry is an example of the "Imperial" type, which Forster describes as "a destroyer. He prepares the way for cosmopolitanism, and though his ambitions be fulfilled the earth that he inherits will be gray" (*HE* 276). The "flux" promoted by "Imperial" types such as Henry both destroys the qualitative distinction between nations and literally turns landscapes into reproducible, blank spaces (with the "gray" of this brave new world contrasting with the parti-colored maps of Empire so common in the early century). Spots of authentic Englishness are being continually erased, Forster suggests, by the "graying" of the country undertaken by crass materialists like Henry Wilcox.

Yet Margaret Schlegel marries him. By making this match, Forster pairs two symbolic registers that would seem to be utterly incompatible: the sense of "space" and the sense of "flux," the appreciation of pastoral England (though Margaret is not a "native" herself) with the acceptance of a global capitalist modernity. As Thacker suggests, these connections can be mapped geographically in *Howards End*, with the "true" spaces of England increasingly threatened by the fluid, fluctuating spaces that surround and threaten them. In his narrative connection of these two worlds, however, Forster achieves a kind of Geddesian synthesis, effectively transforming the paradigmatic scale of social relations from the territorial, bounded homogeneity of the nation to the more hybrid spaces at the interface of country and city. In this way, *Howards End* represents a regional view, albeit one that offers a critique of Geddes' utopianism. In its nostalgia for an enclosed, insular England, Forster maintains a desire for national feeling that Geddes deems merely irrational. Yet, on the other hand, Forster sees a city-country synthesis as already networked to larger, *trans*national spaces in much more expansive ways. As only narrative can demonstrate, the synthesis that Geddes imagines in a purely visual mode involves a much more complicated geography, one that includes personal attachments to multiple, often conflicting, scales of identity.

It is perhaps no coincidence that the oft-cited epigraph to *Howards End*—"only connect..."—could easily be co-opted as a slogan for the modern telecommunication industry.[31] While the phrase is usually understood as Forster's liberal humanist call to repair the fragmentations of modern life—between sexes, between classes, between nations—there also seems to be a peculiarly technological modernity in the phrase, particularly if we read it in the historical context of the early-twentieth-century extension of communication and transportation networks.[32] Even Forster's Edwardian readers would have likely had trouble reading the epigraph without considering the ever-expanding and intensifying means and media of connection between people. Forster's epigraph is especially apt, then: it intimates a desire to preserve rooted, face-to-face human interactions but suggests also that we may be in danger of becoming *too* connected in a more literal sense. A distinction needs to be drawn, Forster implies, between a superficial, merely literal, connection and something more meaningful and profound. The sense of simultaneity in the novel, the feeling of an ever-present "meanwhile," partakes of the same epistemological standpoint as Geddes' regionalism. The idea of connection recalls the "synthetic vision" of regional geography, a "putting together" of things, people, and places in a simultaneous field. For both Geddes and Forster, then, the problem becomes one of scale: what would be the largest spatial field over which such connections could be organic and sustaining rather than merely coincidental and contingent?

Many readings of the novel have suggested that Forster's answer to this question comes in a metaphorical fusion of the ancestral home of Howards End and the imagined community of England. Lionel Trilling has set the tone for such readings, observing in 1943, "Like the plots of so many English novels, the plot of *Howards End* is about the rights of property, about a destroyed will-and-testament and rightful and wrongful heirs. It asks the question, 'Who shall inherit England?' "[33] Forster's apparent identification of the detached country house as an iconic space of English national identity takes part in a wider cultural discourse of the late Victorian and Edwardian periods. As the architect Edward Prior wrote in 1901, "That art of architecture, which in the eyes of other nations is mostly one of cities—of public buildings and public monuments—has to English taste lain in the separate house-building of individuals."[34] One foreign visitor to England during the first decade of the century, the German architectural critic and ambassador, Hermann Muthesius, confirms Prior's view: while on the continent industrial modernity "caused mass migration into the cities, where people became imprisoned in giant multi-storied barrack-like blocks," England provided "dwelling-places for individuals, making them into little separate worlds and concentrating and incorporating all the comforts of life in them."[35] In opposition to the more transient residences portrayed in *Howards End*, the eponymous house takes part in a national myth of domesticity, through which architecture acquires a deepened symbolic resonance. More than just bricks and mortar, Howards End is a trenchant critique of technologized modernity, of which imperialism, in Forster's eyes, is a significant part.[36]

In the novel's Edwardian present, however, Howards End has undergone a significant refurbishment, which separates the house from an inward-looking, pastoral domesticity. The horses have been replaced by motor cars and the paddock has been turned into a garage. The ancestral earth-mother of the house, the "*genius loci*" Ruth Wilcox (née Howard) does not so much die as simply disappear into narrative ellipsis.[37] Howards End has been opened up to the outside world, placed irrevocably into networks of modernity.[38] This is cause for lamentation to the male Wilcoxes, who yearn for a comfortable retreat from the daily commercial dealings of the Imperial and West African Rubber Company in their London offices. Henry Wilcox wishes to remove from city to country, or, put another way, from "Empire" into "England." And although it is Henry who has opened up Howards End to the spaces of modernity by building the garage and pursuing his hobby of motoring, he criticizes the geographical situation of the house, claiming that "the neighborhood's getting suburban" (*HE* 116). For all of the Wilcox disenchantment with Howards End—it has merely become a piece of devalued real estate—it offers the possibility of becoming a halfway house for a new kind of England, one that is constructed less by an insular devotion to ancestral continuity and conservative rural society than it is by (what Forster sees as) a necessary rapprochement between a masculinized, commercial, "imperial" England and its feminized, cosmopolitan, "cultural" sensibilities. If we want to follow Trilling's line of criticism, then, and read Howards End as a spatial allegory of the nation, then we must acknowledge a tension between a symbol so compact and spatially self-contained as a house and the multiple spaces and heterogeneous subjectivities of the "real" England. Forster seems to conclude that something so diverse and multidimensional as a national community cannot be collapsed into an idealized architectural structure and circumscribed social relation.

As the novel proceeds, Howards End becomes less a setting than an object of narrative desire. If we think about the movements of the characters, the space of the novel takes on a regional rather than a domestic scope. Specifically, much of the narrative centers upon the region of southeast England and the Home Counties; rather than think of *Howards End* as a "London" novel, we might properly call it a "Greater London" novel.[39] Wickham Place, the Schlegel residence, is in London, while Howards End is in Hertfordshire, the county immediately north of Greater London. Leonard Bast lives in South London, and he takes an overnight walk across the fields of Surrey, to the southwest of London. Charles Wilcox, the elder scion of the Wilcox family, initially builds a house in Epsom, Surrey, before relocating back to Hertfordshire near the end of the novel. If we think of the novel's center of gravity in the region of the Home Counties, it would seem that the novel presents a fairly unflattering portrait of this region. Just as the representative mode of movement becomes the jarring experience of travel by automobile, the representative space of this region is the suburb, or perhaps more accurately, the becoming-suburban. The spatial designation of "suburbia" coded a number of social anxieties in the late nineteenth and early twentieth centuries. After the death of Ruth Wilcox, Henry refuses to live at Howards End, judging that the surrounding area is "neither one thing nor the other" (*HE* 116). Similarly, at the end of the novel, years after Henry's pronouncement, the Schlegel sisters note as they look southward from Howards End that "London's creeping" (*HE* 289). Howards End, it seems, is perpetually threatened by "suburbia" while remaining just outside of the city itself. With the speed of rail and motor travel, however, the house remains regionally tied to London through the technological expansion of the daily lives of the city into the surrounding villages and hamlets just beyond the visibly urbanized landscape.[40] *Howards End*, then, recasts the connotations of regional place rooted to traditions, folkways, and pastoral landscapes into the emerging modern sense of a "metropolitan area" centered on commerce and trade.

In contrast to the metropolitanized region of Greater London, the lyrical passage narrated from the Purbeck Hills in Dorset offers a description of England that forges an alternative regional connection between the immediacy of the human scale and the abstract realm of the nation.[41] The passage begins chapter XIX as an apparent diversion from the immediate story at hand, the impending engagement of Margaret Schlegel and Henry Wilcox. The amiable voice of the narrator begins by presenting a hypothetical view, offering a description as the voice of experience and knowledge dispensing friendly advice: "If one wanted to show a foreigner England, perhaps the wisest course would be to take him to the final section of the Purbeck Hills, and stand him on their summit, a few miles to the east of Corfe" (*HE 142*). The first question that comes up has to do with the diversionary nature of the passage itself: why, in the middle of the story, would the narrator take the reader aside to dispense advice about the relative merit of different views of the English countryside? We soon find out that in fact the view is being witnessed by one of the Schlegels' German relatives, but this piece of information is delayed, giving us the sense that the view from the Purbeck summit is pure description, exterior to the movement of the narrative. Yet, in standing outside of the novel, it also stands *above* the novel. The narrator speaks directly to us, putting the diegesis on hold, highlighting the description as privileged information, a literal truth standing outside of the figurations of the narrative.

The passage begins simply enough with the conditional phrase "If one wanted to show a foreigner England." Initially, "England" can be read either metonymically as a representative sample of England or literally as the totality of the nation itself, an ambiguity that will become relevant later in the passage. The view that is described is initially rendered a literal, mimetic description of a landscape unfolding in perspectival space. The foreign visitor—and by extension, the reader—is placed within the scene, as he is "stand[ing]" on the summit, where (in terms that resonate with the structuralism of Geddesian regional geography) "system after system" of England "roll together under his feet" (*HE* 142). The location is given in precise geographical terms ("final section of the Purbeck Hills…a few miles east of Corfe") and the subsequent description evokes an area that could conceivably be taken in by the human eye:

> Beneath [the visitor] is the valley of the Frome, and all the wild lands that come tossing down from Dorchester, black and gold, to mirror their gorse in the expanses of Poole. The valley of the Stour is beyond, unaccountable stream, dirty at Blandford, pure at Wimborne—the Stour, sliding out of fat fields, to marry the Avon beneath the tower of Christchurch.
>
> (*HE* 142)

Up to this point, the description reads as if might have been lifted from a Baedeker's guide to Dorset, highlighting the natural features of the countryside as they would be visible from the view at the summit. We have here a slightly larger version of the England-in-miniature of the country house: like Howards End, the view from the Purbeck Hills is seen to enchant, to give off radiant beams that might somehow translate an essence of Englishness to a foreigner. As described above, the view from the Purbeck Hills represents the limits of the local; although the boundaries of this place are not as sharply drawn as the property lines of Howards End, the horizon of vision nonetheless marks off this description as the largest possible representation of a locale that can substitute for a literal, total England. By describing the "system after system" unfolding before the gaze of the viewer, Forster implicitly (and somewhat presciently) evokes the geographical scale of the region based upon the fundamental geographical circumstance of the river. Forster reminds the reader that the cities do not simply appear arbitrarily as an imposition upon a prior "nature"; rather, cities arose and grew precisely because of favorable geographical conditions on rivers, bays, or other waterways. Forster places the modern city, cultivated countryside, and major waterways in a more interdependent context. The language of the "system" suggests that such relationships are part of the deep structure of the nation, with one visually perceptible system standing metonymically for a broader national geography.

But it is what happens at the edges of vision, at the boundaries of the local, that separate this view of England's geography from the localized, contained England of Howards End. The narrator continues the description, moving beyond the horizon of the human eye:

> The valley of the Avon—invisible, but far to the north the trained eye may see Clearbury Ring that guards it, and the imagination may leap beyond that on to Salisbury Plain itself, and beyond the Plain to all the glorious downs of Central England. Nor is Suburbia absent. Bournemouth's ignoble coast cowers to the right, heralding the pinetrees that mean, for all

their beauty, red houses and the Stock Exchange, and extend to the gates of London itself.

(*HE* 142–143)

At this point, mimetic description of the local gives way to an imaginative perception: "the imagination leaps beyond" the visible to the "invisible" regions of Salisbury Plain and Central England. In addition to moving beyond the horizon of the visible, the passage describes "Suburbia," elsewhere in the novel derided as the decidedly non-English England that was an alien encroachment on the sanctity of Howards End. And, again, although the literal limits of vision are marked by the pine trees beyond Bournemouth, what those trees "mean" is similarly described through the leap of imagination that takes us to the very "gates of London." Although we are clearly moving to a different order of perception, trading the immediately visible for what is only imaginatively comprehensible, we are still grounded in a geographically specific location on the summit of the Purbeck Hills. The passage renders what is *literally* invisible from our specific point of view as imaginatively visible through the "leap of imagination" only possible with the figurations of novelistic description. Scales have been confounded: we are both rooted to a local spot and able to see beyond the horizon of the local into the contradictory spaces of England: country and city, pine trees and red houses.

The passage concludes with a rhetorical gesture toward an spatial inclusiveness that cannot be directly represented in the confines of mimetic description:

How many villages appear in this view! How many castles! How many churches, vanished or triumphant! How many ships, railways, and roads! What incredible variety of men working beneath that lucent sky to what final end! The reason fails, like a wave on the Swanage beach; the imagination swells, spreads, and deepens, until it becomes geographic and encircles England.

(*HE* 143)

Though posed in interrogative form, these sentences are punctuated as exclamations, allowing the narrator to account for the totality of villages, castles, churches, ships, railways, roads, and men without enumerating and cataloging each one. Moving beyond the immediate description of Wessex, and even beyond the imaginative description of central and southeastern England, the narrator's description ultimately encompasses all of England in this rhetoric of unquantifiable quantity. Yet, the totality of England is still ascribed to "this view"; that is, to the vantage of the embodied foreigner still standing on the summit of the Purbeck Hills. Geographical perception is here associated with an expansive imaginative faculty, while "Reason" is compared to a resolutely local, confined image: a solitary wave

breaking on a beach. Reason, in other words, can only yield limited spatial knowledge, while imagination has the power to awaken a more qualitative, deeply felt
sense of national identity. The sense of expansive, metonymic regionally-based
nationalism expressed in the Purbeck Hills passage, however, remains at odds with
the insular domestic nationalism elsewhere expressed in the novel. If the condition
of England can be expressed through the overriding symbol of the country house,
then menaces to this England begin to appear everywhere: in the motor cars that
disrupt the leisurely pace of country life, in the rust of suburbia that creeps over
the Hertfordshire hills, in urban interlopers such as Leonard and Jacky Bast (and,
to some extent, the Schlegel sisters themselves). By contrast, the Purbeck Hills
passage represents a national sentiment that is potentially inclusive rather than
exclusive: the country exists *with* the city, the natural *with* the cultural, the traditional *with* the modern.

The geographical positioning of Forster's observer likewise gives us a specific
perspective on England that is neither the disembodied nowhere of cartographic
abstraction nor the idealized pastoral that looks backward from a technologized
modernity. Forster puts us at the extreme edge of south-central England, a well-
chosen location for many reasons. First of all, the geography that Forster projects
is at the coastal margin of England, making its reader/viewer aware of a stark
edge to the landform of the island, while also recalling the long mythology of
England as an "island fortress." The spot is also centrally located on an east-west
axis of the island, placing it at the western edge of the urbanized southeast (and
thus putting it within sight of the conurbation of Bournemouth, Southampton,
and Portsmouth, which leads inexorably to London) but also at the eastern border of the pastoral west, a region that evokes a premodern temporality, a lost
age of peasant yeomen and vernacular speech, village churches and dairy farms.
Significantly, this location on the southern edge between the modern east and
the romantic west excludes both the industrialized north as well as the "Celtic
fringe" of Ireland, Wales, and Scotland (though, of course, Henry and Margaret
will encounter the borderlands of Wales at Oniton Grange, their first house as a
married couple).[42] Forster, in effect, uses Geddes' "situated eye" to map a space
that is, if anything, *between* regions rather than at the center of one. In viewing
these interstitial spaces, Forster highlights the tensions of spatial difference rather
than a self-contained organic structure. Yet, because they can occur—theoretically—within a unified field of vision, they conform to Geddes' regionalist epistemology. In Forster's description, then, regionalism is less about the immanence
of a bounded, self-sustaining place than about a scale of perception determined
by the scope of the human gaze.

Where the symbolism of the house-as-nation demands the operations of met-aphor—the house as a substitution for the nation—the landscape from Purbeck Hills suggests a metonymic relationship between regional vision and national com-munity. Ultimately, these two orders of space—the metaphorical domestic England of Howards End and the metonymic regionalized England of the Purbeck Hills passage—cannot be reconciled within the novel. To begin with, the passage is still marked as extradiegetic commentary, a superfluous graft onto the implied unity of the novel. Although the description of the view is underscored by its mode of direct address from the narrator to a reader, this stands outside of the "condition-of-England" narrative allegorized by individual characters. The import of the pas-sage thus passes over the insensible characters in the novel unable to appreciate its significance. Faced with the identical view, Frieda Mosebach, the literal "foreigner" who visits the scene, can only remark dully "that the hills were more swelling here than in Pomerania" (*HE* 143). Elsewhere, the faculty of geographic imagination is denied even to Margaret, the one character in the novel who seems best equipped to adopt it. At one point, "starting from Howards End," Margaret "attempt[s] to realize England" through a similar kind of imagination. Notably, she fails; as the narrator tells us, "visions do not come when we try" (*HE* 174). The novel itself retreats to a somewhat defensive localism in its conclusion, as the growth of suburbia and the onset of mass culture threaten to leave only a severely depreciated Howards End to its ultimate inheritor, Helen's and Leonard's child. If this conclusion is to be taken as Forster's final word on the condition of England, then we might be justified in understanding the novel as a retreat to a Little Englandism that wishes to stand outside the flux of modernity. Yet, the description from Purbeck Hills haunts this insular conclusion as a wish for another space, one that would combine the know-able landscapes of the regional with the collective abstraction of the national.

As a counterpoint to the perspective from Purbeck Hills, the novel concludes with another view from an elevated position. This time, Margaret and Helen, hav-ing now made Howards End their home, look southward over the property toward London. When Margaret remarks on the sense of belonging she feels in the house, Helen sounds a note of caution:

"All the same, London's creeping."

She pointed over the meadow—over eight or nine meadows, but at the end of them was a red rust.

"You see that in Surrey and even Hampshire now," she continued. "I can see it from the Purbeck downs. And London is only part of something else, I'm afraid. Life's going to be melted down, all over the world."

(*HE* 289–290)

Where the narrator's triumphant vision of southern England from the Purbeck Hills stands outside of the diegetic world of the novel, this less grandiose view is very much within it. The undifferentiated, obsolescent rust looms on the horizon, but it has yet to swallow up Howards End or other remaining islands of Englishness. Rather than advance the case of an insular nationalism as a cultural anodyne for a flattening imperial modernity, then, Forster offers a more subtle form of regionalist critique. The Purbeck Hills chapter of the novel consolidates a chorographic sensibility—a literal "view" of a culturally rooted, epistemologically readable, regional landscape—as a means by which an emergent national identity might be formed. Yet, as the conclusion of the novel demonstrates, this regional view is invariably, inextricably coupled with the abstract space of transnational modernity, and it is precisely at the horizon line where the iconic landscapes of Englishness melt into the reproducible spaces of the modern world that a new England might emerge. As much as Forster might wish it otherwise, the nation is not a pristine, bordered fortress against acquisitive imperialism and deterritorializing capitalism. Not only does England incorporate these spaces, but these modern networks connect the island nation, for better or worse, to the rest of the world.

As Richard Helgerson has argued about the heyday of the chorographical genre in sixteenth- and seventeenth-century England, early modern chorography implied notions of place, locality, and particularity, often in tacit resistance to a monarchical consolidation of nationhood. Chorography became the vehicle for a populist, antistatist nationalism, one that turns on the multiple meanings of the word "country." "The emergence of the country," Helgerson writes, "as a single, if variously significant, term for the focal point of allegiance parallels the emergence of the description, survey, or chorography as an autonomous and widely practiced genre."[43] Forster's view from the Purbeck Hills draws precisely on this ambiguity: to imagine the country (as nation), one must first gain a sense of the country (as landscape, as region, as locality). The vision of landscape "becomes geographic" and is only then able to apprehend, to "encircle" England. Helgerson concludes that chorography is a means to a different kind of nationalism: one from a land-based, particularized vision, as it were: "The dialectic of general and particular that is built into the structure of a chorography in the end constitutes the nation it represents."[44] In the early twentieth-century, nationalism had become too often identified with the outward thrust of imperialism and the areal coverage of a global map with the pink-red of British real estate. The jigsaw-puzzle view of the world accommodated and encouraged such a vision. It was Forster's wish to scale down this global view to its foundations in the embodied human interaction with place, land, and community.

From Regionalism to Perspectival Globalism

Through the twentieth century, various examples of the situated eye have lent themselves to the imagination of the world through the kind of synoptic outlook suggested by Geddes and Forster. One such example can be found in many of the maps and images produced by the American geographer Richard Edes Harrison, whose hand drawn, World War II–era maps substituted Cartesian abstraction for a more pictorial, naturalistic view of the terrestrial earth. "His maps," write Susan Schulten, "resemble a photograph of the earth from a distance. Through this perspective [he] translated a three-dimensional view of the air-age world onto a two-dimensional plane, creating a sense of globularity that ordinary commercial maps could not match."[45] Harrison's maps translated the situated eye into an imaginary viewpoint hundreds of miles from earth, but often at an oblique angle, rendering the image more "realistic" and therefore more immediate. In one sense, Harrison's perspectival views encouraged a kind of postnational sensibility, because his maps typically showed no man-made boundary lines and were drawn with the naturalistic details of mountains, plains, waterways, and other topographical features. Particularly in the context of World War II and its geopolitical conflicts, Harrison's images were explicitly formulated to highlight the proximity of foreign threats to the North American continent, and by extension, to argue against any policy of U.S. isolationism. With titles like "Three Approaches to the U.S." and "Japan from Alaska," Harrison's maps used an "airman's perspective" to suggest the vulnerability of the United States in an era of increasing interconnectedness. In this respect, the situated eye of regionalism expands the intimate proximity associated with the naturalistic vision of regional landscape to a global scale. For Harrison, this was implicitly in defense of a nationalist-imperialist sensibility, though this imperialist message is always indicated by a textual supplement, typically a title or caption indicating threat to the "homeland" of the United States. Without such textual commentaries, the images themselves might just as easily encourage a sense of transnational, transcultural community.

The connection between Forster's view of southern England and Harrison's space-centered perspectives on North America points out one crucial aspect of the elevated vision, however. The expansive, three-dimensional view of the world from an elevated vantage point presumes a certain freedom to reinvent visible space in the crucible of the imaginative eye. To see a world of regions, as Geddes would, or a world of landforms without visible borders and boundaries, as Harrison would, requires the luxury of a "home" space from which one can take the measure of the world. Not surprisingly, Geddes, Forster, and Harrison author their works from within—even as they critique—the perspective of the imperial center.[46] When one comes from a national culture where boundaries are seen either as naturally imposed (in the case of England's "island fortress" image) or divinely ordained (as in post–Manifest Destiny America), questions of cultural identity become matters of choice and agency. The critical gesture of disavowing one's own territorially determined national space is less urgent because one can assume that the very space one wishes to critique is in no jeopardy of being dispossessed. Margaret Schlegel, therefore, can easily decry the homogenizing, abstract cartographic sensibility of English imperialism precisely because the geopolitical dominance that *allows* the English to draw the authoritative maps of the world is the very same power that ensures that the England Margaret wishes to preserve will always be there, waiting to be recovered.

While the chorographic impulses of early-twentieth-century regional representation formed a powerful critique to the fetish of quantifiable territorial space, we should not dismiss the power of cartographic space in the struggle *against* colonialism. If we connect post-Enlightenment cartography as a monolithic means of representation that inevitably flattens, reifies, and depopulates spaces full of things, cultures, and lives, then we concede the institutions and legal power of cartography to those very colonial interests. Anticolonial nationalisms, in particular, have needed to fight their struggles on the terrain of cartography, precisely because a bounded space on the map—a territorial nation-state—is the only form through which sovereignty and self-determination can be realized in the post-Versailles world. In the case of revolutionary Ireland, the institutions of cartography are even more intimately bound up in the struggle for sovereignty, as the first full-scale national survey conducted by the British Ordnance Survey (the governmental mapmaking authority) was undertaken *not* in England, but in Ireland. As I will argue in the next chapter, the British construction of Ireland as a mapped object—a "paper landscape," to use J. A. Andrews's phrase—effectively colonized the very means of arbitrating spatial reality. While Irish nationalist activities concentrated on reclaiming an autonomous culture, language, and institutions, very few thought to engage the spatial construction of Ireland as an object of cartography. James Joyce, however, always a cartophile, realized that the reinvention of Ireland could take place within the very map authored through British rule. In the next chapter, I argue that cartographic space was not only instrumental to Joyce's aesthetic experimentation, but also that the map was a means of representation that demanded reappropriation and reinscription for the project of a national community to find a geographical home. Ironically, Joyce's repurposing of imperial cartography could only happen within the pages of a novel.

3. Internal Colony
The Spectral Cartographies of Ulysses

"I have learnt to arrange things in such a way that they become easy to survey and to judge."

—James Joyce, on the benefits of a Jesuit education

James Joyce: Ironic Cartographer

Where the previous two chapters have explored the imaginative use of metageography as a mode of internal national critique, the remaining three chapters look at how fiction invokes mapped space in the formation of anti-imperial, postcolonial nationalities. The literature of decolonizing national communities frequently makes direct references to cartography; often, the first step toward the inscription of a postcolonial identity comes through an act that Graham Huggan describes as "decolonizing the map."[1] Because the survey and mapping of colonial territories has been a medium of spatial control and social repression, maps tend to be highly symbolic objects in the resistance to imperial power. This chapter suggests that Joyce's Jesuit penchant for survey and judgment was refined in specifically cartographic ways by his attachments to Ireland, the largest internal colony of Great Britain until its independence in 1922. Ireland itself had been exhaustively surveyed by British cartographers in the mid-nineteenth century, an undertaking that produced a series of maps at a scale of six inches to the mile. In *Ulysses*, Joyce becomes an ironic surveyor and cartographer, incorporating the mechanisms and formal codes of cartography to undermine the apparent control of Ireland rendered through the British Ordnance Survey, the agency responsible for mapping the island. In doing so, Joyce reimagines cartography as a fluid, connective mode of representation rather than as a means to render space as fixed and static forevermore. In contrast to the cultural and linguistic foundations of revolutionary Irish nationalism, Joyce instead advocates an Irish sensibility that begins with the brute facts of imperial cartography.

Ireland has always had an ambiguous status within the array of British colonies. Separated from England, Scotland, and Wales by the Irish Sea, it existed before the early modern period as a place apart, a realm of exoticized otherness. Yet because of its adjacency to England and its absorption into the entity of "Great Britain" as far back as the seventeenth century (culminating in the 1800 Acts of Union), Ireland was part of the British state well before Britain's most expansive period of colonial acquisition began.[2] Michael Hechter has famously classified the British-Irish situation as one of internal colonialism, an unequal relationship between a modernized core and underdeveloped periphery within the same state. Hechter posits that an initial economic stratification leads to an exacerbation of cultural differences, and eventually the peripheral, exploited group seeks an ethnic nationalist identification as a way of politicizing their subordinate position within an unequal geographical distribution of economic, social, and cultural power.[3] Without evaluating the relative merits and shortcomings of Hechter's model, I want to emphasize its geographical element, which suggests that the core and periphery can be territorially distinct within the space of the state. The more successful nationalist movements arising from an internal colony are typically able to invoke the emergent nation as a territorially contiguous entity.[4] This potentiality for territorial nationhood is especially subversive to the hegemonic nation-state because the existence of an internal colony offers a counternarrative to the seamless merger of territory and cultural identity posited by most nationalist ideologies. Of the many political and legal mechanisms of the British state deployed to force a resistant Ireland into the space of the nation, cartographic survey was one of the most influential means of coercion. With the Ordnance Survey of Ireland, conducted between 1826 and 1852, Great Britain created the very contour of space within which the stateless nation of Ireland was made to exist. Irish nationalism had to contend with the circumstance that a sovereign Ireland would necessarily be created on a map authored by the British state.

This chapter addresses the ways in which James Joyce imagined an Irish identity through a reinscription of imperial survey and cartography into the form of the novel. Without question, cartographic survey was a discursive practice central to the exercise of British colonial power. "Imperialism and mapmaking intersect in the most basic manner," Matthew Edney writes. "Both are fundamentally concerned with territory and knowledge.... To govern territories, one must know them."[5] Yet, the understanding of a map may be quite different than its makers intended. In *A Thousand Plateaus*, Gilles Deleuze and Felix Guattari distinguish between the cognitive activities of "mapping" and "tracing," positing the former as "entirely oriented toward an experimentation in contact with the real" while understanding the latter as a merely repetitive, rote mimicry. Mapping, they explain, "has to do with performance," while tracing "always involves an alleged 'competence.'"[6] Mapping creates novelty through an experiential relationship between the map reader and map artifact. Seen in this way, mapping describes not merely the action of the cartographer but the imaginative activity of the map reader. Rather than simply "tracing" the legible marks of designated routes and marked spaces, the creative reader of maps in fact *re*-maps cartographic territory to create new connections and structural relationships. "Thus," as James Corner writes, "mapping *unfolds* potential; it remakes territory over and over again, each time with new and diverse consequences."[7] Maps, in other words, retain an open-endedness that cannot be reduced to the intentionality and spatial ideology of the institutions and individuals who "author" them. While maps and narratives are categorically different forms, they do enter into a dialogical relationship with each other. Maps, according to Franco Moretti, "highlight...the place-bound nature of literary forms," setting literature in relation to "real historical space."[8]

Certainly, few texts explore the connection between represented narrative space and "real historical space" more intensively than James Joyce's *Ulysses*. One of the long-standing truisms about *Ulysses* is that it offers a comprehensive and factually precise geography of Dublin on June 16, 1904. This idea, at least in part, originated from Joyce himself in his famous remark to Frank Budgen: "I want...to give a picture of Dublin so complete that if the city one day suddenly disappeared from the earth it could be reconstructed out of my book."[9] With this comment, Joyce would have us believe that his book is as much an archive of geographical fact as it is a narrative of imaginative fiction. If the numbers of scholarly guides to "Joyce's Dublin" are any testimony, literary critics have not actively challenged this understanding of the novel.[10] Readers continue to accord *Ulysses* an epistemological authority akin to that of the map: the novel claims to present a totalizing archive of factual knowledge about a particular "real-world" physical space. Joyce seems to have been aware of the particular discursive power of cartography within a larger economy of knowledge, as the relationship between the topographical precision of *Ulysses* and the rhetoric of cartography is more than coincidental. As Budgen noted of the composition of the "Wandering Rocks" chapter of *Ulysses*, Joyce composed the chapter "with a map of Dublin before him on which were traced in red ink the paths of the Earl of Dudley and Father Conmee." Budgen continues: "To see Joyce at work on the 'Wandering Rocks' was to see…a surveyor with theodolite and measuring chain."[11] Likening the precise spatial plotting of the chapter to the surveyor's practice of marking and measuring territory, Budgen draws our attention to the importance that Joyce placed on geographical accuracy in *Ulysses*. The novel's composition is elevated beyond mere imagination; in Budgen's description of the painstaking detail with which Joyce arranges interlocking narratives on a coherent grid of time and space, Joyce's writing is equated with the rigorous method and precision of scientific practice. The true modernist *auteur*, Budgen's narration suggests, is no longer merely a writer fabricating stories from the stuff of imagination but a cartographer ordering the world according to rational laws of scientific truth.

This chapter, however, questions the assumption that Joyce's reliance on mapping is merely a modernist aesthetic strategy designed to give his novel the legitimating weight of objective scientific facticity. While scholars have been all too eager to plot *Ulysses* onto a map of Dublin, few have remarked on the rhetoric of cartography that Joyce himself deployed in the composition of the novel. Two historical circumstances render this question especially relevant to an understanding of this cartographic rhetoric. First, the maps that Joyce used in the creation of *Ulysses* would have been derived from the comprehensive British survey of Ireland taken during the early nineteenth century and would have thus represented Ireland through the spatial perspective of an imperial gaze. Second, while Joyce consulted maps of Dublin during the composition of the novel, the topography of Dublin was being violently altered by the events that led to the independence of Ireland in 1922. By drawing on the form of the map, therefore, the novel necessarily constructs a specific cultural and political geography of Anglo-Irish relations, one distinctly at odds with the organicist cultural nationalism of the Celtic Revival and its associated linguistic and cultural programs.[12] Rather, Joyce's use of cartography in *Ulysses* narrates a nation with the potential to emerge not just in the realm of culture, but also on the most factually authoritative of documents: the map. Although the precision and detail of Joyce's topographies are frequently hailed as hallmarks of Joyce's modernism, the apparently precise representation of Dublin sets up a formal oscillation between the abstract visual space of the map and the local knowledges of narrative, finally drawing attention to the absences inherent within each mode of representation. Cartography promises a surveying view, but this vantage is distant, abstract, and ahistorical. Narrative, conversely, can project individual movements through time and space but ultimately must rely on partial views and situated knowledges. *Ulysses* frequently represents spaces that hover between these two perspectives but ultimately only exist in the negative space between literature and geography, narrative and historical space. This optic is particularly well suited for presenting the geopolitical situation of the internal colony: it both recognizes the discursive power of the cartographer as the ultimate arbiter of sovereign statehood while at the same time projecting narratives that cannot logically be mapped onto the imperial state. Joyce therefore opens up a tension from which the map can be a point of departure for the articulation of a "positional" nationalism, one that cannot pretend to organicist or romantic origins.

I begin by looking closely at the Ordnance Survey of Ireland as a part of what Thomas Richards has called the "imperial archive." Crucially, the maps generated by the survey, while claiming to be produced according to objective science, in fact present a vision of Ireland as an immanent, fully visible object of study detached from the long, tortured history of Anglo-Irish relations. After considering the epistemology of the maps inherited by Joyce, I turn to two chapters of *Ulysses* that offer a critique of the rhetoric of presence figured in the Ordnance Survey maps of Ireland. "Wandering Rocks" seems to abandon narrative in favor of geography in its portrayal of the interlocking paths and overlapping itineraries of scores of Dubliners. The chapter's form invites (indeed, almost necessitates) the consultation of a map to render the fragmented narrative into conceptual coherence. The continual references to the toponymy of Dublin suggest the chapter's investment in cartographic precision. Yet, by promising the spatial exactitude of the map but delivering the fleeting itineraries of narrative, "Wandering Rocks" points out the failings of cartography as a science of spatial representation. Despite its inherent gaps and failures, however, maps are not false, useless objects in the spatial economy of *Ulysses*. Even maps produced for the express purpose of imperial administration can be read differently depending on the cultural position of the reader. Each reading, in other words, creates that map anew with different associations, itineraries, and destinations. In "Ithaca," for example, Leopold Bloom reads the Ordnance Survey map not as a positivist object of knowledge yielding a transparent, factual account of the world but as a "negativist" object of desire giving rise to projection and fantasy about different possible relationships between geographical space and community. Read through Bloom's eyes (and Joyce's text), the map can therefore be understood as an aesthetic object that prompts an ironic consciousness of geography and spatiality.

Ireland in the Imperial Archive

> "We're making a six-inch map of the country. Is there something sinister in that?"
>
> —Owen, an Irish translator working for the British Ordnance Survey in Brian Friel's play *Translations*

As recent work in the history of cartography has made clear, maps convey an impression of scientific accuracy and distanced objectivity that frequently masks the interests involved in their production.[13] The cartographic historian J. B. Harley, in his seminal essay "Deconstructing the Map," points out the inherent textuality of even the most "scientific" of maps. Since the eighteenth century, the practice of cartography has been governed by what Harley calls "a standard scientific model of knowledge and cognition," which assumes "that the objects in the world to be mapped are real and objective, and that they enjoy an existence independent of the cartographer; that their reality can be expressed in mathematical terms; that systematic observation and measurement offer the only route to cartographic truth; and that this truth can be independently verified."[14] The form of cartography encodes these assumptions: once data enters into the form of the map, it instantaneously acquires the aura of fact and reality. Yet Harley reminds us that the map's apparent factuality is in fact a by-product of its rhetoric: "The steps in making a map—selection, omission, simplification, classification, the creation of hierarchies, and 'symbolization'—are all inherently rhetorical."[15] Recent studies in both critical geography and postcolonial theory have uncovered the complex power/ knowledge relations that inhere within the rhetoric of mapping, leading to a reassessment of cartography in general and imperial cartography in particular. As Harley points out, much of the scientific rhetoric of post-Enlightenment cartography was used to maintain systems of state and imperial domination. "In modern Western society," Harley writes, "maps quickly became crucial to the maintenance of state power—to its boundaries, to its commerce, to its internal administration, to control of populations, and to its military strength."[16] To "state power" might be added "imperial conquest," as cartography also created knowledge used for the subjugation and administration of aboriginal populations and colonial territories. Writing of British imperial cartography in particular, Matthew Edney points out that "maps came to define the empire itself, to give it territorial integrity and its basic existence."[17] Maps were not merely neutral representations of imperial territory; by submitting these territories to the common language of latitude and longitude, they forced the heterogeneity and chaos of far-flung colonial places into a seamless graticule of abstract, instrumentalized space.

While debate ensues about if and when Ireland was a "legitimate" colony of the British Empire, and whether Ireland should be considered as an external colonial possession or an internal peripheral region,[18] it is clear that the comprehensive mapping of Ireland by the British Ordnance Survey from 1826 to 1852 was a part of a larger British imperative to consolidate systematic control of its colonial possessions through the conversion of physical territory into archival knowledge. Along with the contemporaneous Great Trigonometrical Survey of India and subsequent surveys of East Africa, the Irish Survey, as it came to be called, aimed to create a definitive map of a colonial space, wiping away all vestiges of the haphazard, local geographies of towns, estates, and counties. The Survey succeeded to the extent that the maps that were produced remained the "official" maps of Ireland until well after independence. Most mass-produced maps from the 1850s until the 1920s were derived from the survey, including those appended to the 1904 edition of Alexander Thom's *Irish Almanac and Official Directory*, the legendary source of the topographical detail of *Ulysses*.[19] While the maps of Dublin in Thom's *Almanac* seem harmlessly neutral and factual, the cartographic archive from which Joyce derives the Dublin of *Ulysses* was produced through the material and discursive practices of colonialism. Moreover, while Joyce was drafting much of the novel, Dublin was a colonial battleground whose geography was being rapidly and violently transformed through revolutionary uprising and civil war. The possibility that much of Dublin might "suddenly disappear" was not merely speculation; much of the city was in fact destroyed between the Easter Rebellion of 1916 and the establishment of the Free State in 1922. As Enda Duffy has shown, Joyce was well aware of the cataclysmic events taking place in Ireland as he wrote his book on the Continent.[20] Although Budgen's mythologizing account shows Joyce in the guise of the detached, scientific cartographer presiding masterfully over geographical space, Joyce's use of cartographic method should also be read as an inquiry into the imperial production of knowledge.

The Ordnance Survey, originally a wing of the British military charged with maintaining supplies and ammunition to troops, became principally responsible for topographical survey and cartography in the late eighteenth century. Setting its sights on Ireland shortly after the Acts of Union in 1800, the Ordnance Survey was commissioned to create a comprehensive map of Ireland, scaled at six inches to the mile, for the immediate purpose of providing equitable taxation for property owners on the island, most of whom were Anglo-Irish Protestants. While the explicit rationale for the survey suggested a modest bureaucratic aim, the survey was emblematic of a changing conception of imperial space brought about by advances in cartographic technology. The mapping proceeded by trigonometrical survey, or triangulation, which used the laws of mathematics to convert physical terrain into a series of triangles, the exact locations of which could be determined through the calculation of angles relative to a precisely measured baseline. With triangulation, mapmaking was given the air of epistemological infallibility and scientific precision so central in establishing the modern cultural authority of the cartographic image. Triangulation also fixed any point within the graticule of longitude and latitude that described the shape and size of the globe. By promising a science of location into which any point on the terrestrial earth could be compared with any other point, cartography used trigonometrical survey to create a homogeneous global space in which any location could be expressed through two numerical values. The maps of Ireland created by the Ordnance Survey were thus, by definition, part of a uniformly abstract space that was particularly well suited to rendering the disparate colonies of the British Empire with the common language of latitude and longitude. Like the Great Trigonometrical Survey of India, which was undertaken at roughly the same time and with many of the same technologies and personnel, the Ordnance Survey of Ireland was a part of a larger British imperial project: the systematic and scientific possession of territory by means of codified spatial knowledge.[21]

The survey of Ireland would become part of what Thomas Richards has called the British "imperial archive," the popular fantasy image for the comprehensive knowledge supposedly possessed by the British imperial state during the nineteenth and early twentieth centuries. As Richards argues, narratives of the British Empire were unique in their imagining of an empire "united not by force but by information."[22] Given its global scope and the seemingly endless outline of its frontiers, it was unthinkable that Great Britain could effectively rule its territories through wholesale military occupation. Richards posits that, in the absence of a stable interior space through which the Empire becomes one with the nation, new means of administration and control were needed. The archive was the imaginative space where the various fragments of the Empire could be made whole, and information was the medium that filled out this space with meaning. Importantly, the archive was only a *fantasy* of totality, of complete possession, and the seemingly perfect infinitude of knowledge within its imaginative walls was an illusory effect of the staggering amount of heterogeneous data collected in its service. Although the idea of the perfect archive was ultimately a fiction, Richards notes the power of such fictions, claiming that, with the imperial archive, "Britain had devised a mythology of knowledge that played a global role in consolidating the British Empire as a secure symbiosis of knowledge and power."[23] By projecting the convincing illusion of infinite knowledge, Great Britain assumed a very real geopolitical power over spaces and cultures ill equipped to resist the British will-to-information.

Consisting of various fields of knowledge such as anthropology, biology, sociology, climatology, and geology, the imperial archive demanded some kind of master text, a sort of epistemological Rosetta Stone that could enable the translation of one field of knowledge to another. Because the Empire was by nature a spatial field of power with virtually all of the knowledges in the imperial archive depending upon some spatial distribution, it fell to geography to provide this master language of the archive. Maps, in particular, became the visual shorthand for the breadth of imperial knowledge as well as the scope of the Empire's territorial claims. As Matthew Edney suggests, maps were the perfect metaphor and icon for Enlightenment models of positive knowledge, heuristically organizing discrete pieces of data within a unified conceptual space. "The Enlightenment conception of archive-construction," Edney writes, "was clearly shaped by a cartographic metaphor. Within the abstract space of the archive, each new observation could be located in its proper *place*."[24] Maps were not only metaphors for any spatialized knowledge, but they also marked the boundaries past which intellectual inquiry had not yet pushed. As Edney puts it, " 'white space' in the archive indicated gaps in knowledge, much as it was assumed to do on maps, and so indicated arenas for further investigation."[25] Maps, by transforming the heterogeneity of place into the abstraction of space, quite literally created a grid—or more properly, a graticule—onto which other imperial sciences could be plotted and inscribed.[26] Cartographers could create maps to convey different fields of data, including topography, population distribution, vegetation types, land use, and so on. This was certainly true of the Ordnance Survey's mapping of Ireland: as J. H. Andrews observes of the Ordnance Survey maps, "it was their facility for receiving further information that made the six-inch maps so useful to scientists and scholars."[27] Moreover, maps could be created at any number of scales to accommodate any type of spatial distribution ranging from the geopolitical order of nations to the detail of landownership in a remote townland. As Edney puts it, "The space of the map was not bounded and limited but was extensible and as potentially all-encompassing as British power and knowledge could make it."[28] The map, then, was both a synecdoche of the archive and a grid for all of its data; it both represented and measured the British Empire.

To establish its representational authority, however, cartography had to clear away the flotsam of heterogeneous, unsystematized knowledges, thus creating at least the effect of an archival *tabula rasa*. The ideal construction of archival knowledge as the inscription of data on an imaginary map depends upon the a priori "emptiness" of the archive itself; that is, the map must be conceptually "blank" before information can be placed and ordered within its frame. This emptiness is, of course, a fiction—it is impossible to locate a point of origin, either temporally or spatially, from which a coherent project of imperial archive building begins. Yet, as Michel Foucault argues in *The Archaeology of Knowledge*, there must be some imaginary "ground zero" that enables the project of archive construction within a conceptual space, a point from which knowledge can emerge as a positive, categorizable entity. This "condition of reality," as Foucault terms it, is both an essential premise to the existence of the archive and the fictive moment of origin from which scientific knowledge emerges.[29] Although such "conditions of reality" are always illusory and retroactively constructed, the blank spaces on the map— the *terrae incognitae*—visibly suggested that archives were waiting to be compiled in spaces not yet explored. Imperial mapping thus worked within an economy of knowledge that privileged the blank map as a ground on which systematized knowledges could be inscribed. Yet, such blankness, of course, never really existed. Like the adult Marlow musing on the map of Africa, the explorer always arrives after some prior knowledge has been established. Given the proximity of England and Ireland as well as Ireland's long-standing status as an internal colony of Great Britain, the fiction of Ireland's archival emptiness was perhaps even more difficult to maintain than in geographically distant colonies. Ireland was no unknown land; it had already been mapped many times over (by both English and Continental cartographers) before the Ordnance Survey began its efforts.[30] These efforts were not sanctioned by a state apparatus, however, and none were accomplished systematically, using the scientific method promised by triangulation. For the early-nineteenth-century British cartographic establishment that presided over the newly incorporated Ireland, the motive for creating a comprehensive map based on trigonometric surveys was in a sense to cleanse the archive of its haphazard, variant, local knowledges and to replace them with a homogeneous, scientific informatics of the state.

To accomplish this, the creators of the Ordnance Survey chose a scale and a style that would suggest both scientific austerity and aesthetic pleasure. Put another way, the Ireland of the Ordnance Survey is both familiar and foreign, a comforting image of a recognizable English spatiality and an object of ethnographic otherness. At six inches to the mile—the smallest scale at which property lines could still be clearly drawn—the maps present sufficient detail to suggest a sort of aerial landscape painting rather than the abstract grids, lines, and points common on smaller-scale maps. At such a large scale, the Ordnance Survey etches a placid, idyllic topography whose visual specificity creates a convincing portrait of an ordered and peaceful nation under the guiding hand of a benevolent colonial administration. In particular, the map's emphasis on Ascendancy manor houses helps to project a kind of unionist geography in which the picturesque country-side is given shape and order by the individual estates. In a detail of the map of County Kilkenny, for example, estate houses are rendered in great detail with trees, hedgerows, and gardens indicated on the map along with the houses of the estate. In such panels, the breach between a strictly topographical map and a map of a socially inscribed landscape becomes clear. Along with features such as moun-tains, streams, and fields, the houses themselves are presented with the man-made details of landscape and architecture, such as shrubs and garden pathways. The geography of the Ascendancy manor house is made to seem natural and timeless. Estate names are also prominently displayed on the map, further naturalizing the Ascendancy class as a quasi-topographical feature of the land itself. By including the homely details of estate grounds and field borders, the maps hint at the placid, picturesque realism of a Constable painting within the abstract symbolic language of post-Enlightenment scientific cartography. The head of the Survey in Ireland, Thomas Larcom, acknowledged the artful quality of the survey, though he identi-fied its aims with a different genre. The Survey, Larcom wrote, would provide a "full-face portrait of the land" of Ireland.[31] Moreover, as Mary Hamer points out, landowners could control representations of their own properties. Hamer writes that "landowners were allowed to be the sole source of authority for the name of their demesnes and were allowed to define their own demesne boundaries."[32] Just as members of the gentry frequently commissioned portraits that would flatter the patrons, so could members of the Ascendancy "author" the image of their own lands within the conventions of cartographic representation. As part landscape painting, part portraiture, the maps evoke a topography that is fixed forever in time, thus repressing the chaotic historical circumstances of Ireland during the years of the map's production from 1826 to 1852. In the Ordnance Survey maps, a unionist Ireland is captured in amber, portrayed in an imaginary moment of idyl-lic peace and ordered stability under the beneficent hand of British rule.

The fact that the years of the Ordnance Survey mapping encompass the great famine of the 1840s draws attention to the historical contingency of the image of Ireland presented in the six-inch maps. By the time the survey was completed, many of the earlier maps were no longer accurate, given the changes of landscape brought about by the famine. Cottages, estates, and even villages were deserted; net-works of incomplete "famine roads" were built as public works projects; and larger metropolitan areas such as Dublin and Cork swelled with new public buildings, including workhouses for the waves of destitute immigrants from the countryside. Yet the geography of the Ordnance Survey served as the template for virtually all professionally produced maps until well after independence. Eavan Boland's 1994 poem "That the Science of Cartography Is Limited" speaks specifically about the "famine roads," built at the behest of the Survey but frequently never completed and, therefore, never worthy of a place on the map. Boland's poem introduces a register of space that commingles the history of the starving Irish peasants with the homogeneous, timeless space of cartography, a space that can only be recognized by its cartographic absence: "the line which says woodland and cries hunger/ ... will not be there."[33] Imperial cartography is not merely a "limited" science but one whose conventions obscure histories of struggle and inequity. The Ordnance Survey mapping of Ireland, according to Boland's poem, literally erases history from the map. The aesthetics of presence embodied in the maps thus compensates for the necessary absences, fissures, and blind spots in the imperial archive. The mass of visual detail helped to cover over the specific choices of represented objects and the transience of topographical features that had changed over the history of the Survey, rendering an ever-changing cultural space as a permanent and naturalized landscape.

A passage from Elizabeth Bowen's *The Last September* captures this combination of the picturesque and the abstract, though it reflects an emerging sense among the late Ascendancy class that such pristine geographies were becoming quickly endangered by the historical struggles that they repressed. Bowen's novel portrays the last years of the Ascendancy era, depicting one particular County Cork big house under threat by an increasingly radical Republican peasantry. This theme is focused through a coming-of-age story of an Anglo-Irish teenager, Lois Farquar, and her brief love affair with an occupying British soldier, set against the backdrop of the escalating War of Independence. At one point early in the novel, Lois returns to her family's estate, Danielstown, after a visit with a peasant family whose son is a suspected rebel. As Lois descends by automobile from the Cork hills toward her family's estate, her elevated view of the landscape surrounding the big house hints at an awakening political consciousness. Initially, Lois's view approximates the abstract, God's-eye objectivity of cartography: "To the south, below them, the demesne trees of Danielstown made a dark formal square like a rug on the green country."[34] The picturesque view of the "formal" arrangement of Danielstown soon leads to a creeping sense of dread, however.

> Looking down, it seemed to Lois they lived in a forest; space of lawns blotted out in the pressure and dusk of trees. She wondered they were not smothered; then wondered still more that they were not afraid. Far from here, too, their isolation became apparent. The house seemed to be pressing

low in apprehension, hiding its face, as though it had her vision of where it was. It seemed to huddle its trees close in fright and amazement at the wide light lovely unloving country, the unwilling bosom whereon it was set.... Seen from above, the house in its pit of trees seemed a very reservoir of obscurity.[35]

In this elevated view, the homeliness of Danielstown, an avatar of the cartography of timeless presence suggested by the Ordnance Survey maps, gives way to an *unheimlich* sense that such a stable spatial arrangement might in fact be near an end. While the house is "press[ed] low," feeling "fright and amazement," however, it is not simply positioned against a negative space of chaos and disorder. What threatens the house is the "wide light lovely unloving country," the specter of an Ireland uncoupled from the stewardship of the Ascendancy class. In a sweeping glance at the landscape, then, Lois begins to realize her precarious political position. She finds herself in a "wide light lovely" country that is yet "unloving" toward her and the class she represents. Her cartographic vision does not yield assurance but instead gives her an intimation of the coming destruction of Danielstown and a cognitive mapping of her own class obsolescence.

Lois's vision of the big house under siege from a countryside no longer falling under the visual—and thereby political—order of the Anglo-Irish ruling class accords with many nationalist mythologies of a peasant reclamation of the land in the name of an organic national identity. The break between an occupying colonial class and an awakening nationalist movement would seem to be less legible in the city, of which one would expect to find maps depicting signs and symbols of modernity—population densities, networks of streets and railways, and cultural destinations. What, then, of the Ordnance Survey maps of Dublin, which were so meticulously studied by Joyce in his composition of *Ulysses*? Certainly a cartographic project scaled at six inches to the mile would not be able to project the bucolic landscape suggested in the maps of more rural areas. The scale chosen for the initial survey, however, offers the perfect size to mediate both a picturesque naturalism and an encompassing colonial gaze. Cities are shown at a scale that reveals such details as the shapes of buildings and the landscaping of parks while being at a sufficient distance to also include the surrounding countryside. Even the sheet containing central Dublin represents the heart of the metropolis surrounded by the Dublin Bay to the east, the rambling Phoenix Park to the northwest, and undeveloped agricultural land to the north and south. Dublin appears bounded and circumscribed by rural Ireland on three sides with Dublin Bay on a fourth. Moreover, just as the touches of naturalism associated with the Ordnance Survey

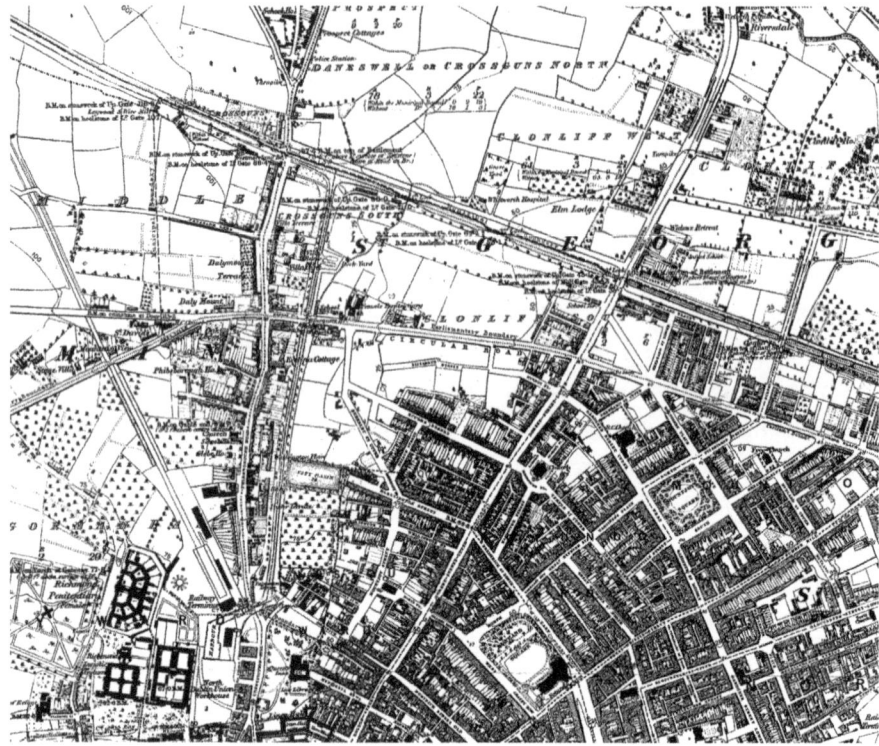

Figure 3.1. Detail from Ordnance Survey map of Dublin, Ireland. Reproduced from the 1846 Ordnance Survey map. Reproduction courtesy of the Newberry Library.

style portrayed a bucolic rural Ireland outside of history, so too does Dublin appear as a static space, neatly framed by the countryside and interspersed with parks, schools, and churches. Dublin is rendered less as a modern international metropolis and capital city than a provincial, if thriving, market town outside of, or at least marginal to, the scope of modernity. The autonomy that Joyce wished to ascribe to Dublin—to present it to the world as a great European city—is undercut by its representation in the Ordnance Survey maps as a merely large provincial town.

In fact, the Ordnance Survey maps of the city show precisely the method through which Joyce could gesture toward a politicized Irish sensibility—a kind of nationalism from below—outside the objectified, picturesque Ireland under the benevolent sway of British imperial stewardship. As the maps show, Dublin was a bounded finitude, a city of which it was, in fact, theoretically possible to know every street, landmark, and point of interest. Joyce's plotting of the novel could thus conceivably encompass enough of the city to create the metonymic suggestion of wholeness. Ironically, by anchoring his narrative to a classic mode of representational abstraction and reification—post-Enlightenment cartography—Joyce could borrow the modern, scientific factualism of the map as a way to lend verisimilitude to the portrayal of a self-contained community. In *Ulysses*, Joyce presents a city small enough to be the world's largest *Gemeineschaft* but large enough to suggest that the community of Dublin could stand for the potentiality of nationhood.

Mapping Coincidence

Following Frank Budgen's characterization of Joyce as a writer-cum-mapmaker, scholars and critics of *Ulysses* have delighted in reading the novel through the lens of geography, producing maps, itineraries, and surveys of the "real-world" Dublin to which the text continually refers. Until recently, most critics have seldom questioned the status of the map as a means of representing space; the map is a mirror of nature rather than a culturally determined representation.[36] Two studies of *Ulysses* in particular have made extensive use of maps: Clive Hart's and Leo Knuth's *A Topographical Guide to "Ulysses"* (1975) and Michael Seidel's *Epic Geography* (1976).[37] Hart's and Knuth's book, as its title suggests, is less a work of criticism than a survey in its own right: its primary purpose is to provide a catalog of places to which the novel refers. Included with the text are several maps, drawn at different scales ranging from a national projection of Ireland to an architectural diagram of 7 Eccles Street. While Hart and Knuth do comment on Joyce's aesthetic transformation of geographical knowledge, they do not question the "factual" status of Thom's *Almanac* and the accompanying Ordnance Survey maps. Seidel's study has a more ambitious aim: to compare the geography of Joyce's Dublin to the classical Mediterranean geography of the *Odyssey*. While Seidel's study also suggests the aesthetic dimensions of geographical knowledge, it too accords an objective quality to the map, as much of its substance is devoted to explicating the maps that compare the space of chapters in *Ulysses* with their corresponding episodes of the *Odyssey*. Both studies ultimately rely on an aesthetic of presence similar to that established by the Ordnance Survey maps: the cartographic space of Ireland is a self-evident representation of reality, which Joyce reworks into fiction in order to give his text a similar aura of presence and facticity. In the following section, I will argue the opposite claim of "Wandering Rocks" in particular: that Joyce invokes the precision of cartography to draw attention to its absences, opacities, and representational failures. In doing so, the chapter sets up an oscillation between a surveying gaze and a situated perspective to show the inherent limitations of both map and narrative in providing a true account of geographical space.

As I discussed in the introduction, maps and narratives have a complementary relationship, albeit one that has changed throughout their respective histories. The history of cartography has moved from an acknowledgment of the narrative quality of maps to the suppression of any traces of narrative from the timeless stasis of post-Enlightenment cartography. Michel de Certeau comments on the originary intertwining of maps and stories in pre-Enlightenment cartography, invoking the itinerary as a formal mode that combines the temporal qualities of storytelling with the spatial imperatives of mapmaking. As a result of the scientific turn in cartography (embodied by such institutions as the Ordnance Survey), "the map has slowly disengaged itself from the itineraries that were the condition of its possibility."[38] The scientific rhetoric of cartography helped to erase temporality from the map by excising iconic figures such as ships, animals, monsters, and other characters that implicitly referred to the specific journeys involved in both the production of geographical knowledge and the future use of the map as a wayfinder. "The map," de Certeau concludes, is "a totalizing stage on which elements of diverse origin are brought together to form the tableau of a 'state' of geographical knowledge."[39] De Certeau's central metaphor is telling: modern maps present a static, totalizing "tableau" of an unchanging geography when their origins in fact suggest they are better thought of as a stage on which any number of performances, voyages, or itineraries might take place. While it is true that any map implies both a rhetoric internal to its form and ideological factors in the circumstances of its production, map readers are not necessarily restricted to the passive viewing of an unchanging "tableau." Rather, each reading of a map is a walk upon the stage, a unique narrative that changes with each imagined or actual itinerary.

In "Wandering Rocks," Joyce remaps the Dublin of the Ordnance Survey map to inscribe particular routes and itineraries, writing the city's geography through the spontaneous performances of its citizens rather than the frozen tableau of abstract space. As Budgen makes clear in his account of Joyce's composition of the episode, the paths of Father Conmee and the Viceregal cavalcade—representing the twin oppressors of Ireland, according to Stephen—are the two orienting lines on the map of Dublin. Between the narration of these relatively purposeful journeys, however, are seventeen other episodes, each distinguished by section breaks, portraying characters moving about the city along more aleatory or diffuse paths. Within these episodes, fragments from the other narrative itineraries are interspersed without any explicit or graphic transition between the "main" episode and the interpolated fragment. One of the threads running through the chapter is the constant reference to the particulars of geographical space. The episode, which takes up fewer than thirty pages, contains (by my count) nearly two hundred top-onyms of nations, counties, towns, streets, rivers, buildings, and other geographi-cal features. In a sense, the episode's narrative elements serve as a pretense for the presentation of geographical space, as the map of Dublin (either physical or mental) becomes a necessary text to integrate the disjunctive events of the chapter into a systematic whole. The narrative depiction of the various meanderings of the novel's characters can only be resolved into a coherent totality through their imag-inary or actual plotting into cartographic space. "Wandering Rocks" thus forces the reader into a detached, aerial, surveying viewpoint, yet the narrative itself does not yield an overarching perspective with which to arrange story information into a meaningful pattern. We are made privy to any number of simultaneous scenes but without any explicit contextual frame into which they may be placed; that is, the narration gives us the power to witness any scene but denies us the ability to "survey and judge" these isolated episodes. For that, we need a map.

While "Wandering Rocks" constantly directs the reader to the totalizing frame of the map, the map's aerial view subsequently returns the reader to the street-level particularities of narrative. The narrative forces us into a dialectical mode of read-ing, book in one hand, map in the other, constantly shuttling between the two if we hope to plot the chapter both temporally and spatially. The map of Dublin and the disjunctive narratives of its inhabitants are necessary complements of each other, each revealing the limits of the other's representational abilities. Without the map, we have only fragmented routes and heterogeneous episodes that only occasionally intersect, and we are overburdened with place names that are not put in any explicit relationship with each other.[40] Yet if we plot the movement of char-acters onto the map in order to gain a totalizing perspective, we risk reducing the multidimensional contours of the narrative into a two-dimensional visual image. The reader's perspective fuses both dimensions of the chapter, mediating the indi-vidual and the collective, the lived experience of the street and the abstract space of the map. "Wandering Rocks," then, is as much an itinerary as it is a narrative. An itinerary—defined both as a recollection of a journey or a planned route—inscribes the temporality of individual experience onto the space of the map. By presenting Dublin not as an organic community (in which inhabitants are linked by essentialized bonds such as class, religion, race, or kinship) but as a series of individual itineraries bound only by their coincidence in space and time, Joyce suggests that the cartographic image of space is less an authoritative representa-tion of the boundaries of community than a heuristic tool to unify conceptually what is necessarily multiform and disparate; it only becomes possible to fuse both survey and local knowledge if one maintains both judging distance on and inti-mate familiarity with a collective social body.

The oscillating perspectives of "Wandering Rocks" reveal the inherent fictional-ity of an organic national community, an idea echoed by Joyce himself. Responding to Frank Budgen's argument for Irish Home Rule, Joyce remarked that "Ireland is what she is...and therefore I am what I am because of the relations that have existed between England and Ireland. Tell me why you think I ought to wish to change the conditions that gave Ireland and me a shape and a destiny?"[41] Joyce here argues that Ireland's existence owes as much to its contact with England as it does to any a priori, primordial national character. Whatever Irish nationhood may be, it does not precede but only emerges within the agonistic relationship between colonizer and colonized. This implied criticism of an essentialist nation-alist politics of purity and essence is amply supported by the novel's equation of the one-dimensional vision of the Cyclops to the single-minded Fenian nationalism of the Citizen. The Citizen's idea of Irish nationalism, based on essential, immanent qualities of Irishness, allows for no ambiguity or multiple loyalties: one is either Irish or an outsider. As the Citizen exclaims to Bloom in a moment of fury, "*Sinn fein amhain!* The friends we love are by our side and the foes we hate before us" (*U* 251). While Joyce parodies the Citizen's chauvinist nationalism as a dangerously extreme stance, the larger point seems to be that all nationalisms based on a poli-tics of purity lead down the slippery slope toward a potentially violent exclusion of difference. Opposed to both the ethnographic stereotypes voiced by Haines and the militant Fenianism of the Citizen, the narrative perspective seems to under-score Bloom's more prosaic idea of a nation as "the same people living in the same place" (*U* 272). Bloom's improvised definition (soon revised to include people in "different places") is more astute than even he realizes: he suggests that nations are not organic but contingent communities. Bloom describes the nation as a literal co-incidence, a cultural identity created through nothing more than a simultane-ous residence in a geographically circumscribed location. Bloom's idea of national community is based on relation rather than essence, present circumstance rather than past history. The map, therefore, does not represent a preexisting community; it creates that community by abstracting a unified space out of a multiplicity of individually experienced places.

The sequence of episodes in "Wandering Rocks" illustrates Bloom's definition of community as a co-incidence. Between the circumscribing paths (and narra-tives) of Father Conmee and the Viceregal cavalcade, the sequence of episodes and interpolations within episodes adheres to no overarching logic that might suggest a community of citizens sharing essential characteristics of cultural identity. The logic initially used to justify the "jumps" from one character and setting to another in "Wandering Rocks" seems clear enough at the beginning of the episode. After the long narration of Father Conmee's itinerary from Gardiner Street toward Artane, we first cut to Corny Kelleher speaking with the constable, then to the "onelegged sailor" singing for alms. Both of these scenes are encountered by Father Conmee on his walk, and we would therefore assume that the subsequent episodes will follow from their relation to Conmee in his journey. In the fourth episode, however, this pattern is broken: we move to the Dedalus household, which is removed from any of the previous characters by at least half a mile. This shift signals a liberation from a sequence of episodes based on immediate spatial contiguity, and suddenly the principles of "cross-cutting" become much more artificial and abstract, where they are discernible at all. In addition, this episode marks the beginning of the interpolated intrusions that offer brief glimpses of other episodes in the chapter without any narrative explanation or visual distinction (in contrast to the three asterisks that separate the larger episodes).[42] A sequence that begins with an organizing principle of physical contiguity quickly throws off this rationale with no discernible governing logic to take its place.

While the totality of the episodes, including their interpolated "intrusions," does not constitute a coherent system, there are local examples of scene shifts that work according to a conceptual rather than spatial logic. While Boylan is arranging to have champagne sent to Molly Bloom, the narration cuts to Bloom, described as a "darkbacked figure under Merchant's arch" who "scanned books on the hawker's cart" (*U* 187). The connection seems obviously justified by its connection of Molly's paramour and husband and more specifically in the currency they use to obtain Molly's affections: Boylan sends food and drink, while Bloom searches for softcore pornographic novels. Similarly, the theme of mechanistic technology connects Tom Rochford's device to alert tardy theater patrons of a show's progress and Miss Dunne's "clicks" on the typewriter keyboard (*U* 188). The connective logic can be linguistic as well as thematic, as in the transition from the "Barang!" of the "lacquey's bell" in front of the auction house to the "Bang" of the "lastlap bell" at the Trinity College track race (*U* 195). Even the co-incidence of character names can lead to connections, as if the chapter's movement were determined by the sequencing of Thom's *Almanac* rather than by any narratively motivated reason. The name "Dudley," for example, occurs three times, first referring to "the reverend Nicholas Dudley C.C. of saint Agatha's church," then to the Viceroy, William Humble, Earl of Dudley, and finally to one of the citizens passed by the Earl of Dudley's cavalcade, "Mr. Dudley White, B.L., M.A." (*U* 207). In all of these coincidental linkages between the various citizens of Dublin, the episode draws attention to connections of which none of the characters can possibly be aware. The reader is the *only* consciousness with access to the linking elements of the individual episodes and characters, suggesting that any community represented by the chapter is an arbitrary rather than organic formation, resolved only by the surveying and judging gaze of the reader who can plot these diverse itineraries on a map of Dublin.

Despite the insistence on connections that exist in the coding of the text rather than the represented world of the novel, Joyce does not suggest that the coincident community of "Wandering Rocks" is an ahistorical, purely formal category only to be embodied in the abstract realm of fictional representation. In fact, the chapter uses the device of the narrative "cutaway" to imply histories of political and cultural struggle embedded within the topography of the city. For example, as Miss Dunne types the date—June 16, 1904—on her typewriter keyboard, we cut to the following scene without any visible breaks: "Five tallwhitehatted sandwichmen between Monypeny's corner and the slab where Wolfe Tone's statue was not, eeled themselves turning H.E.L.Y'S and plodded back as they had come" (*U* 188). The explicit mention of the date (the only place in the novel it is directly mentioned) calls to mind what Benedict Anderson refers to as the "calendrical coincidence" of newspapers, which mark "the steady onward clocking of [the] homogenous, empty time" of the modern nation.[43] As Anderson has argued, the calendar is to the time of the modern nation what the map is to its space: an arbitrary means by which nations interpellate subjects into a common imaginative space. Yet, in counterpoint to the historical presence of a specific temporal moment indicated by the date typed by Miss Dunne, we are shown a spatial absence: the "slab where Wolfe Tone's statue was not." A foundation had been laid in 1898 for a statue of the eighteenth-century Irish revolutionary, but the statue was never completed.[44] The syntax conjures the unbuilt statue only to negate its existence with the trailing word "not." The statue is constructed and dismantled in the space of a sentence, and for the briefest moment Joyce imagines a Dublin in which the martyred Tone is given a proper memorial. The map prompts this alternate Dublin but cannot represent it, bound as it is to a factual record of an existing topography. Narrative, however, can provoke a play between the presence implied by geographical and historical mimeticism and the absences suggested through language. If maps mark the coincident space of national community—as calendars record the "steady onward" movement of its time—then narrative has the unique power to evoke alternate histories and transformed spaces.

"Wandering Rocks" uses the rhetoric of cartography not to totalize and circumscribe the space of community but to evoke an imaginative space in which history might have turned out (and might still turn out) differently. In fact, "Wandering Rocks" suggests the *necessity* of the colonist's map as a means to articulate the coincident community of late colonial Dublin. None of the characters in the chapter have more than a fragmentary glimpse of the collective social existence of Dublin on June 16, 1904. The chapter's narrative point of view, on the other hand, by implying the map as a staging ground for representing the simultaneous experience of unrelated Dubliners, expresses community *through* the medium of cartographic knowledge. From this perspective, the imagined community of Dublin, and by extension Ireland, only exists in the mind of one who can "survey and judge" from a distanced viewpoint. The ambivalence that Joyce felt toward Ireland—as reluctant patriot and willful exile—can be read in the shifting point of view in "Wandering Rocks." To belong to a place, Joyce suggests, one must have both intimate knowledge and skeptical distance, the particulate experience of the street along with the synoptic view of the map. Communities are not made out of anterior essences that are then given spatial form through geographical knowledge; there is no collectivity prior to its spatialization on the map, even if that map is part of an imperial archive. As Bloom would eagerly tell us, maps give us a fictive sense of being "the same people" precisely *because* we live in "the same place." "Wandering Rocks" thus shows the possibilities for combining cartographic and narrative knowledge; neither perspective yields an ultimate truth, but the simultaneity of multiple points of view brings out new "relational structures" between the spatial conditions of late colonial Ireland and the possibilities for the emergence of spaces that might escape the objectified realm of the imperial archive.

Graphs of Desire

While "Wandering Rocks" affords the reader the power to jump from the street-level perceptions of the characters to the larger scale of the urban map, the boundaries of the community are still limited to the scale of the city. The community presented in "Wandering Rocks" is a *polis* rather than a *patria*; its parameters are described by the immediate physical environment of the urban milieu rather than the larger, more abstract realm of the nation.[45] Because of this circumscription, the nomadic movements that seem to bypass or ignore the local instantiations of imperial power might merely be absorbed into a larger geography of imperial rule; for all of the chapter's wanderings, they still take place in the gulf between the "banks" of church (Father Conmee) and state (the Viceroy). As Joyce himself made clear to Budgen, these lines circumscribe the geographical as well as narrative movement of the chapter.[46] In spite of its use of coincidence rather than essence as the basis for community, the chapter's topography is still bound to the particular frame and scale of the six-inch Ordnance Survey map of Dublin, itself produced with the aim of maintaining British administrative control of Ireland. One could plausibly argue, then, that the disjunctions visible at the urban scale are simply invisible in the smaller scale of the composite national map. Dublin is reduced from a multiplicity to a singularity, from a network of streets to a self-contained point. In this reduction, whatever is anomalous or disorderly is simply reduced to a unified image of order.

Later in the novel, however, we are introduced to spatial scales both beyond and within the local, particularly through the ruminations of Bloom in the penultimate "Ithaca" chapter. As Marjorie Howes has argued, the notion of geographical scale is central to two other works by Joyce: "The Dead" and *A Portrait of the Artist as a Young Man*. Howes writes that in these narratives, the interplay between "local, regional, and international scales" foreground the nation as a "problematic" rather than a naturally emerging geographical scale in its own right.[47] "Ithaca," however, presents spatial scales that range far beyond the familiar cartographic registers of the local, regional, national, and international. The radical play of scales shown in "Ithaca" forces the reader to question the choice of scales commonly found on "political" maps. Scale, as Denis Cosgrove argues, is not a by-product or effect of mapping; rather, it is a constitutive feature of any cartographic representation. "Enlarging or reducing the space generated and occupied by phenomena alters their form, their significance, their relations of meaning with other phenomena."[48] Cartographic rhetoric asks us to "see through" different scales to imagine that any topographical location can be mapped at any possible scale. Yet, maps at different scales are distinctly different representations, conveying increased or decreased quantities of graphic and linguistic signs and different relationships between visual elements.[49] "Ithaca" takes us on an imaginative journey from the bedroom to the cosmos and back again, a range of scales that effaces the epistemological priority of national and imperial geographies such as those generated by the Ordnance Survey. Such a journey, I argue, causes a spatial disorientation that is ultimately left unresolved, because the chapter ends with a representation of a space that cannot be assimilated to any discernible scale.

For Leopold Bloom, maps are not merely indexes to "real-world" space; they provide a vehicle for the imaginative extension and intension of space beyond and within the realist scale of the city. As Joyce shows in "Ithaca," maps can function as catalysts for the transformation of the spatial orientation of the individual subject, using geographical knowledge as a staging-ground for the possible rather than as an archival record of the actual. Cosgrove amplifies this self-projective aspect of mapping as "the creative probing, the tactical reworking, the imaginative projection of a surface," going on to claim that the map "excites imagination and graphs desire, its projection is the foundation for and stimulus to projects."[50] Bloom (whose mind, incidentally, teems with "projects" for individual and social improvement) uses the projections of cartography to imagine possible futures in which individual identity slides across spatial scales from the minute to the cosmic, no longer bound to the conventions of the "political" maps of nations and empires. While "Wandering Rocks" asks the reader to resolve the radical disjunctions of narrative by referring to the unifying field of the map, "Ithaca" represents knowledge in terms of aleatory connection rather than archival totalization. Within this economy of knowledge, the map no longer assumes its privileged place as the record of an ontologically foundational space. The cartographic precision of many of the earlier chapters of *Ulysses* therefore needs to be contrasted to the more abstract registers of space in "Ithaca."

In "Ithaca," we find that Bloom's first conscious memory of narrative is inextricably connected to its emplotment on a map. As his father narrated his life story as "a retrospective arrangement of migrations and settlements in and between Dublin, London, Florence, Milan, Vienna, Budapest, [and] Szombathely," the six-year-old Leopold "had accompanied these narrations by constant consultation of a geographical map of Europe (political)" (*U* 595). Bloom uses the map to make his father's narrative his own, just as the novel's representation of Dublin becomes our opportunity for *re*mapping, and consequently projecting ourselves, into the narrative. For Bloom, mapping offers the experience of projecting himself into his father's itinerary, using the map as a point of connection between his possible futures and his father's experienced past. The adult Bloom views maps with a similar attraction in their ability to extrapolate utopian possibility from everyday reality. As he contemplates a possible journey away from Molly and from Dublin, the questioning voice asks: "What considerations rendered departure desirable?" The answer refers specifically to the medium of cartography: "The attractive character of certain localities in Ireland and abroad, as represented in general geographical maps of polychrome design or in special ordnance survey charts by employment of scale numerals and hachures" (*U* 597). The syntax here is vague, suggesting that what renders the places "attractive" is not necessarily any inherent quality that they possess but their visual qualities "as represented" on the map. The detailed attention to the artful conventions of cartography—polychrome design, scale numerals, and hachures (shading to indicate mountains or other topographical variations)—further highlights the graphic conventions of the map rather than the immanence of the places to which it refers. For Bloom, clearly, the map is more than simply a static representation of space; it inspires both aesthetic contemplation and imaginative projection.

Bloom's meditation on the "attractive character" of maps leads him to imagine a voyage with many possible itineraries, both local and international. He first considers voyages to places in Ireland—including the "windy wilds" of Connemara, the "Golden Vale of Tipperary," the Aran Isles (*U* 597)—that perhaps describe a typical list of Irish tourist destinations that might be frequented by cultural nationalists and amateur ethnographers alike. But unlike Haines, the Citizen, or (perhaps more appropriately) Miss Ivors in "The Dead," Bloom also envisions travels to any number of places outside of Ireland for reasons that range from the immediately personal to the inscrutably abstract:

> Ceylon (with spicegardens supplying tea to Thomas Kernan, agent for Pulbrook, Robertson, and Co, 2 Mincing Lane, London, E.C., 5 Dame street, Dublin), Jerusalem, the holy city (with mosque of Omar and gate of Damascus, goal of aspiration), the straits of Gibraltar (the unique birthplace of Marion Tweedy), the Parthenon (containing statues of nude Grecian divinities), the Wall street money market (which controlled international finance), the Plaza de Toros at La Linca, Spain (where O'Hara of the Camerons had slain the bull), Niagara (over which no human being had passed with impunity), the land of the Eskimos (eaters of soap), the forbidden country of Thibet (from which no traveller returns), the bay of Naples (to see which was to die), the Dead Sea.
>
> (*U* 597–598)

The first thing that one notices about Bloom's imagined destinations is their diversity. From the Holy Land to Wall Street, from ancient Greece and Rome to the mysteriously vague "land of the Eskimos," Bloom's itinerary covers East and West, ancient and modern, religious and secular. His reasons for travel are similarly eclectic: some are obviously personal (Gibraltar) and some presumably religious or historical (Jerusalem, the Parthenon, the Dead Sea). While Ceylon and Tibet seem motivated by his Orientalist proclivities, the inquisitive Bloom is not content to rest on exoticizing stereotypes of a "distant East." After mentioning the "spicegardens" of Ceylon, Bloom immediately connects this fantasy to its source in his own daily life, noting the circuits of exchange through which the "exotic" products of empire must pass to be available for consumption in Dublin. Similarly, Bloom's wish to visit Wall Street might be understood as yet another of his desires to see the inner workings of all exterior phenomena. However, the narrative suggests that such an impulse to see beneath the planimetric projection of the map might in fact prompt a more critical, nuanced view of the "invisible" global economic system emerging in the wake of the more cartographically visible regime of European imperialism.[51] The significant omission in Bloom's list of itineraries is England, suggesting that that the everyday landscape of colonial rule has not gained sovereignty over Bloom's fantasies of travel. The maps lead Bloom from Ireland directly to his destinations throughout the world; unlike the tea that Bloom drinks, he need not pass through the imperial capital to recirculate into other places.

Although the speculative voyage that Bloom plots for himself ultimately extends to the most cosmic spatial scales, "to the extreme limit of his cometary orbit, beyond the fixed stars and variable suns and telescopic planets," it eventually returns to the intimate, domestic space of his conjugal bed, where Molly sleeps (*U* 598). While the "conventional" map initiates these imaginative wanderings, Bloom transforms cartographic space by destroying its scale. Bloom travels from 7 Eccles Street in Dublin, through Ireland, the world, and eventually through the cosmos before returning to the confines of home. After this sojourn, the narrative merges the domestic location of the bedroom with a much larger scale of global space, as in the description of Bloom's and Molly's positions in bed: "Listener [Molly], S.E. by E.: Narrator [Bloom], N.W. by W.: on the 53rd parallel of latitude, N., and 6th meridian of longitude, W.: at an angle of 45° to the terrestrial equator" (*U* 606). The intimate zone of home is plotted on the abstract graticule of the globe, forcing the reader into an expanded version of the oscillating vision of "Wandering Rocks." Instead of a movement from city street to urban map, we shuttle from the most personal of scales, the bedroom, to the widest possible geographic area, the globe. This more extreme oscillation imaginatively removes the novel from the "political" map of nations that had circumscribed its space in earlier episodes. The dissolution of spatial scale is ultimately rendered in the chapter's final character. The questioner concludes with a one-word query, which is answered with an ambiguous graphic mark:

Where?

•

The chapter's concluding mark is an abstract location in a mapless space, a point with no context and no scale. The point that answers the question "Where?" could equally refer to the mind of Bloom, the bedroom of the Bloom residence, 7 Eccles Street, Dublin, Ireland, Europe, and so on. By decontextualizing the "point," Joyce uses a common cartographic symbol to draw attention to the inherently arbitrary representation of any place. Without the formal elements of cartography—scale, projection, framing, iconography—the graphic mark floats in an abstract non-space emptied of any referential meaning.

The disruption of scale both recalls and rewrites the multiple spatial identifications of the young Stephen Dedalus in *A Portrait*. Daydreaming during his geography lesson at Clongowes Wood, Stephen lists several realms of identification that extend concentrically from the immediately personal to the distantly abstract, from his affiliation with the school, Clongowes Wood, to the largest imaginable scale, the universe. Just as the young Stephen intuitively places his own identity within a number of spaces and contexts in his geography lesson at Clongowes Wood, moving outward from the classroom to the universe, so does "Ithaca" suggest the same concentricity of Bloom. Marjorie Howes writes that "his formulation offers a model of the relations among scales as orderly and commensurate, with each scale neatly enfolding the smaller ones."[52] While Howes understands Stephen's list to give implicit priority to the scale of the nation, I would argue that the passage suggests a certain "play" with scales that predates Stephen's inauguration into a predominantly national identification. For Stephen, Ireland is but one item in the list, one scale at which to map one's identity onto a spatial field. In his valedictory moment, Bloom likewise becomes a subject who cannot be fully assimilated into a scale of geographical space associated with a dominant register of identity. Although the scales of Bloom's identities expand to the far reaches of the universe, his journey is not a universalizing one wherein each move to a higher scale effaces the differences or schisms of the previous one. The graphic mark at the end of "Ithaca" undoes spatial scale in an even more radical way than Stephen's geography lesson. Where Stephen's ruminations are narratively contextualized within the environment of the school, a place where students are socialized into national subjects, Bloom's mark is a point of no return, a sign that can never be resolved into a stable referent. If geographical knowledge is customarily seen as positivist knowledge—data about the world that have an existence and truth independent of the observer—then Joyce suggests that, in narrative at least, cartography might instead be looked at as a "negativist" knowledge of signs without natural topographical referents or grounded spatial meanings.

Post-Enlightenment cartography imagined itself an ideal form of representation, a way to reduce the diverse knowledges of the world into an abstract image of clarity and scientific neutrality. One of the most important lessons of recent critiques of cartography is the recognition of the social inequity concealed by the seductive abstraction of mapping. Yet despite cartography's history of complicity with imperial conquest and domination, maps are perhaps more fluent than many critics have allowed, encoding relations of cultural exchange rather than simply the top-down exercise of power. Just as maps can confer the power of possession of a territory, they can likewise become a means to imagine new articulations of space. In this, the imperial map is akin to the colonizing tongue: both are sign-systems that are deployed to order the chaos of the real; both attempt to establish a *langue* that would govern possible expressions of *parole*. Yet, just as official languages inevitably mutate into unsanctioned dialects, pidgins, and other "minor" versions, the map is also open to deterritorialization and resignification. As Deleuze and Guattari suggest, writing and mapping share the power to imagine "realms to come." The incorporation of cartographic rhetoric in *Ulysses* need not be seen as an imperial complicity, nor can it be reduced to a revolutionary postcolonial mapping of resistance. As much as Budgen's account of Joyce seems designed to confer the aura of science on the act of writing, this reading relies on the common conception of the cartographer as an engineer, surveying and inscribing territory from a safe distance. Budgen's portrait thus inadvertently turns Joyce into an imperialist *manqué*, surveying and mapping Ireland in his desire to present the nation to the world as a commodified object of knowledge.

In fact, Joyce comes as close as possible to representing the form of the emergent nation-state within a finite, bounded work of fiction. We are kept from the plentitude of the Andersonian imagined community by those antirealist elements that reduce the human fullness of a national society to the formalism of its cartographic existence. Cartography represents both the ground and limit for the narratives of the nation. On the one hand, the map provides an authoritative geographical entity that facilitates the possibility of a territorial, sovereign statehood; on the other hand, the potential infinitude of individual narratives inevitably gives way to the wider abstractions of a coherent, bounded surface onto which they can be mapped. In representing Ireland during the waning years of its colonial period, therefore, *Ulysses* plots the uncertainty of postcolonial nationhood as a negative dialectic between the realism of the map and the realism of fiction.

4. Island

Rhys, Kincaid, and the Myth of Insular Sovereignty

It is often forgotten how large the distances are in the West Indies.

—Hume Wrong, *Government of the West Indies*, 1923

The stone had skidded arc'd and bloomed into islands:
    Cuba and San Domingo
    Jamaica and Puerto Rico
    Grenada Guadeloupe Bonaire

—Kamau Brathwaite, "Calypso"

Water, Water Everywhere

Kamau Brathwaite's poem "Calypso" offers an origin myth that rewrites the pattern of most national narratives. Brathwaite does not describe an origin that explains a singular, homogeneous national culture; rather, his description of a skidding stone leaving behind the individual islands of the Caribbean archipelago relies purely on a cartographic image. To look at a map of the Caribbean is to see the figure that Brathwaite composes: the larger islands of Jamaica, Cuba, Hispañola, and Puerto Rico moving to the east, then arcing southward in a line of smaller islands toward the South American coast. Contrary to the sober opinion of Hume Wrong, an early-twentieth-century Canadian historian and diplomat, Brathwaite imagines the Antillean islands as mythologically and geologically connected, each arising from the common "bloom" of the arcing stone. Moreover, "Calypso" rewrites centuries of European colonization in the Caribbean, the results of which separated island cultures along the linguistic and national cultures of their imperial masters. As with Joyce, Brathwaite uses a cartographic image to offer a counterargument to imperial conceptions of territorial acquisition and possession. Brathwaite invites us to reconsider notions of distance and proximity across the negative space of the ocean. Are the islands of the Caribbean separated and isolated by the gulf between, as Wrong would have it? Or does the ocean serve as a medium of connection and means of community?

Focusing largely on late and postcolonial texts that respond to the culturally dominant island nation of England, this chapter argues for a view of the island-ocean relationship that erodes the myth of the English "island story." Reading two island writers in particular, the Dominican Jean Rhys and the Antiguan Jamaica Kincaid, I posit a countervailing worldview based upon the perspective of the "peripheral" island. Rather than forming a rock-solid terrain in the midst of unstable, threatening fluidity, the island functions as a way station, a momentary repository of economic, historical, and cultural currents. Island stories do not and cannot conform to modes of linear narrative and the circumscribed settings of the knowable community. In the case of Jean Rhys, the triad of islands depicted in *Wide Sargasso Sea*—Jamaica, Dominica, and England—are haunted by an absence and deferral that is signified by the oceanic space referred to in the title of the novel. Rhys destabilizes the normative island of Britain by introducing Jamaica and Dominica as alternative island-realms, in the process upsetting spatial binaries and turning all three islands into "elsewheres." Rhys's lingering nostalgia for an idealized England is thoroughly undercut by Jamaica Kincaid in her satirical travel essay, *A Small Place*. For Kincaid, the island of Antigua (along with its related islands of Barbuda and Redonda) is almost overloaded with presence, a riot of cultures, economies, and populations that have found their way to and through the "small place" of Antigua. By layering complex geographies and cultural lines of force, Kincaid explodes the myth—often invoked in the cause of Caribbean postcolonial nationalism—of the island as sovereign political territory and national culture. Both Rhys and Kincaid, I argue, force us to question one of the governing assumptions of islandness: that the happenstance of a landform bounded by water authorizes both a cultural and political sovereignty. Rather, for each author, islands are stripped of their ontological "reality" and are placed into an ambiguous and uncertain relationship with the waters that surround them. These reversals of a geographical figure-ground relationship translate to an aesthetic defamiliarization of narrative place, a vertiginous discontinuity that recalls modernist experimentations with narrative space, including those previously discussed by Conrad, Greene, Forster, and Joyce.[1]

In geography, the imaginative transformation of oceans from ground to figure was a consequence of Britain's success as a maritime empire. In his widely influential 1890 book, *The Influence of Sea Power upon History*, Alfred Mahan argued that the dominance of the island, or water-bordered nations, is predicated upon how such nations can turn their surrounding waters to national advantage. Great Britain was a textbook example of a nation transforming its maritime space into an extension of its lands through economic and military control. Because Britain is "so situated that it is neither forced to defend itself by land, it has, by the very unity of its aim directed upon the sea, an advantage as compared with a people one of whose boundaries is continental."[2] Halford Mackinder, the geopolitical thinker we encountered in the first two chapters, applied some of Mahan's insights in his 1902 geography textbook, *Britain and the British Seas* (note that even the title annexes the oceans to British territory). In describing the geographical position of Britain as an reason for its rise to world hegemony, Mackinder posits a kind of cognitive paradox whereby the British Isles are at once bounded *and* extended by the sea. "Britain," Mackinder writes, "is possessed of two geographical qualities, complementary rather than antagonistic: insularity and universality. Before Columbus, the insularity was more evident than the universality. ... After Columbus, value began to attach to the ocean-highway, which is in its nature universal. Even the great continents are only vast islands and discontinuous; but every part of the ocean is accessible from every other part."[3] Through possession and control of the world's seas, the "national character" of British insularity is extended throughout the globe, allowing the British Empire to both retain its particularity, cast as inward-looking, local "Englishness," and to justify its imperial project in the name of the "universality" granted by access to the sea. Mackinder thus uses the quasi-scientific language of physical geography to provide political legitimation for the extension of empire across the seas.

This view of oceanic space effectively treats it as a continuation of geographical territory, as Mahan and Mackinder imaginatively annex the spaces of the ocean to the British Empire. The "naturally" seafaring British manage to widen the scope of their tiny island such that any shore around the world may be claimed as an extension of British sovereignty. Yet, as Mackinder suggests, this is not a reversible situation; the inflow of others across the sea to Britain is to be met with the defenses of an island fortress, protecting a national insularity from the world. In Mahan's and Mackinder's epistemology, the paradigmatic island of Britain is a culturally sealed zone able to exert its influence and power in an outward way but never participating in any kind of free-flowing exchange. Mackinder imaginatively domesticates and territorializes the potentially threatening, ungovernable space of the sea in an effort to justify and naturalize centuries of overseas British colonization. Such a myth requires an irreducible binary of land and sea, most vividly expressed in that emblematic English image of the Dover cliffs ascending in a vertical escarpment from the English Channel. Most interfaces between island and sea are not so well defined, admitting liminality and movement to the border between land and water, which made it all the more necessary to protect and police. In his influential essay "The Geographical Pivot of History," Mackinder goes as far as positing the large, multicontinental landmass of Asia, Europe, and Africa as the "world-island," around which the peripheral "islands" such as the Americas, Australia, and the South Pacific were arrayed. Mackinder felt that the "heartland" of the world-island, namely Russia, and Eastern Europe, and parts of China, was the emerging seat of global geopolitical strength in the world.[4] In fact, Mackinder's paper, while to some degree presaging the emerging power of the U.S.S.R., functioned as a renewed call to vigilance for threatened sea-based powers, of which Great Britain was the most significant. Mackinder's ideas, while positing a new kind of world order based upon the dialectic between land and sea, did so primarily to once again justify British imperial designs.

One set of islands on the periphery of Mackinder's world picture was beginning to articulate cultural identities that challenged his wide-scale vision of a world-island threatened by subversion from within its heartland. The Caribbean archipelago, with its arc stretching northward in tiny islands from the Venezuelan coast of South America and veering west toward the larger islands of Puerto Rico, Hispañola, Jamaica, and Cuba, had been since the time of Columbian contact a zone of traversal and circulation. Historians and theorists such as Paul Gilroy, Édouard Glissant, and Antonio Benítez-Rojo have brought attention to the Caribbean as a crucial locus of the "Black Atlantic," a site of ambivalent relation with European colonial metropoles, and a region of cross-cultural and multilingual interchange between its own islands. In the Caribbean, the distinction between islands and oceans is never as sharply drawn as it is in Mackinder's geopolitically inflected worldview. Water is never simply negative space but rather is an medium for an obscured historical memory, a symbol of distance and detachment from "civilization," and a pathway both permitting the incursion of hostile external forces and facilitating escape into a larger world.

Between Worlds

Published in 1956, two years before the establishment of the West Indies Federation, Samuel Selvon's novel of Caribbean émigrés in England, *The Lonely Londoners*, would seem to suggest the community of feeling that culminated in (admittedly short-lived) pan-island West Indian sovereignty. The novel's protagonist, Moses Aloetta, becomes a de facto leader of an immigrant community in London, assisting its new West Indian arrivals no matter what their island of origin. Ever conscious of English racism and the wish to not arouse resentment for the establishment of "West Indian" neighborhoods, Moses finds housing and work for new arrivals throughout the city. "And so like a welfare officer," Selvon writes, "Moses scattering the boys around London, for he don't want no concentrated area in the Water—as it is, things bad enough already."[5] The alliances of Moses and his band of West Indian brothers (for, significantly, women are marginal to this community)[6] are largely formed in response to an identity that is forced upon them through the common experience of English racism. This provisional solidarity is consistent with a history of West Indian nationalist movements, which have almost always taken root among émigré communities rather than within the islands themselves. Beginning with the mutiny of several West Indian battalions fighting in Italy for the British Empire during World War I, and the subsequent formation of the Caribbean League by noncommissioned officers from these battalions, pan-island nationalist consciousness was largely driven by the resistance to racism directed at black West Indians abroad.

Yet interisland rivalries would never be completely dissolved in a pan-island nationalism. There are suggestions in Selvon's novel that the islanders' fellow feeling has its limits. Early in the novel, as Moses waits for a new *arrivant* in Waterloo Station, he is approached by a news reporter who, assuming he is also a recent émigré, asks him what the conditions are like in Jamaica. Moses plays along, albeit with a weary resentment. "Now Moses don't know a damn thing about Jamaica— Moses come from Trinidad, which is a thousand miles from Jamaica, but the English people believe that everybody who come from the West Indies come from Jamaica."[7] Although coming from the second largest of the British West Indian colonies, Moses still recognizes that, in the hazy geography of British consciousness, "Jamaica" could stand in for an entire archipelago that most white Britons couldn't be bothered to learn about in more precise detail. Although Moses's resentment is expressed in comic tones, the fear that local island identities would be swallowed up—politically, economically, and culturally—by the larger, more heavily populated islands was a main line of resistance to federation nationalism. Conversely,

Jamaican politicians worried that the relative poverty and economic stagnation of the smaller islands would make Jamaica a de facto welfare state for the smaller islands in the federation. And it was Jamaica that took the first step toward the dissolution of the federation by withdrawing in September 1961. Subsequently, most of the islands (or groups of islands that were culturally bound in one way or another) began to seek sovereign nationhood on their own.[8]

Without resorting to a geographical determinism that would suggest the failure of federation can be blamed simply on the considerable distance between the islands, I would like to consider how geography might have worked against the establishment of a form of transoceanic sovereignty. In the history of Western representation, the relationship between islands and the bodies of water that surround them has been understand in terms of the opposition between order and chaos, figure and ground, positive being and its dark, lethal negation. Within a Western tradition of metaphysics, it has been very difficult to think of water as a connective, binding substance.[9] Water is the negative space that divides and separates, enabling cultures to neatly partition "here" from "there," "us" from "them." Islands, by contrast, provide an image of self-containment and unity that can seem naturally, geologically predestined. In the case of the British West Indies, island populations as geographically distant as Jamaica and Trinidad were implicitly asked to adopt a sense of national identity analogous to post-Enlightenment European models based upon territorial contiguity. Hume Wrong, however, reminds us "how large the distances are in the West Indies," just as the Trinidadian Moses Aloetta, several decades later, proclaims with irritation that "he don't know a damn thing" about an island a thousand miles away. The prospects of the federation were disadvantaged at its inception because it projected a Western metaphysics of nationhood onto a geography that resisted the bounded, territorially contiguous geography that authorized such versions of national identity. A pan-island, transoceanic identity might require a "derivative" form of nationalism, to echo Partha Chatterjee's thesis on India, but it could never simply mimic a territorially based Western identity. We therefore need to look at how the Caribbean archipelago has functioned within a metropolitan European consciousness before we can understand what this identity might look like.

In the view of metropolitan Britain, the islands of the Caribbean archipelago have long been understood as curiously multiplied, inverse images of the British island nation. As the habitual use of the initial Columbian misappellation "West Indies" suggests, the Caribbean islands stood for the indistinct, proliferating "elsewheres" of metropolitan imperial culture.[10] Lumped together conceptually in the minds of Britons, they nevertheless were seldom seen as any kind of unified culture or community. As J. R. Seeley wrote in the early 1880s of the future threat of anti-colonial nationalism in different British colonies, dismissing possessions within the Caribbean archipelago as beneath his concern: "In the West Indian group such difficulties for the present do not take a serious form, because the colonies are in the main dispersed in small islands and have no community of feeling."[11] Seeley expresses the late-nineteenth-century absence of meaning attached to the West Indies: seen only as "dispersed... small islands," they occupied far less of the British popular imaginary than colonial possessions in sub-Saharan Africa or India, for example. Ironically, as the twentieth century brought about the increase of cultural traffic across what Paul Gilroy has described as the "Black Atlantic," Caribbean writers arguably became more immersed in the cultures of Anglo-American modernism than writers from other colonial territories, including India, Africa, and South America. Yet the Caribbean still functioned as a geographical gap in the minds of metropolitan subjects, and its peoples and cultures were often assimilated to Africa through the racialized discourse of primitivism.[12] This geographical neglect of the Caribbean has laid the groundwork for a late-twentieth-century tourist epistemology, within which one island is interchangeable with another, as long as all feature the requisite picturesque sunsets, beaches, and other tropical attractions.[13]

From an Anglo-American metropolitan perspective, the Caribbean has been represented according to a trope that Antonio Benítez-Rojo refers to as the "repeating island." Writing against a conventional geography and historiography of the Caribbean as a series of disjunctive locales, separated by the emptiness of water and the differences of language, Benítez-Rojo understands the region not in an abstract, linear history but through an embodied island sensorium, noting the common layer of experience provided by the "geographical accident" of the Caribbean archipelago. The Caribbean, he writes, is to be found in a condition of "discontinuous conjunction" marked by "unstable condensations, turbulences, whirlpools, clumps of bubbles, frayed seaweed, sunken galleons, crashing breakers, flying fish, seagull squawks, downpours, nighttime phosphorescences, eddies and pools, uncertain voyages of signification."[14] Benítez-Rojo begins to articulate a kind of experiential sovereignty to the Antillean archipelago, offering a counter-narrative to the segmented imposition of distinct European national cultures and languages.[15] Benítez-Rojo extrapolates this coherence:

> Within the sociocultural fluidity that the Caribbean archipelago presents, within its historiographic turbulence and its ethnological and linguistic clamor, within its generalized instability of vertigo and hurricane, one can

sense the features of an island that "repeats" itself, unfolding and bifurcating until it reaches all the seas and lands of the earth.[16]

Rather than work within the linear causation of history, which tends to separate and isolate individual territories and link them conceptually to their respective metropolitan centers, Benítez-Rojo provides an image of a pan-Caribbean identity based on the geographical and cultural entity of the island, whose "repeated" form blurs and obscures individual island identities within a European epistemology.

Benítez-Rojo offers a view of the Caribbean archipelago primarily as a conceptual negation of Eurocentric imaginative geographies. Many late-twentieth-century Anglophone Caribbean writers, however, have attempted to reverse and complicate the relationship between the British island myth and the marginal, dispersed nonplace of the Caribbean archipelago. The Barbadian poet and critic Kamau Brathwaite, for example, would dispute Seeley's claim that the Caribbean islands have no "community of feeling." Drawing upon the shared history of slavery for the great majority of Caribbeans of African origin, Brathwaite proposes the concept of "nation language" to describe the generative interaction across all Caribbean islands between "submerged" West African languages and the colonial languages of English, Spanish, French, and Dutch.[17] In his poem "Calypso," Brathwaite presents an origin myth that imagines the archipelago coming into existence from a common source, a stone skimming across the surface of the ocean, leaving behind spots in the water which "bloomed into islands." Brathwaite locates the history of the islands in terms of mytho-geological connection, rather than the dispersal imposed from without by the different national cultures of the colonial states. This staging of a distinctly Caribbean identity does not depend upon the moment of European contact to be called forth into existence. Similarly, other writers have drawn upon the islandness of the Caribbean to express a geo-cultural identity outside of the master/slave paradigm.

Édouard Glissant finds a potential solution to these perpetual problems of isolation in the notion of Caribbeanness (*antillanité* in the original French). Like Brathwaite's pan-Caribbean notion of "nation language," Glissant argues for a recognition of common experience across the diverse spaces and cultures of the archipelago. Unlike Brathwaite, however, Glissant is reluctant to trace this common memory back to Africa; he unequivocally favors *antillanité* over an Afrocentric *negritude*. Glissant locates Caribbeanness in the "multidimensional nature" of diversity.[18] Firmly entrenched in the present "world of the Americas" rather than across the distant sea to the colonial metropole, the Caribbean islands must negotiate a common identity across the geographical barriers of water and the discursive barriers of linguistic difference. What Glissant does *not* advocate is a formal legislation of a sovereign body; rather, "the dream is kept alive in a limited way in the cultural sphere."[19] This is less a world-regional or supranational identity than a contingent, networked, quasi-national political sovereignty. This view advocates an Andersonian imagined community, yet this collective identity is self-consciously located in the circumstances, performance, and expression of the present rather than in the originary myths of the past. This model of sovereignty self-consciously attends to concepts of spatiality, but not in a way that fetishizes the enclosed, self-sufficient governance of the territorial nation-state. Rather, it seeks new models of relational space based on common cultural and historical experience; rather than a singular areal territory fused to the earth, Glissant proposes a more flexible space akin to Benítez-Rojo's "repeating island." Theoretically, the challenge to the formulation of a pan-Caribbean identity has largely been a geographical one: how can diverse islands find mutual interest across the negative space of water? How can water become a means of connection rather than separation and isolation? In the wake of "failed" pan-Caribbean nationalist movements and institutions, a number of writers have explored the difficulties of establishing a geographically coherent cultural identity that would neither fully identify with a former colonial master nor reduce its horizons to an island nationalism that borrows the myth of the self-contained island. Rather than simply mimic models of Western territorial sovereignty, which would claim a self-contained cultural and political autonomy for each island, many postcolonial writers of the Caribbean have adapted modernist aesthetic strategies to deconstruct such island mythologies. Jean Rhys and Jamaica Kincaid, in particular, advise us to be suspicious of a perspective that would isolate islands from the cultural, historical, and geographical currents that link them to a larger world.

Repeating Islands: *Wide Sargasso Sea*

As Mary Lou Emery has persuasively argued, Jean Rhys's portrayal of Antoinette Cosway in *Wide Sargasso Sea* transforms the modernist narrative problematic of identity—who is Antoinette?—to a question of cultural location—"From what place does she speak?"[20] Emery points out that an aesthetic of dislocation and otherness, usually associated with metropolitan modernist narratives, acquires a particularly anticolonial resonance in Caribbean writing. This reconfiguration of modernist alienation into an incipient postcolonial dislocation is given a geographical specificity in *Wide Sargasso Sea*, but the geography of the novel is easily lost within its oneiric, uncanny prose style. The novel's coordinates—Jamaica, Dominica, and England—complicate the dualities and binarisms often associated with postcolonial fiction: center and periphery, metropole and colony, civilization and wilderness. Invoking three island spaces in their disconnected, uncertain geographical relationships with each other sets in motion a new chain of associations and resonances that ask the reader to consider interisland as well as transatlantic networks of power and control. *Wide Sargasso Sea* uses the figure of the "repeating island" to spatialize a critique of the island landform as a template for a bounded, coherent cultural space—the model of which is, of course, England. The novel also invites us to consider the idealized, normative island to be a gendered space of disembodied, Cartesian masculinity. Rochester, the avatar of this magisterial perspective, finds himself troubled by the proliferation of "repeating" islands that escape stable, normative systems of meaning. The novel asks us to attend to the space that troubles Rochester's gaze—though it yet may appear hazy and indistinct, it points toward an emergent sovereignty based upon a reconfigured relationship between land and water.

Wide Sargasso Sea begins, like so many English novels, with an Englishman going out to sea. Yet, Rhys gives us no fortune-seeking Robinson Crusoe, or even the philosophical ambivalence of Conrad's Marlow. Instead, *Wide Sargasso Sea* begins with the story of Mr. Luttrell, a former slavemaster and plantation owner, whose fortunes have come to ruin after the 1833 Emancipation Act, which freed all remaining slaves in British colonies, including Jamaica, where the narrative of *Wide Sargasso Sea* commences. Of Luttrell, we only learn that "one calm evening he shot his dog, swam out to sea, and was gone for always" (*WSS* 9). For members of the Caribbean plantocracy like Luttrell, life after Emancipation seems impossible to contemplate. Rhys suggests that, for the "decadent" society of English Creoles, living in Jamaica is only possible within the privileged relation of colonial dominance, the maintenance of English identity only guaranteed by the enslavement of non-English bodies. Even the English sanctity of the home cannot be retained after Emancipation, as "no agent came from England to look after [Luttrell's] property" (*WSS* 9–10). In a reversal of the archetypal sailor's tale (a trope suggested by the name of the estate, Nelson's Rest), the home is no sacred *terra firma* promised after a life of seafaring. The novel ties the emancipation of the slaves, and thus the liberation of anticolonial energies, to the onset of a world that simply cannot be made sense of through English systems of reference. In most novels of English seafaring adventure, the outlying island—be it Caribbean, South Pacific, or simply imaginary—can at least be conceptually grasped by overlaying the island image of England itself upon the mysterious *insula incognita*. In these replays of the Crusoe myth, the geographical form of the island—a bounded, self-contained land bordered only by undifferentiated space of the sea—functions as a template for the cultural location of the mobile subject. As Chris Bongie has put it, the island can be figured as "the site of a debilitating or dangerous isolation," but it can also acquire more positive associations as a place of "defined boundaries and desirable self-sufficiency."[21] In Defoe's *Robinson Crusoe*, the island quickly moves from the former to the latter. Robinson's first responses to his debilitating isolation are precisely the defining of boundaries and the attainment of self-sufficiency. After he regains his wits, he immediately endeavors "to view the Country, and seek a proper Place for my Habitation"—a simultaneous mapping of the territory and centering of the self.[22] Surveying the island and building a home (which he takes to calling his "country house") come across as attempts to recreate a miniature of the "civilized" England. Rhys suggests that, in the post-Emancipation era, such recenterings are no longer possible, and Luttrell's return to the sea implies the end of any chance of mapping Jamaica as an England-in-miniature.

If Jamaica (and other Anglophone Caribbean islands) can no longer have England as their referential island home, then what will become of those Creoles who remain behind, particularly the novel's Creole protagonist, Antoinette? Rhys's ambivalent response is coded through one word: after the family has been ostracized by both newer English arrivées and the island's recently emancipated black population, Annette Cosway, Antoinette's mother, laments, "Now we are marooned" (*WSS* 10). The word itself suggests multiple, contradictory associations. The first, and dominant meaning refers to the sense of abandonment and isolation felt by Annette Cosway as her ties to her former Creole plantocratic society are rapidly disintegrating in the post-Emancipation era. Going back to 1726, according to the *Oxford English Dictionary*, the verb "maroon" denoted the following: "To put (a person) ashore on a desolate island or coast, to be left there esp. as a form of punishment."[23] The word implied an abandonment beyond the ken of civilization, specifically on an island distant from any known territory. Yet, behind this obviously Anglocentric implication of being stranded in the "wild," the word also recalls the communities of runaway slaves who escaped to the mountainous regions of Jamaica, other West Indian colonies, and the Americas.[24] As Mary Lou Emery points out, Annette "inadvertently... alludes to places in the island's history that Antoinette might inhabit and the wild, unexplored parts of the island that may help her survive."[25] Even in the family's moment of demise, Emery argues, Rhys suggests alternative identifications that might reorient an English colonial epistemology toward an incipient anticolonial Caribbean sensibility. Because their eyes are trained on the distant colonial metropole, however, the Cosways can only construct their social position as stranded outcasts. Although Rhys gestures toward an emergent anticolonial sensibility based upon a trans-Caribbean rather than transatlantic orientation, the white Creole characters in the novel are still held within the cultural orbit of an England that has stranded them on the proverbial deserted island.

Within this outdated center-periphery model, however, Rhys constructs an alternative geography. Rhys sets each of the three parts of *Wide Sargasso Sea* on different islands—Jamaica, Dominica, and England, respectively—with no spatial transitions between the three sections of the novel. The first part ends on Jamaica with a young Antoinette awaiting her English suitor, Rochester; the second begins after Rochester and Antoinette have made their honeymoon trip to Jamaica and ends as they prepare to leave for England; and the third part begins at Rochester's country home, Thornfield Hall. The tripartite geography of the novel undercuts a conventional duality typically associated with the symbolism of the distant island; rather than an inverted image of England and Englishness, the Caribbean presents an image of bifurcated otherness, with islands that in and of themselves cannot be resolved into a singular reflective image of England. In *Wide Sargasso Sea*, Rhys leaves Dominica unnamed, allowing us to see it in an unspecified, unstable, yet essential relation with, first, the Jamaican setting of the novel's first part and, later, the English setting of the novel's conclusion.

Rhys's use of dual narrators further underscores the sense of disconnection implied in the spatial movement of the narrative: part I is narrated entirely by Antoinette; part II, by Rochester (with an interlude narrated by Antoinette); and part III again by Antoinette.[26] As with its discontinuous spatiality, the novel engages in a serial narration, with the world of the novel seen through two perspectives that never merge. Knowing that each chapter takes place on a different island intensifies the sense of estrangement and disconnection in these spatial jumps, as if each episode cannot be reliably placed in the same narrative space as the others. Rhys figures each section of the novel as an island in its own right, radically, almost ontologically, sundered from the other sections. The spatial and narrative discontinuities are brought forth in one telling exchange between Antoinette and Rochester, as related through Rochester's point of view:

> "Is it true," she said, "that England is like a dream? Because one of my friends who married an Englishman wrote and told me so. She said this place London is like a cold dark dream sometimes. I want to wake up."
>
> "Well," I answered annoyed, "that is precisely how your beautiful island seems to me, quite unreal and like a dream."

"But how can rivers and mountains and the sea be unreal?"

"And how can millions of people, their houses and their streets be unreal?"

"More easily," she said, "much more easily. Yes a big city must be like a dream."

"No, this is unreal and like a dream," I thought.

$$(WSS\ 47–48)$$

Even as we have already seen Antoinette identifying with an imperial Englishness (most acutely through her wistful affection for the "Miller's Daughter" painting), her experiential being is still grounded in the home space of the islands. Antoinette here answers back to Rochester's imperial epistemology wherein England is solidly anchored to "reality" and exotic colonial landscapes smack of the dreamlike and unreal. Antoinette, despite her earlier fetishization of Englishness, is not cowed into Rochester's way of thinking, and the exchange ends at an impasse; neither recognizes the claim of the other on what constitutes reality and what is merely a dream. Yet, we still see the power of Rochester's Anglocentric worldview here, because it is he who has the last word. This, however, takes place within the interior, nonverbal space of the first-person narration, as his final response to the "she said" of Antoinette is the monologic, unanswerable "I thought." Rochester retreats into a disembodied Cartesian perspective here, needing to rest his identity on the unanswerable foundation of interior cogitation. This exchange focuses the formal and thematic struggle of the novel as a war between contending realities, neither of which seems able to be assimilated to the other.

In her staging of the narrative and epistemological conflict between Antoinette and Rochester, Rhys recognizes that a specific symbolic geography of colonialism arises in the English conquest of the island realms of the West Indies, one distinct from the colonial discourse surrounding larger expanses of territory. Going back to such touchstone texts of the English Renaissance as More's *Utopia* (1516) and Shakespeare's *The Tempest* (1611), the island has been a stock setting for the English imagination of other worlds. Likewise, Renaissance cartographies of England solidified its popular image as an island nation. As Richard Helgerson points out, the frontispiece of Camden's 1607 atlas *Britannia* marginalized images of the allegorical personification of Britain in favor of a cartographic image of the island itself.[27] It stands to reason, then, that the imaginative projection of alternate worlds, societies, and cultures would likewise take on a similar geographical form to that of the home nation. Islands function in the English imagination as mirrored, yet inverted, spaces of home. Their lack of contiguity to any recognizable landmass places them at an indefinite distance, both geographically and imaginatively, from the charted, domesticated, known spaces of the island homeland. Islands therefore exist in a relationship to English images of empire that larger landmasses, such as India and sub-Saharan Africa, for example, cannot. As canonical texts such as Conrad's *Heart of Darkness* and Forster's *A Passage to India* demonstrate, landmass colonies are often figured as impenetrable, vast, and overwhelming to the British observer. Islands can be grasped conceptually—they are bounded, localized places in a recognizable geographical form—so their mystery and exoticism need to come from different sources. Rhys suggests that the island-form of the West Indian colonies troubles English perception because it implies a quality typically associated with a dominant English geographical consciousness: self-reliant, borderless sovereignty. Not sovereignty in a political sense—at least not yet—but sovereignty in the sense of a life-world and experiential mode of being that cannot seamlessly be folded into and interpreted within a colonial epistemology.

Early in the novel, Rhys complicates the perception of the West Indian colony as a satellite only oriented toward the imperial home of England. Layers of conflicted history and cultural traversal are revealed in Antoinette's *in medias res* opening narration:

> They say when trouble comes close ranks, and so the white people did. But we were not in their ranks. The Jamaican ladies had never approved of my mother, "because she pretty like pretty self " Christophine said.
>
> She was my father's second wife, far too young for him they thought, and worse still, a Martinique girl. When I asked her why so few people came to see us, she told me that the road from Spanish Town to Coulibri Estate where we lived was very bad and that road repairing was now a thing of the past.

(9)

The society that Antoinette describes is highly stratified, including recent white arrivals from England ("the Jamaican ladies"), the older English plantocracy (Antoinette's father), white Creole imports from Martinique (her mother), and, through Antoinette's quotation, the servant classes of African origin (Christophine, who, as a former slave from French-held Martinique, forms part of a submerged bond between black interisland migrants across colonial cultures). Antoinette likewise gestures toward the different imprints of European national cultures on the islands, as the English name "Spanish Town" memorializes the Spanish control of Jamaica from 1525 until 1655, when it was taken by the English. The distrust between the English Jamaican population and the Francophone import from Martinique further transposes European rivalry on the archipelago of the Caribbean. Finally, hanging ghostlike in the deep recesses of cultural memory is the Carib word "Coulibri," which, as Judith Raiskin points out, "derives from a Carib word for the Antillean Crested Hummingbird."[28] Traversed as it is by a multitude of social, racial, linguistic, and national strata, the Jamaica presented on the first page of *Wide Sargasso Sea* complicates and contradicts the idea of the Caribbean island as a colony wholly absorbed into an English worldview.

The ontological sovereignty of the islands is most vividly portrayed through Rochester's narration in part II, particularly his perception of the islands as an opaque, unknowable space. Significantly, Rhys transfers the scene from Jamaica to Dominica in this section of the novel, moving the locale from the most well known of British West Indian colonies to one of the least known (Dominica had been made a Crown colony only in 1805, approximately thirty-five to forty years before the novel takes place). Dominica also has an ambivalent connection with Englishness, given its long Francophone history and its geographical situation between two of the larger French Caribbean colonies, Guadeloupe and Martinique. Just as Rochester is never directly named in the narrative, so does he never utter the name of the island, only referring to it as "one of the Windward Islands," as if each might be interchangeable with another (*WSS* 39). Rochester seems perceptually incapable of making sense of the island, because his only descriptions of Dominica can be spoken through adjectives of excess. After describing the island as "an extreme green," Rochester muses inwardly: "Everything is too much, I felt as I rode wearily after her. Too much blue, too much purple, too much green. The flowers too red, the mountains too high, the hills too near" (*WSS* 41). Rochester can only make sense of the island colony as a distorted, inferior mirror of England, as he derisively judges the honeymoon estate to be "an imitation of an English summer house" (*WSS* 42). For Rochester, then, the islands either make sense in terms of their relation to England and Englishness, or not at all.

In part II of *Wide Sargasso Sea*, race becomes the axis on which the difference between the knowable and the unknowable is played out. Rochester's inability to place his phenomenological experience of the islands into a stable geographical and cultural frame necessitates two metonymic reductions: the unknowable island of Dominica becomes the more tractable body of Antoinette, and the myriad geographical, cultural, and linguistic differences that traverse the Caribbean archipelago are reduced to the primordial, binary difference of race. In effect, Rochester's inability to undertake a legible cognitive mapping of the island results in his subsequent "mapping" of Antoinette. With the eye of a surveyor, he "watched her critically," taking note of her "long, sad, dark, alien eyes. Creole of pure English descent she may be, but they are not English or European either" (*WSS* 39). As H. Adlai Murdoch points out, the term "Creole" does not function as an explicit racial marker, but it certainly leaves such questions open. Glossing the *OED* definition, Murdoch writes that "what is stressed is the absence of any specificity of origin or any reference to skin color. ... As a result of this discursive and locational slippage, a creole person can be either white or black, colonizer or colonized, as the term articulates an essential ambiguity that both mediates and ruptures ... dominant designations of difference."[29] The open-ended flexibility of the term "Creole," then, serves as an index of the constantly shifting, doubling, and morphing of the islands in relation to a self-contained English cultural identity. In other words, the sovereignty of the islands outside of English frames of reference can only be named by a term that itself escapes colonial systems of meaning predicated on understanding the islands simply as degraded, inverted images of Britain, the normative "home" island.

Ultimately, Rhys can only express the disharmony between the singular locus of Britain and the multiple locations of Caribbean islandness through images of subjective and textual absence and dislocation. Antoinette expresses this sense of personal dislocation most acutely through the text, as she multiply identifies with both the everyday reality of her white Creole identity and the desired wish image of perfect Englishness. Shortly after her mother marries Mr. Mason, a "new" Englishman (i.e., without a slaveholding past), Antoinette and Mason engage in a conversation that forces the reader's recognition of the split between English and Creole identities. When Mason dismisses Aunt Cora's excuses for not helping the Cosway family during post-Emancipation troubles as "nonsense," Antoinette responds:

> "It isn't nonsense, they lived in England and he was angry if she wrote to us. He hated the West Indies. When he died not long ago she came home, before that what could she do? *She* wasn't rich."
>
> "That's her story. I don't believe it. A frivolous woman. In your mother's place I'd resent her behaviour."
>
> "None of you understand about us," I thought.
>
> (*WSS* 18)

In the conversation with her stepfather, Antoinette casts Mason as an alien "you" and herself as part of a Creole "us," inwardly recognizing the gulf of experience separating her from the Englishman who attempts to legitimize her mother and family *as* English rather than Creole. Antoinette's identity, however, seems to hover in the abyssal gulf between the loci of the Caribbean islands and England, as she expresses desires for an idealized English femininity through her gaze upon the "Miller's Daughter" picture, which depicts "a lovely English girl with brown curls and blue eyes and a dress slipping off her shoulders" (*WSS* 21). This leads to a visual comparison between her idealized "English" self in the picture and the two poles between which Antoinette is forced to fashion her own identity: "Then I looked across the white tablecloth and the vase of yellow roses at Mr. Mason, so sure of himself, so without a doubt English. And at my mother, so without a doubt not English, but no white nigger either" (*WSS* 21). In this doubling of parent figures, the confident, self-possessed but inauthentic stepfather and the beautiful-but-damaged Creole mother, Antoinette reduces her condition to these models for selfhood. The only way Antoinette can express her mother's identity, however, is through negation: being a Creole West Indian is a function of being *neither* English nor a "white nigger."

In what seems like Antoinette's final, desperate effort to anchor herself to the stable location of Englishness, she consults a geography book. Trying to grasp England as a positive, factual entity, she is once again thrown back into the gulf between her native Caribbean sensorium and the abstractions of an England she only knows through linguistic and visual representation:

> I will be a different person when I live in England and different things will happen to me…England, rosy pink in the geography book map, but on the page opposite the words are closely crowded, heavy looking. Exports, coal, iron, wool. Then Imports and Character of Inhabitants. Names, Essex, Chelmsford on the Chelmer. The Yorkshire and Lincolnshire wolds. Wolds? Does that mean hills?
>
> (*WSS* 66)

The distance and discontinuity of England affords Antoinette the opportunity, she believes, to transform herself utterly. But the obscure, unknown signifiers of England remind her of her dependent condition: she will be going to England only as Rochester's bride and legal possession. Christophine interrupts Antoinette's reverie, giving us a glimpse of one whose identity is *not* anchored to a distant northern island. When Christophine asks Antoinette if she believes that "there is such a place" as England, Antoinette rephrases her question, giving it a different cast: "You do not believe that there is a country called England?" (*WSS* 67). Raiskin reads this exchange as an illustration of competing codes of power: "When Christophine distances herself as a black Caribbean from the spiritual 'place'-England, Antoinette switches the terminology to one of politics and fealty."[30] Having no identification with the "cold thief place" of England, Christophine can easily undercut Antoinette's idealization. Yet Antoinette's insertion of the political designation of England as a "country" shows a subtle assertion of her power to usurp Christophine's situated, empirical questioning of England's existence. The reader, however, sees Antoinette slipping into the cracks of homelessness. While Christophine can live within the present of inter-Caribbean existence, Antoinette will forever remain alien to both the island culture she leaves behind and the island culture she hopes to attain.

For this is where the concluding section of the book places Antoinette: in a "cardboard" England that in no way squares with her idealized dream vision. The split between her circumstance as a prisoner in Thornfield Hall, Rochester's estate and her earlier vision of England as "chandeliers and dancing ... swans and roses and snow" could not be more stark (*WSS* 67). Instead, Antoinette experiences England as "a cardboard world where everything is coloured brown or dark red or yellow that has no light in it" (*WSS* 107). She refuses to acknowledge the difference between her beautiful dream and the less pleasant reality: "They tell me I am in England but I don't believe them. We lost our way to England" (*WSS* 107). Antoinette recalls the moment in transit across the wide Atlantic, depicting a space we only see through retrospective narration yet which gives the title to the novel. Captive on the ship that will bring her across the Sargasso Sea to her new place of residence, she wishes for escape: "I smashed the glasses and plates against the porthole. I hoped it would break and the sea come in" (*WSS* 107). After being given a sedative, Antoinette wakes to a different reality: "When I woke it was a different sea. Colder. It was that night, I think, that we changed course and lost our way to England" (*WSS* 107). Even the boundless flows of the sea are territorialized, as Antoinette goes to sleep in warm Caribbean waters and wakes in the cold, alien seas associated with Europe and England. Fittingly, it is in the Sargasso Sea, the famously static, stagnant region of the mid-Atlantic, where the fulcrum of Antoinette's split identity is located. As Antoinette carries the candle that will presumably set fire to Thornfield Hall, blind Rochester, and end her own life, the novel concludes with a word, "passage," that not only signifies the middle space of the ocean separating the culturally located spaces of the Caribbean and England but also recalls the larger historical milieu of the Middle Passage. Even as her novel is centered on the cultural and interpersonal relations between an Englishman and a (presumably) white Creole woman, Rhys calls up the ghosts of the countless journeys of slave ships from the West African coast to the Caribbean islands. Rhys points toward what Édouard Glissant will call the "submarine" unity beneath the apparent discontinuity of the Caribbean islands. Reading through Glissant, Ian Baucom elaborates the uncertain spatiality of the submarine in opposition to a grounded, land-based identity: "For if the subject of this post-colonial submarine again manifests itself as a rootwork, and as a route-work, this subject finds itself wonderingly—grounded not 'in some primordial spot' but in the uncertainties of imperial water."[31] Antoinette can only be located within this uncertainty, which is no location at all. The novel seems to present an impossible geography: the space of comparison and correlation between the disparate worlds of England

and the Caribbean is a space of absence, sleep, stagnation, erasure, captivity, and death. Rhys can therefore only gesture toward a more complex metageography wherein England is not necessarily the sun around which other colonial satellites simply orbit. *Wide Sargasso Sea*, for all of its complications and revisions of an English worldview, is still structurally locked in an agonistic embrace with the mother island. Even as the text gestures toward an alternative metageography outside of English dominance, the very premise of the novel—its intertextual response to *Jane Eyre*—reproduces a world in which England yet remains the *omphalos*, the island at the center of it all.

An Island Is the World: *A Small Place*

Rhys's treatment of the island metageographies of England and the West Indies uses modernist narrative techniques of absence, silence, ellipsis, and indeterminacy to decenter and denaturalize the worldview that imagined Caribbean islands as inverted or degraded forms of Britain. Jamaica Kincaid's travel narrative-cum-satire, *A Small Place*, treats the cultural history of a different Anglophone Caribbean island, Antigua, in a much different manner.[32] While Kincaid is likewise critical of a dominant English worldview, she evolves a more contemporary, more complex narrative of an island-bound spatiality. Where Rhys's Antoinette is characterized by her divided allegiances to both the distant hegemon of England and the lived experience of the Antilles, Kincaid's speaker has decisively moved beyond a crippling nostalgia for an idealized version of Englishness. At one point, echoing Rhys's language of the "real" England forever out of reach or located in dreams, Kincaid muses about the possibility of two Englands, the "ill-mannered" England of the Antiguan colonists and "the England that was so far away, the England that not even a boat could take us to, the England that, no matter what we did, we could never be of" (*SP* 30). Yet, where Rhys still conveys a residual nostalgia, Kincaid projects nothing but disenchantment. At one point, she relates a conversation with an Englishman, in which she angrily tells him that Antiguans were made to celebrate Queen Victoria's birthday. When her interlocutor responds that, at his English school, they only celebrated the day of Victoria's death, Kincaid's narrator fires back: "'Well, apart from the fact that she belonged to you and so anything you did about her was proper, at least you know she died'" (*SP* 31). Certainly, one could argue that Rhys's ambivalence speaks to her (and Antoinette's) status as a white Creole, while Kincaid speaks as a black Antiguan. In this sense, Kincaid speaks not as a descendant of Antoinette but rather of Christophine, who neither identifies with nor pines for the "cold thief place" of England. Kincaid, however, offers more than simply a defiant indifference to Englishness. Though the deleterious effects of English rule in Antigua do not escape her critical eye, she is more alive to the multiple cultural locations that overwrite the "small place" of Antigua. England is simply one of the many geocultural coordinates with which contemporary Antigua contends.

Both *Wide Sargasso Sea* and *A Small Place* reflect upon the position of small Caribbean islands within a larger geopolitical sphere. Where Rhys signifies displacement with respect to a metropolitan center and dominant imperial culture, however, Kincaid's version of displacement has no such nostalgic "home," instead projecting a world of networks and cultural flows consistent with the postmodern geographies described by Fredric Jameson, Edward Soja, Arjun Appadurai, and others. In her recasting of a "small place" as a location within a much more complex web of other places—Britain, Europe, the United States, the Middle East, the West African coast—Kincaid provides an example of what the feminist geographer Doreen Massey has called "a global sense of place."[33] But, as with previously discussed examples by both geographers (Mackinder, Reclus) and writers (Forster, Joyce), Kincaid adopts one of the principal methods of geographical modernism: a discontinuous scale bending that juxtaposes the local (an island that can be circumnavigated by car in an afternoon) with the national (a nation-state that takes its formal place in a world order) and the supranational (multinational capital, First World tourism, migrations of labor, the transatlantic history of slavery). By juxtaposing the fiction of island sovereignty with the transnational lines of force that traverse the island, Kincaid offers a scathing critique of the myth of the sovereign, self-determining island nation.

The resonance of Kincaid's scale bending centers on the multiple meanings suggested by the term "a small place." First, her description of Antigua as "a small place" refers simply to the island's geographical size: "twelve miles long and nine miles wide," as she writes several times during the text (*SP* 9). Through her narration of the essay's first section in the second person, addressed to a North American or European tourist, Kincaid conveys a literal sense of Antigua that plays into such tourist perceptions. As a comparatively tiny island (even for the island nations of the Caribbean archipelago), Antigua is represented as an escape from the "real world" of North America and Europe, an island getaway. Our *entrée* into the text is via the means of transport that most Europeans and Americans will use to enter Antigua: by airplane. "As your plane descends to land, you might say, What a beautiful island Antigua is—more beautiful than any of the other islands you have seen, and they were very beautiful, in their own way, but they were much too green, much too lush with vegetation" (*SP* 3–4). Echoing Rochester's inability to find a qualitative language for the Caribbean islands, Kincaid's tourists are likewise only able to define differences in islands through degree, rather than kind. Each is categorically interchangeable, with differences only in the lushness of vegetation (the lack of which, for Kincaid's tourist, signifies the pleasure of sunshine rather than the disaster of drought). This initial perspective underscores the sense of an island playground disconnected in space and time from the quotidian everyday of the metropolitan subject.

Yet it becomes clear that Kincaid intends a deeper irony in her deprecating description of Antigua. While, according to a two-dimensional cartographic vision, Antigua might seem small, marginal, inconsequential, barely (if at all) visible on a global scale, Kincaid means to show that the "small place" of Antigua is overwritten by layers of history and vectors of geography that render it a crucial, if often forgotten, part of larger networks of cultural-historical traffic. Where Rhys opposes the irreconcilable presences of radically different island cultures to the abstract, liminal nonspace of the sea, Kincaid imagines the sea as a material space of access, traversal, and exchange. The sea, for example, conventionally seen as a means of separation and distancing in the tourist discourse that Kincaid mocks, is given a substance and materiality designed to challenge the assumptions of the Euro-American reader. Miming the imaginary tourist's impressions, Kincaid recreates a prose "postcard" view of the Caribbean Ocean: "That water—have you ever seen anything like it? Far out, to the horizon, the colour of water is navy-blue; nearer, the water is the colour of the North American sky. From there to the shore, the water is pale, silvery, clear, so clear that you can see its pinkish-white sand bottom. Oh, what beauty!" (*SP* 12–13). The beauty of the tropical ocean assumes more sinister tones as Kincaid reinserts the postcard sea into the more quotidian systems of exchange that undergird the tourist's euphoria. "You must not wonder," Kincaid writes,

> what exactly happened to the contents of your lavatory when you flushed it. ... Oh, it might all end up in the water you are thinking of taking a swim in; the contents of your lavatory might, just might, graze gently against your ankle as you wade carefree in the water, for you see, in Antigua, there is no proper sewage-disposal system.
>
> (*SP* 14)

To be sure, Kincaid employs shock value here to make a point about the disjunction between tourist and local economies and infrastructures; the reality that subtends the imaginary "postcard" view of Antigua is simply one of an economically crippled nation with no sustainable sources of prosperity other than tourism. This separation is easy enough to maintain on land, where spaces are engineered carefully so as not to bring the tourist face to face with the quotidian Antigua. The sea, however, for all of its beauty, is also a repository for the waste created by a tourist economy, and Kincaid expresses this through the unseemly picture of the tourist wading in his own excrement.

Kincaid's demystified, material portrait of the sea suddenly takes on a different cast, however. As if to reassure the tourist fearful of swimming in his own waste, Kincaid remarks: "But the Caribbean Sea is very big and the Atlantic Ocean is even bigger; it would amaze even you to know the number of black slaves this ocean has swallowed up" (*SP* 14). Kincaid calls the reader back to a past that precedes both the present postcolonial moment of globetrotting tourism and the earlier age of formal British imperialism, taking us back to the epoch of the forced labor removed from Africa and enslaved on the sugar plantations of the Caribbean islands. Specifically, Kincaid invests the beautiful Caribbean waters with the haunting, sunken presence of countless African slaves thrown overboard during the Middle Passage. Kincaid's narration invokes the specter of the drowned slave, but its placement is peculiar, offhanded, almost an aside between her musings on sewage and her analysis of the economy of seafood in Antigua. The casual tone of the remark allows it to be part of a shared history of the Caribbean islands but not one that necessarily usurps the tragicomedy of the islands' present circumstance. Kincaid's reference to the drowned slaves sets in motion a chain of "transversal" histories of the Atlantic-Caribbean waters, as Ian Baucom puts it in his reading of Glissant. Baucom writes, "The coral-become bodies of those slaves drowned in the Middle Passage ... link the waters washing the coast of Martinique with an eighteenth and nineteenth century history of the Caribbean, with the past and present legacies of the triangular trade, with the Victorian and Edwardian underdevelopment of Africa, Rastafarian and Pan-Africanist narratives of return, the poetry of Aimé Césaire, Afrocentric curricula, and the commodification of Kente cloth."[34] Kincaid gestures toward the endless metonymy of these geographical and historical coordinates. Her Antiguan ocean is many things other than the playground of the bourgeois tourist: it is the neocolonial present in which sewage floats freely, from which fish are sold to American companies and then resold to restaurants that might be only yards from the shore of their original habitat, and over which hurricanes arrive to batter an already dilapidated infrastructure. The sea is also the repository of history, the ever-present reminder of the human embodiment of the politics and economics of slavery.

Along with the history of the Middle Passage and plantation slavery, the lingering presence of British colonization looms in the background of Kincaid's portrait of Antigua. Kincaid's version, however, is far removed from that obscure, if imaginary, object of desire that Antoinette projects onto her idealized version of

England. Nor is the English presence of *A Small Place* the contending, immediate oppressor featured in the work of the first generation of immigrant black British writers, as it is in texts such as Selvon's *The Lonely Londoners*, Buchi Emecheta's autobiographical novel *Second Class Citizen*, or Linton Kwesi Johnson's dub poem "Inglan Is a Bitch." The England of Kincaid's work has certainly left its mark—"we lived on a street named after an English maritime criminal, Horatio Nelson, and all the other streets around us were named after some other English maritime criminals" (*SP* 24)—but a generation's distance from the last vestiges of direct English rule in Antigua give Kincaid some distance on the epoch of formal colonialism. While the English are "such a pitiful lot these days," Kincaid bristles at the imperial nostalgia that characterized so much of the Thatcherite 1980s, when *A Small Place* was written. Kincaid makes explicit what Rhys leaves just beneath the surface of her text—that the violence of English colonialism, particularly in its cultural hegemonics, arises not from power but from lack and loss: "And so everywhere they went they turned it into England; and everybody they met they turned English. But no place could ever really be England, and nobody who did not look exactly like them would ever be English, so you can imagine the destruction of people and land that came from that" (*SP* 24). Ian Baucom frames this dissonance between the simultaneous imperative and inability of the English to reproduce the special places of the nation in the far reaches of colonial space. Baucom asks whether the empire was "the domain of England's mastery of the globe or the territory of the loss of Englishness?"[35] Kincaid's frank analysis of the futile reproduction of Englishness in the colonies functions as an exposition of Rochester's need, in *Wide Sargasso Sea*, to draw a crude picture of a house and insert the stick-figure representation of his bride within it. The drunken Rochester can only comfort himself with the thought that at least "it was an English house" (*WSS* 98). The *coup de grâce* of Kincaid's dismissal of Englishness lies in her refusal to acknowledge that colonial rule was based upon considerations of politics or race; rather, "the English were ill-mannered, not racists" (*SP* 34). Not only does this portrayal diminish the historical power of the English colonial project, but it also levies a criticism at the one supposed trait of upper-crust Englishness that can still draw credit around the world: good manners. Although at least one-fifth of *A Small Place* is devoted to the effects of English rule on Antigua, Kincaid conveys the impression that, even as the residue of colonization remains, contemporary Antigua no longer contends with the British Empire, only with the relics it has left behind.

Other coordinates and traversals determine the conditions of existence of Antigua, and these cannot be reduced to a Manichean binary of metropole and periphery. For example, Kincaid notes the pervasive presence of Levantine Arab capital, particularly from Syria and Lebanon. But how to place an immigrant population that has brought capital but not "culture" to the island? "In the Antigua telephone directory, the Syrians and Lebanese have more business addresses and telephone numbers than any of the other same surnames listed," yet "they have no cultural institutions in Antigua, not even a restaurant" (*SP* 63). These émigrés have no identifiable position in a cultural hierarchy defined by race and nationality: they "are called 'those foreigners' even though most of them have acquired Antiguan citizenship. North Americans and Europeans are not foreigners; they are white people. Everybody is used to white people. The Syrians and Lebanese are not 'white people'" (*SP* 63). Kincaid makes the point here that racial identity, economic capital, and social power cannot be completely correlated on a spectrum of power. Though, according to Kincaid, Syrian and Lebanese nationals regularly lend the government of Antigua money, they occupy an ambiguous, undefined space in the social makeup of the island. Though initially arriving at the turn of the nineteenth century, the Syrian and Lebanese populations of Antigua remain beyond the pale of a dualistic postcolonial epistemology. Kincaid implies that this diaspora is but a metonym for other diasporic populations—East Indian, Chinese, and South African, for example—that continue to traverse the Caribbean islands.

Beyond and beneath the history of the Atlantic passage, British imperialism, and the continued circulation of overseas populations and capital, Kincaid suggests the most recent influence upon the island's cultural geography may be its most pervasive. Kincaid links the Syrian and Lebanese presence on the island to a pervasive American economic, cultural, and military imperialism. To paraphrase Derek Walcott (himself adapting Graham Greene), Kincaid portrays elements of Antigua as "quietly American." The Levantine developers build condominiums whose prices, Kincaid tells us parenthetically, are quoted in United States dollars (*SP* 62). Every government official in Antigua seeks medical care for serious illness not in St. John's, but in New York (*SP* 8). A calypso singer's sister's decapitated body is found "near the island's United States Army base" (*SP* 63). Teenagers in Antigua are now familiar with the popular cultural "rubbish of North America" (whereas her generation had been familiar with the "rubbish of England") (*SP* 44). And Kincaid speculates that, given the corruption of the Antiguan government, a revolutionary populist leader might arise, just as Maurice Bishop did in Grenada in the late 1970s. Kincaid predicts a similar end for such a figure, with one crucial difference: "He'll do Maurice Bishop-like things and say Maurice Bishop-like things and come to a Maurice Bishop-like end—death, only this time at the hands of the Americans" (*SP* 74). Not only does the United States hold economic and cultural sway over much of Antigua, it stands ready to intervene in the island's political affairs if they become troublesome to its interests in the region. Noting that Antigua's army is only useful "as a decoration," Kincaid makes it clear that Antigua's fate rests in the hands of a much larger state entity; if an anti-American regime somehow managed to seize power, the "quietly" American presence would suddenly become as loud as helicopters and gunfire.

After spending so much time describing the flows of people, culture, and capital that traverse the islands, the language of territorial nationality can only be used ironically to describe Antigua. When Kincaid declares that Antigua "has no enemies," she resorts to the language of sovereign statehood to describe Antigua's international standing (*SP* 72). After first European contact, the extermination of indigenous populations, the importing of slave labor, the occupation of an imperial power, the immigration of diasporic populations, the rule of corrupt politicians, and the flows of overseas capital, it seems odd to read that Antigua has no "official" conflicts with other nation-states. In this disjunction between the language of sovereign statehood and the landscape of history and everyday life, Kincaid once and for all punctures the myth of sovereignty that attaches to Caribbean nation-states. On the stage of world affairs, Antigua is a bit player, little more than an ineffectually decorative army, a quaint national flag, and an endearingly tiny Olympic team. Though possessing the formal sovereignty of a territorial nation-state, this condition isolates Antiguans from the more complex geographies that determine their day-to-day existence. Where the myth of the island nation sustained the British ideology of empire, the transference of that myth to the Caribbean nation-state only produces isolation. "For the people in a small place," Kincaid writes, "every event is a domestic event" (*SP* 52). She intends a double meaning here: events are both absorbed into the fabric of everyday life, and they only resonate on the shores of the island nation itself. "The people in a small place cannot see themselves in a larger picture, they cannot see that they might be part of a chain of something, anything" (*SP* 52). If "the people" have conventionally been the agent of national subjectivity and the site of enunciation in which the quotidian is transmuted into the world-historical, then Kincaid's Antiguans are rendered mute. *A Small Place* argues, however, that this enunciation must come in an entirely different register. This must be a subjectivity freed at last from the language of national identity and that might yet be able to see the chains that link Antiguans to the world rather than bind them to a limited, flattened view.

Conclusion

The territorial nation-state, *A Small Place* suggests, holds no promise for the securing of sovereignty, rights, and collective freedoms. Throughout her text, Kincaid illustrates many of the conditions that, according to Glissant, prevent the articulation of cultural and political sovereignty in the Caribbean:

> The historical balkanization of the islands, the inculcation of different and often "opposed" major languages…the umbilical cords that maintain, in a rigid or flexible way, many of these islands within the sphere of influence of a particular metropolitan power, the presence of frightening and powerful neighbors, Canada and especially the United States.[36]

Glissant articulates a list of historical consequences that have, implicitly, arisen from the imposition of not only formal colonialism but from the transfer of European notions of national independence and state sovereignty. The model of the nation-state implants a standard of sovereignty and an "official" language, both of which orient the Caribbean island nation more toward its former colonizer than toward the proximate islands in the archipelago. The "postcolonial" era of the Caribbean thus implies a double alienation from a meaningful pan-island sovereignty within a larger sphere of politics and culture. First, the residual cultures of empire continue to maintain divides that cut along the language and imported cultures of the former colonizers: here the Spanish-speaking islands, here the British West Indies, here the French Antilles, here the Dutch. And, perhaps more fundamentally, the assumption that nation-states must be bounded, terrestrial, territorial entities limits Caribbean islands to a form of sovereignty that inevitably atomizes and disempowers individual islands on a political level, leaving them open to the cultural, economic, and social forces of neo-imperialism and multinational capital.

As much as Rhys and Kincaid offer metageographical models of the island that revise its conventional symbolism as a bounded, self-contained place of unified identity and sovereignty, these worldviews inevitably must convert the negative space of the sea into a positive, meaningful category. Deriving a cultural identity from a geographical space of negation is no easy task. Gary S. Elbow points to a condition of the Caribbean that, from a social scientific perspective, remains a barrier to a pan-island imagined community. "One could argue," Elbow writes, "that a part of the region's identity is derived negatively—the Caribbean does not fit conveniently into either of the generally recognized hemispheric cultural macro-scale regions [North, Central, South, or "Latin" America], therefore it has acquired a separate identity."[37] From a positivist perspective, the lack of a clear continental or world-regional scale would seem to hinder attempts at a pan-Caribbean cultural sensibility. Yet, from the perspectives of writers and theorists such as Rhys, Kincaid, Glissant, and Benítez-Rojo (each of which, it should be noted, comes from a different cultural and linguistic tradition), the negative space opened up by the impossibility of a circumscribed, territorial definition of the Caribbean is precisely the space of potential enunciation. The sea that washes the islands ultimately cannot be said to either unite or divide the islands of the archipelago. Rather, it suspends, always refracting and frustrating attempts to complete a cognitive map of the islands once and for all. As Glissant has written, the unity of the Caribbean is "submarine," and it can only be understood as a shifting nexus of currents in an ocean that washes all the shores of the world.

5. Boundary

Nehru, Ghosh, and the Enchantment of Lines

While many postcolonial literatures respond to similar conditions of political, economic, and cultural imperialism, geography plays a significant role in how specific traditions of postcolonial fiction represent narrative space differently across world regions. In the case of the Caribbean, for example, the symbolic understanding of the island as a self-contained, organically whole space can be manifest in the structural discontinuities of *Wide Sargasso Sea*, or it can prompt an ironic demystification of such insularity, as we see in *A Small Place*. Moreover, in the case of former British colonies in the West Indies, many novels address the mythology of Britain's "island story," which implicitly renders the insular exceptionalism of English island nationalism as the standard against which *all* nationalisms should be measured. Fictions that come from partitioned nations, on the other hand, must contend with a different kind of geographical circumstance. Where islands, in their clear separation from the surrounding negative space of water, can seem naturally, organically preordained spaces of cultural unification, partitions are arbitrary, all-too-cultural demarcations of difference. Nation-states created out of a partition retroactively attach the wholeness of a primeval national mythos to a political space that is created within the messy, arbitrary workings of history. Literatures that address the conditions of partition inevitably confront the blunt, determining fact of the boundary line as a circumstance that separates and fragments communities, introduces cartographic abstraction into lived social space, and serves as a frequent catalyst for interpersonal and intercommunal conflict. Not surprisingly, fiction arising out of cultures of partition uses the boundary line as a significant thematic and structural element. This chapter addresses the imaginative form of the boundary in the political and geographical discourse of partition in the Indian subcontinent. I look closely at the writings and speeches of Jawaharlal Nehru, the Congress Party leader and the first prime minister of independent India, showing how his attachments to cartographic overview imply a critique of the territorial partition that he was called on to execute and enforce in 1947. The chapter then moves to an analysis of post-partition fiction, examining how Amitav Ghosh uses the cartographic "accident" of the boundary as a central thematic and structural element in his 1988 novel *The Shadow Lines*.

In many ways, this chapter (not coincidentally) recalls many of the same concerns as chapter 3. As Ireland was fighting for, and ultimately winning, its sovereignty from the British Empire, Indian nationalists both in the subcontinent and in the British Isles were following this war of independence closely. In the early twentieth century, Elleke Boehmer writes, "nationalists and anti-colonialists kept a keen eye on resistance unfolding in other regions of the empire." Ireland and India formed one connection within what Boehmer labels "cross-nationalist circuitry."[1] In particular, Ireland and India shared a common problem pertaining to the imagination of a sovereign state: a population deeply divided by religion. Ultimately, the broad geographical distribution of dominant religious communities—Protestants in the north and Roman Catholics in the south within Ireland; Hindus in the central subcontinent and Muslims in the eastern and western sections within India—led political leaders on all sides to the ultimate solution of creating separate nations. When the Irish Free State was declared on December 6, 1922, it was a foregone conclusion that the six counties of Ulster, having been given the option, would secede from the Free State and return to Britain. This in fact came to pass the very next day. On August 15, 1947, India was only created as a sovereign state by the partitioning of East and West Pakistan. Both Ireland and India, therefore, were born with an acute consciousness of boundary lines, a circumstance that poses an eternal problem to organic nationalism. Lines of partition are drawn, not divinely ordained, and thus they can never be easily or fully dissolved into the myth of nations as predestined, timeless fusions of culture and territory. The lines of partition are inscriptions that inevitably expose the nation as a humanly authored fiction. Yet, within states where the making of boundaries exists within the full glare of contemporary history rather than the hazy origin stories of national myth, boundary lines are arguably invested with even *more* power than in more "established" states.

Why, then, do many postcolonial states continue to cleave to the lines of partition rather than skeptically view them as the arbitrary cartographic markings of so many bureaucrats, commissions, and surveyors?

Certainly, the connection between the British Empire and the partition of new nation-states is no accident. In his study of the literature regarding partition in Ireland and Palestine, Joe Cleary writes, "As a general rule...it would seem that partitions are most likely to occur where—as a consequence of colonial rule or of total military collapse in times of war—societies have lost control over their own political destinies and are vulnerable to the wills of external superpowers."[2] While I agree generally with this claim, it does not quite account for one of the most fascinating and troubling aspects of the negotiations that led to the partition of India. Even though the emerging political arena in early-twentieth-century India had been under the watchful, paternalistic eye of British authority, the Indian leaders involved in the decision to undertake partition were in fact encouraged by the British *not* to do so. As late as April 1946, only sixteen months before the end of the Raj, many British officials were hopeful that a secular, unified India would emerge. Certainly, the departing British had sown the seeds for partition in the separation of Muslim and Hindu electorates (in the 1935 Government of India Act) and in the tacit encouragement of religious, class, and gender divisions during their entire occupation. Yet to explain the partition as the simple authorship of a line by British bureaucrats drastically oversimplifies what was a far more complex historical situation. The fact remains that until after it had already occurred, partition seemed for many a viable option to secure freedom and autonomy for those living in the Indian subcontinent, and some parties hoped, naïvely, that the two nations might join again as a united India. Partition was always seen as a provisional solution, bearing out the words of the Irish diplomat Conor Cruise O'Brien that partition is "the expedient of the tired statesman."[3]

One dimension of partition that has not been sufficiently examined is the way in which Western ideas of political and cultural space were imported into late and postcolonial India, thereby giving indigenous political elites a very specific, limited range of options through which they could imagine cultural and national autonomy.[4] These spatial forms come not just out of the history of Western political ideas, but also out of aesthetic and cultural expressions of space that can be broadly connected to certain formal aspects of Anglo-European cultural modernism (Jawaharlal Nehru, with his time spent in Cambridge and London during the 1910s, best exemplifies this merger of international political thought and metropolitan cultural modernism). The idea of the territorial nation-state evolved conjointly with modernist revolutions in space and politics more generally. The territorial nation-state sits at an intersection between modernist philosophies about the materiality and substance of space, emerging geopolitical ideas of a global world order, and finally, the increasing popularity of cultural relativism conveyed through the social sciences, particularly as they used colonial spaces as sites for research and fieldwork. I conclude this chapter with a reading of one of the few critiques of the Indian partition that meditates on the philosophical, aesthetic, and political considerations and consequences of boundary drawing in Amitav Ghosh's 1988 novel *The Shadow Lines*. Because Ghosh pays close attention to the form and aesthetics of partition—particularly in his almost philosophical analysis of the importance of "lines"—he offers a way of understanding partition that both places it in a wider global context and avoids the too-common trap of reading the separation of India and Pakistan exclusively through a narrative of blame.

Given the model of international politics that placed such value on the form of the territorial nation-state, those in the subcontinent who favored partition believed that it would once and for all sunder the opposing communities, permitting each to pursue its national interest independent of the other. Yet, perhaps because the partition of the subcontinent precipitated the creation of two *new* nation-states, the emerging national narratives of both Pakistan and India tended to be cast primarily in terms of this binary opposition rather than entrance into a broader community of nations.[5] In other words, the act of separation was so fundamental to the creation of both India and Pakistan that citizens of each nation had a difficult time imagining an autonomous existence without reference to the other. The popular version of the argument for partition was called the "Two Nations" theory, suggesting the paring down of the political landscape into a simple, Manichean opposition between a Muslim Pakistan and a Hindu India. Once the political debate was cast in these terms, focus was inevitably placed on and directed toward the act of division. The narrator of *The Shadow Lines* summarizes this particular worldview by looking retrospectively at partition approximately thirty years after the fact: "They had drawn their borders, believing in that pattern, in the enchantment of lines, hoping perhaps that once they had etched their borders upon the map, the two bits of land would sail away from each other like the shifting tectonic plates of the prehistoric Gondwanaland" (*SL* 233). Ghosh captures the unconscious naturalization that attended the construction of the two partitioned states: the idea that, once separated, two nations drawn apart by partition could make a political division seem almost geological in its permanence. Ghosh's narrator comes to this moment of ethical reflection by looking at, and literally reinscribing, a map. Although this act of resistance is perhaps no more effective than that of Toba Tek

Singh, who refuses to budge from the border, Ghosh's narrator models a subjectivity for whom the active interpretation of political cartography can point the way toward a more fluid, malleable conception of the world.

Boundary Discourse and the Logic of Partition

In June 1947, after years of negotiation between the British and both Hindu and Muslim political representatives in India, a plan was announced for the British departure from India and the subsequent partition of British-held territories into a Muslim-majority state, to be called Pakistan, and a secular, though predominantly Hindu, state of India.[6] The plan was presented to the public by the final Viceroy of India, Lord Mountbatten; the leader of the Muslim League, Mohammed Ali Jinnah; and the leader of the Hindu-dominated Congress Party, Jawaharlal Nehru. Amazingly, the date set for Independence was the 15th of August of the same year, only about ten weeks from the initial announcement. Three weeks after the unveiling of the plans, on the 30th of June, the Boundary Commissions for the Punjab and Bengal were formed, to be chaired by a lawyer from England who had little knowledge of the subcontinent, Sir Cyril Radcliffe. Radcliffe assumed responsibility for the execution of the political plans into cartographic reality. The line that Radcliffe drew sundered provinces, cities, villages, and families, leaving approximately sixteen million Muslims in the Hindu-dominated state of India, fifteen million Hindus in Muslim Pakistan, and five million Sikhs as a minority in both new nation-states.[7] When Radcliffe was asked later in life about his role in the partition, he replied in a deceptively straightforward way: "Jinnah, Nehru, and Patel told me that they wanted a line before or on 15th August. So I drew them a line."[8] This reply boils down a centuries-long history of conquest, violence, diplomacy, and geopolitical struggle into a simple, even naïve, act of inscription. Radcliffe represents his own role in the events of partition as a functionary, a mere scribe who simply executes the will of others, be it for better or worse. Radcliffe's statement also brings up the vexed issue of historical agency in the case of partitioned territories, an issue that runs throughout the course of twentieth-century geopolitical history. Who is accountable for the sundering and division that inevitably accompany partition? In the case of the subcontinent, was it Radcliffe, who simply drew a line? Was it Lord Mountbatten, the final Viceroy of India, who decided that the only way to resolve the hopeless situation was to set a date for partition, hold to it with a characteristically British stiff upper lip, and then leave the two nations to sort it out among themselves? Was it Mohammed Ali Jinnah, the leader of the Muslim

League, who advanced the "two nations" theory by insisting on separate Muslim and Hindu states? Was it Jawaharlal Nehru, who by contrast advocated a secular state whose dominant party happened to have a decisive Hindu majority? Was it Gandhi, who popularized the emergent nationalist movement in the preceding decades? Or should we go back to Robert Clive, perhaps the first British man in India who recognized the consolidating power that could be achieved in India by playing Hindu, Muslim, and Sikh populations against each other? The apparently simple act of "drawing a line" reduces our view of complex cultural spaces and histories to the flattened abstraction of cartography. Because we see partitions most clearly on the two-dimensional surface of the map, we are tempted to flatten their complex circumstances into something as tangible, persuasive, and definitive as a boundary line. We are encouraged, I would argue, to apply conventional ideas of authorship in the complex historical circumstances of partition. Radcliffe intimates that the concept of authorship extends beyond textual and verbal utterances into the material world of political geography. In other words, by so adamantly denying his *own* authorship in partition, Radcliffe gives credence to the idea that the partition was in fact "authored," even if this authorship was a collaborative effort. The visual simplicity of the line seems to call for an equally simple interpretation of history, one that can clearly pinpoint the party or parties responsible for such massive political and social division.

While the lines that most novelists write do not generally result in the death and displacement of hundreds of thousands of people, literary and territorial writing are both inscriptions that translate the abstraction of a sign-system into performative—and frequently transformative—acts in the material world. The attribution of authorship in something like a partition, like the question of historical blame, is not so easily parsed. As the complex and often contradictory historiography of the partition of India suggests, attributing authorship to any one person, or even any one group, is an enterprise destined for failure. Yet most observers continue to apply literary modes of authorship to moments of political, historical, and geographical change. In the case of partitions, decisions are generally made through the negotiation and compromise of a number of interest groups of variable influence. In many scenarios, an arbitrating party has the final say on precisely where lines of partition are drawn and also about which regions, communities, and even neighborhoods will become part of the separate states. In the case of partitions in Ulster, Palestine, and the Indian subcontinent, the arbitrating power happened to be the departing British colonial regime. It would be inaccurate to suggest that the British simply imposed a clearly defined intention in their division of India and Pakistan. But it would be equally erroneous to suggest that the Congress Party, the Muslim League, and the British Raj were equal players in the great game of partition. Clearly, conventional models of authorship cannot explain both the centuries-long histories that led to the separation of the two states, nor can it explain the need to use a particular form—the bounded territorial unit—as an archetype for political, cultural, and religious unity.

Partition, arising out of an instrumentalist boundary discourse of early-twentieth-century political geography, inevitably reduces social complexity to formal unity, forcing a static, two-dimensional, cartographic solution to problems that exist in the dynamic fullness of culture. The act of partitioning two new sovereign nation-states reduces diverse social and cultural relations by mapping them onto a circumscribed territorial unit. The partitioned nation appears as a preordained realm, divorced from its very real geographical and historical contexts. Once this division is made, even imaginatively, a primary cultural identification is seen to derive from the formal unity of an enclosed territory. Pakistan is *Muslim* Pakistan, Ulster is *Protestant* Ulster, and so on. Thongchai Winichakul refers to this territorial image of a national culture as the "geo-body" of a nation, which he defines as "an effect of modern geographical discourse whose prime technology is a map."[9] But, far from being a flat, bloodless abstraction, the geo-body becomes a "source of pride, loyalty, passion, bias, hatred, reason, unreason."[10] The idea of the geo-body imputes organic, living, breathing existence to what, in fact, are geographical abstractions. In the discourse leading up to the partition of the subcontinent, the language surrounding the partition could move very quickly from the abstract, instrumentalist language of the state to the organic, embodied imagery of the national geo-body. This metaphorical embodiment of territory found its way into popular debates about partition, as many anti-Muslim voices in favor of partition likened it to a "surgery" that would "cut off the diseased limb" of Muslim culture.[11]

Taken to its extreme, the logic of partition proposed that the territorial space of the nation should approximate as closely as possible the boundaries of the largest possible culturally homogeneous community. The most effective partition would therefore be one that maintained the smallest minority constituency within the new national borders. This logic, of course, leads to two inextricable problems: first, the difficulty of preserving rights for the necessary minority communities, and second, the material conditions of cultural settlement, which even in the smallest possible administrative units disperses Hindu, Muslim, and Sikh communities next to, and within, one another. As Robert K. Schaeffer has argued, "No matter how carefully they might be drawn, boundaries between divided states left too many people on the wrong side. The same ethnic population would be part of a majority or a minority depending on where the line was drawn. The result was the creation of a territorial basis for irredentist claims."[12] In partitioned states, minority communities are frequently targets for surveillance and repression. As Cleary points out, minority populations pose a de facto threat to national security and stability: "Since the assumption that subtends partitionist thinking is that ethnically homogenous states will be more stable than ethnically heterogeneous ones, the policy tends to see 'minorities' in an intrinsically negative light as a problem that has somehow or other to be resolved."[13] Needless to say, such suspicion could justify the most brutal repression. In the case of the partition of the subcontinent, the inscription of the boundary would have a direct bearing on the makeup of minority communities in each state and the calculus of violence and bloodshed visited upon these communities. As twentieth-century geographers, political scientists, and governmental officials were coming to realize, boundary drawing, while dealing with geometrical abstraction, had very material consequences.

In early-twentieth-century military and political treatises on the subject, boundaries were increasingly defined by the mutual antagonism of each bordering nation, and they came to enshrine a permanent friction rather than a permanent peace. By the time of the partition in the subcontinent, the study and practice of boundary drawing had become a burgeoning field of practical cartography. Forged by necessity in the theater of imperial competition, the discourse of boundaries was the pragmatic obverse to the idealist visions of organicist nationhood. Where "true" nations were thought to express their identities through a natural occupation of a given territorial realm, disputed colonial spaces were seen simply as parcels of land to be negotiated through treaty or warfare. With the occupation of most of the terrestrial earth by the end of World War I, however, the instrumental view of boundary making clashed with the organicism of romantic European nationalism. Thomas Holdich, a colonel in the British Army and an eventual president of the Royal Geographical Society, comments on this new importance of boundaries in a world traversed by imperial nation-states:

> Thus it came about that within the space of half a century the white man found himself face to face with a new proposition in race expansion. He was no longer up against the black or brown man...but it was the white man of another nationality than his own who blocked his way. Under such conditions the defining of territories and of frontiers became a necessity, and unscientific as were many of the boundaries then detailed on paper they anticipated the necessity for practical demarcation and answered the purpose of preventing collisions for a time. Never was there such an era of

boundary-making in English history as during the past forty years, nor do we appear to have reached the limit yet.[14]

Writing during World War I, Holdich sees the boundary as a line that existed for defense and the exclusion of outsiders. The boundary is no longer posited as a cultural limit from within; it is a militarized zone to keep enemies out. "The ideal artificial frontier of the future," Holdich writes, "would then be represented and demarcated by long lines of trenches, supported by fortresses of varied size and importance, with a lateral system of railway communication in its rear which would ensure the rapid concentration of troops at any threatened point."[15] Though it isn't surprising that Holdich's military background would lead him to such a view about the function of boundary lines, the similarity between his description of "ideal" frontiers and the miserable trenches of the Western Front suggests that a state of antagonism and potential warfare will be the rule of boundary lines, not the exception.

Twentieth-century boundary discourse was also an unquestionably Western mode of representation. A British contemporary of Holdich's, C. B. Fawcett, wrote that "the tendency toward precise demarcation is universal among civilized powers."[16] Linking the desire for geographical precision with ideas of racial hierarchy, Fawcett posits that "the territories of savage tribes or barbarous states had precise limits only where they were bounded by the sea, or a great river, or some other very definite and strong natural barrier." By contrast, "the territories of modern civilized states are almost everywhere enclosed by lines which have been carefully demarcated, even in areas which have little or no intrinsic value."[17] "Precision," which ultimately speaks to a governmental and capitalist reification of the land, is here justified as a marker of advanced civilization and given hints of a kind of moral superiority as well. Yet even the technicians of boundary drawing admitted that the desire for precision could lead to a bloodless abstraction, which manifested itself in the fetish for straight lines. "Nothing but the necessity imposed by ignorance," writes Holdich, "can justify the adoption of the straight line."[18] A 1945 guide to boundary drawing advises the following: "It is tempting to place a ruler on a map and draw a line which is to be a boundary. Such a boundary, however, may be disharmonic with the facts of land and people. Widespread use of geometrical boundaries testifies to absentee, office-bound boundary making."[19] Even while precise boundaries were seen as a necessary precondition for the maintenance of civilized order between nation-states, the concern over the crude abstraction of the straight line suggests that boundaries could and should legislate cultural divisions. In other words, extra care was given to boundary drawing simply because

political cartographers had such a faith in their ultimate efficacy. Indeed, the need
for precise boundaries was a precondition for the entry of any new, decolonized
nation-state into the emergent world order.

Unsurprisingly, the discourse of boundary lines tends to reduce the complex
identities and affiliations of the everyday to a black and white abstraction. The
political parties that negotiated the settlement—Jinnah's Muslim League, and
Nehru's Congress Party—represented only a very small portion of the entire elec-
torate, much less all of the affected populations of the subcontinent. Religious
communities outside of the Hindu/Muslim binary, most notably the Sikhs in the
Punjab, but also Parsees and Christians throughout the subcontinent, were left
with little to no influence over the process of partition. Other categories of identity, such as gender and caste, were likewise subordinated in the negotiations for
a Hindu/Muslim partition. Recent histories have of course sharpened the view of
the English role in partition, which was obviously more influential than Radcliffe's
quote suggests. The British, in granting local self-government to its Indian states,
set up separate electorates for Hindus and Muslims, thereby denying the possibility of a formal, abstract equality among Indians. The structures of political participation in India were already divided along religious lines, so it follows that
each group would see its primary affiliation as communal rather than national.
Eventually, Lord Mountbatten, the final Viceroy of India, set a firm date for the
transfer of power, which had the effect of both forcing the hand of Hindu and
Muslim interests while also causing each group to retreat further into their respective antagonistic, uncompromising stances. Finally, on August 15, 1947, India and
Pakistan each became sovereign nation-states, although in some cases the boundary lines were not revealed until days, and sometimes weeks, later.

The fetish of boundaries, itself generated by the insistence on territorial sovereignty for each state, had direct consequences for the definition of the "nation."
The "two nations" theory of a Hindu India and a Muslim Pakistan, popularized by
Jinnah, exploited an ambiguity in the idea of nationality. One vision of nationhood
claimed its foundation in communal autonomy for both Hindu and Muslim populations; the other vision identified the nation as an entity whose *sine qua non* was
territorial sovereignty. Frequently, communal and ethnic nationalisms attempt
to align these two ideas, but, as Joya Chatterji points out, notions of communal
autonomy and territorial sovereignty do not always line up. "The first emphasizes
the rights of the people of a community to self-determination, rights which in
theory could be achieved within a single state. The second stresses the bounded
space within which a community is sovereign, and could be realized only by a territorial separation."[20] Jinnah's initial claim, for example, that Hindu and Muslim

India were two distinct "nations" is based on the idea of religious and cultural separatism. Hindus and Muslims, he posits, do not share religious and cultural beliefs and therefore constitute two different national units, which must of necessity find their expression through different political structures. In the several years before the end of the British Raj, Jinnah himself never openly agitated for territorial partition, refusing to apply this communalist definition of "nation" to the material and bureaucratic separation of two territorial nation-states. Others, however, assumed that Jinnah's "two nations" theory aligned communal autonomy with territorial sovereignty, following the implication that two "nations" necessarily meant two bounded, distinct nation-states. Jinnah's refusal to clarify his position on the question of territorial sovereignty was manipulated into an argument for partition on both sides. Jinnah, as the chief spokesperson and de facto political leader of an incipient Pakistani state, came to be identified with the cause of partition. Hindus and others wishing against partition generally assumed that Jinnah's wish was for a separate state, leading to responses that pointed out the impossibility of a logical and just separation of Muslim from Hindu territories. In 1944, Nehru himself pointed out the absurdity of the "two nations" logic in his book *The Discovery of India*, wondering: "Why only two I do not know, for if nationality was based on religion, then there were many nations in India. Of two brothers, one may be a Hindu, another a Moslem; they would belong to two different nations. These two nations existed in varying proportions in most of the villages of India. They were nations which had no boundaries; they overlapped."[21] Although he attempts to argue against the use of religion as a principle for partition, Nehru in fact makes the point of pro-partition interests: that any idea of a nation without a bounded, sovereign, territorial state will simply be unworkable.

Nehru, Modernist Cosmopolitanism, and the Geography of Destiny

Nehru's "tryst with destiny" speech is widely acknowledged as a canonical document of the postcolonial archive, the measured, articulate utterance of a newly decolonized nation in its moment of official origin.[22] As Partha Chatterjee has argued, Indian nationalism was a "derivative" version of European nationalism, even if the country's unique circumstance as both a former colony and a place of religious, cultural, and ethnic diversity necessitated a revision of such ideologies. In many ways, Nehru's speech echoes many motifs of Western nationalist rhetoric, including the feminine personification of the nation, the proclamation of the nation's existence from time immemorial, and, of course, the preordained "destiny" that India would one day become a sovereign, independent state. Nehru's rhetoric of romantic nationalism, at first glance, is difficult to square with many of his pre-Independence speeches and writings, which have a decidedly cosmopolitan perspective. The distinction between romantic nationalism and modern cosmopolitanism is not simply an ideological contrast; these can be tied directly to spatial, geographical models of the nation-state within the world. Nehru's early career as a politician and advocate for Indian Independence negotiated the tension between, on the one hand, a modern cosmopolitan sensibility that projected a "global India" on the international state and, on the other, a unified nation-state inhabiting a coherent cultural identity within the borders of a demarcated territory. Even while Nehru remains committed to a modern India looking beyond its borders toward the world, the practicalities of nation formation and the exigencies of partition often drew his rhetoric inward toward a more conventionally territorial stance. Either of these stances lends a specific meaning to the boundary: it is either a portal to other nations, and consequently the world, or it is an ontological limit point beyond which exists only the negation of the nation's organic immanence and presence.

Because it figured so prominently in the speeches and texts surrounding partition, I want to consider the language of national "destiny," particularly in its relationship to geographical territory. Many, if not all, modern nationalist movements use the language of destiny to describe retroactively the achievement of sovereign independence and to posit the future utopia toward which the new nation always strives. The idea of destiny is an essential component to the narration of the nation-state; it might in fact be understood as the prerequisite for casting the nation into a narrative in the first place. "Destiny" is both conclusive and elusive, and so it must be endlessly deferred but never forgotten or cast aside. It exists as a qualitative goal to give shape and purpose to the everyday "homogenous, empty time" that Anderson has posited as the characteristic temporality of the nation.[23] If the ultimate destiny of a nation is always put off toward some future moment, the expression of destiny in the here and now demands a more tangible, material form. This expression is necessarily spatial: the moment of Independence promises an enclosed, common space for diverse individual and communal destinies to be worked out under the sign of the nation. The territoriality of destiny stands in for its impossible temporality; the fact of a finite, bounded, geographical space is the compensation for the endless deferral of the nation's ultimate arrival in a state of pure Being. Nehru, as the leader of the Congress Party and the first prime minister of India, perhaps gave the most famous voice to the language of destiny in his famous "tryst with destiny" speech at the moment of Independence on August 15, 1947. Upon a first reading of the speech, we can interpret Nehru's invocation of destiny as a conventional romantic nationalist use of the term. Nehru, however, was anything but a romantic nationalist, and his writings during the pre-Independence period speak to a remarkably shrewd self-consciousness about his own political discourse. Part of Nehru's challenge in moving from being a party spokesperson for an emergent independence movement to becoming the national leader of a newly created state involved a careful recalibration of the idea of national destiny so that it could accommodate a nation that had been founded in a moment of rupture and fragmentation.

Nehru emerges as a modern, and arguably modernist, figure representing, paradoxically, an emergent nation defined primarily through its opposition to a modernized West. In his autobiography, *Toward Freedom*, Nehru describes a distinctly cosmopolitan education. Attending Harrow and Cambridge in the years before World War I, Nehru was an eager student of the cultural and political thinkers of prewar Europe. Along with liberal doses of Wilde, Shaw, and Nietzsche, Nehru immersed himself in the political questions of the day, especially gravitating to the Irish nationalist and women's suffrage movements. As he notes of a 1910 visit to Ireland, "the early beginnings of Sinn Fein attracted me."[24] Certainly, the connection between Ireland and India would have been keenly felt by Nehru, as evidenced by his response to the Easter Week uprising in 1916, which, "by its very failure attracted, for was that not true courage which mocked at [*sic*] almost certain failure and proclaimed to the world that no physical might could crush the invincible spirit of a nation?"[25] Nehru notes that, in 1916, he was a "pure nationalist, my vague socialist ideas of college days having sunk into the background."[26] Yet his self-description as a "pure nationalist" was itself participating in one of the cultures of modernism: what Elleke Boehmer refers to as "the colonial facilitation of nationalist interconnection."[27] As colonial elites congregated in the metropolis, in this case London, the conditions of their respective home territories were much discussed and compared. As Boehmer writes, "London, pullulating with secularist, anarchist, socialist, avant-garde, and freethinking circles...thus formed an important meeting ground for Indian, Irish, African, and Caribbean freedom movements."[28] Nehru was certainly a part of this scene, contemplating and comparing Indian and Irish nationalisms within a distinctly modernist milieu.

It is therefore no surprise to find Nehru citing another anticolonial nationalist intellectual who was immersed in the cultures of metropolitan modernism, W. B. Yeats. Early in his wide-ranging historical and cultural work, *The Discovery of*

India, Nehru muses on the personal stresses and struggles of a political life, imagining himself in the position to the speaker in Yeats's "An Irish Airman Foresees His Death":

> Perhaps I ought to have been an aviator, so that when the slowness and dullness of life overcame me I could have rushed into the tumult of clouds and said to myself:
>
> > I balanced all, brought all to mind,
> > The years to come seemed waste of breath,
> > A waste of breath the years behind
> > In balance with this life, this death.[29]

Nehru's citation of Yeats encompasses multiple levels of political and cultural reference. Through this citation, Nehru aligns himself with Yeats, another secular nationalist from a privileged background working to overcome sectarian divisions in the struggle against imperial colonialism and the formation of a newly independent nation-state. Along with his stated affinities with the Irish nationalist movement, the citation of Yeats implies Nehru's conviction that the emergence of nations is an isomorphic process that happens similarly in different parts of the world. Also, by citing an Anglo-Irish high cultural poet, Nehru addresses himself to a transnational audience that is familiar with the authors and texts of European high modernism, using literature as a means for a transcultural identification above and beyond the political sphere. Nehru puts forward his credentials as a cosmopolitan intellectual, suggesting that Yeats's poem is part of a common international culture, able not only to transcend national boundaries but to dissolve the more entrenched conceptual boundary between the Occident and Orient. This appears to be a prime example of what Boehmer calls "resistance in interaction," a productive intertextuality between two nationalized intellectuals, each involved in his own anti-imperial struggle, that avoids being routed through the dominant imperial culture.[30]

Yet, for all of the aesthetic and political kinship implied, Nehru explicitly identifies himself not with the poet-figure but with the speaker of Yeats's poem, Robert Gregory. Gregory, the son of Yeats's friend and benefactor Lady Gregory, was an Irish aviator fighting for the British in a struggle *between* imperial powers. The Irish airman's soliloquy brings together two salient themes: a politicized passive resistance to serving in the name of the imperial master and a modernist psychological isolation and social alienation (indicated most powerfully in the lines "Those that I fight I do not hate/Those that I guard I do not love").[31] In addition to the cultural transnationalism of borrowing an anticolonial text to underwrite the struggle for an Indian nationalism, Nehru also yokes modernist psychological alienation with a resistant passivity analogous to *satyagraha*, Mohandas Gandhi's program of nonviolent resistance to colonial authority. Though piloting a British aircraft, the speaker of Yeats's poem has inwardly declared his own *non serviam* to the colonial master. Nehru likewise communicates an anticolonial resistance that is both wholly individualized and imagined through the mise-en-scène of modernity. In a text whose goal is to outline the historical and cultural rationale for a secular Indian nation-state, however, Nehru's affinity with Yeats's alienated war pilot stands out as a moment of aesthetic self-consciousness. Nehru seems here to fashion himself not simply as a political leader but as a tortured soul and poet *manqué* as well, an uncharacteristically Prufrockian moment for a figure so devoted to the public spheres of politics and culture.

Nehru's gesture toward this detachment, however, seems more politically motivated than a mere projection of a cosmopolitan cultural elitism. Crucially, in his autobiography, Nehru locates his phase of "pure nationalism" in the enthusiasms of a youthful past. Taken with his citation of a poem written in the pre-Independence climate of Ireland, we can imagine that Nehru's individualized expression of a desire to withdraw from the public sphere is likewise grounded in a youthful angst. The enthusiasms of both radical nationalism and alienated individualism seem like two sides of the same coin of youth. At the time of the composition of his autobiography (from 1934 to 1936) and of *The Discovery of India* (in 1944–1945), however, Nehru was the figure most identified with the project of a modern, secular Indian nation-state. Narrating his own life as a bildungsroman of sorts, Nehru translates this individual arc of self-development into the broader process of national awakening. With the famous proclamation of India's "tryst with destiny" at the moment of Independence in 1947, Nehru completes the imaginative transformation that fuses his own biographical narrative to that of the nation-state. Just as, in the bildungsroman, the beginning of the protagonist's narrative is also the ending, the moment of enunciation that is the precondition for the retrospective narrative itself, Nehru, both standing apart from and standing in for India, completes his transformation from Congress Party leader to prime minister, a change already implied by the intellectual distance and subjective voice that characterizes both his autobiography and *The Discovery of India*. As Partha Chatterjee points out, Nehru knew that he was not an organic intellectual rising from the masses, and much of Nehru's writing is quite self-conscious in its worrying over his ability to represent a nation that he wasn't even quite sure he knew and from which he often felt distinctly apart.

Another significant dimension of Nehru's citation of Yeats is its mise-en-scène of technologized modernity: Nehru finds in the aviator piloting an aircraft an apt image of detachment. As David Matless has argued, the view from a plane flying above a landscape was intriguing in the early decades of air travel, not simply as "a god's eye-view, a position of anonymous, remote, and objectifying power, but a specific human position produced through new kinds of travel."[32] Nehru himself had a longtime fascination with flying, as a symbol of both national and global progress. After being among the crowd at Le Bourget airfield in Paris when Charles Lindbergh landed at the end of his famous solo transatlantic flight, Nehru breathlessly wrote in the Hindi-language daily *Aaj*, "England is full of Indians who, allured by the Bar, medicine, or jobs, stay there undergoing all sorts of humiliation in London or Edinburgh. If even a few of them would dare to learn flying and shun the idea of jobs, they could be of so much benefit to India."[33] Nehru believed that the establishment of an aviation industry in India would strengthen the military, build the economy, and encourage cultural exchange across the diverse regions of the subcontinent. In a 1948 speech delivered to a meeting of the International Civic Aviation Organization, Nehru hailed the advent of air travel as a landmark not simply in its potential for national "development" but in terms of human history. "It is a major event," he declares, "that the human being crawling about on the surface of the earth, more or less in a two-dimensional way, suddenly leaps up to the third dimension."[34] Nehru would have joined the chorus of early-twentieth-century technophiles who, in the words of Stephen Kern, praised the airplane for its "uplifting of human consciousness" and "its capacity to unify people and nations."[35] The aircraft, for Nehru, was a personal symbol of his own attachment to a cultural and political cosmopolitanism. In fact, Nehru admits that his "chief regret" was that he "did not become an aviator."[36] Nehru's airborne removal from the world, then, is not simply a technologized instance of modernist detachment; it provides a means for such personal inwardness within a context of a technology used for the greater good.

Even coming secondhand from the words of an Irish poet, this imagined airborne detachment allows Nehru a position from which he can look upon India as from high above and imaginatively map its diverse cultures and spaces. Just as Joyce saw himself in the position of a surveyor in writing about the Dublin of *Ulysses*,[37] Nehru also uses the pose of detachment to give expression to a nation that no situated perspective could grasp. The point of such a surveying gaze is not necessarily a desire for imperialistic control but simply for the usable knowledge of a cognitive map. Such images, whether in a cartographic or narrative form, allow for the grounded subject with limited perspective to take part in a larger whole. In

The Discovery of India, Nehru attempts such a survey, describing the various ethnic and cultural groups of India as if pointing to them on a map:

> It is fascinating to find how the Bengalese, the Marathas, the Gujratis, the Tamils, the Andhras, the Oriyas, the Assamese, the Canarese, the Malayalis, the Sindhis, the Punjabis, the Pathans, the Kashmiris, the Rajputs, and the great central bloc comprising the Hindustani-speaking people, have retained their peculiar characteristics for hundreds of years, have still more or less the same virtues and failings of which old tradition or record tells us, and yet have been throughout these ages distinctively Indian, with the same national heritage and the same set of moral and mental qualities.[38]

Nehru posits a retrospective unity within the cultural diversity of the subcontinent; indeed, in this formulation the nation of "distinctively Indian" people has existed for centuries, waiting only to find its full expression in the form of the modern nation-state. By phrasing the differences in the subcontinent in terms of the "superficial" distinctions of culture rather than the more profound differences of religion, Nehru avoids, perhaps disingenuously, the dualistic Hindu-Muslim opposition that proved decisive in the partition of the subcontinent. When Nehru does bring up the question of religious communalism, he subordinates it to an a priori national unity: "An Indian Christian is looked upon as an Indian wherever he may go. An Indian Moslem is considered an Indian in Turkey or Arabia or Iran or any other country where Islam is the dominant religion."[39] Notably, Nehru doesn't confront the question of what religious communalism means *within* India. Nehru separates the spheres of religion and culture, assuming an "Indian" identity separate from and prior to a religious affiliation, even though religious separatism was the very engine driving the formation of the two partitioned nation-states.

Nehru can make the case for a kind of federated India because, in his mind, the nation-state itself is simply a harbinger of a broader global community. Objecting to the plan of partition on the grounds that smaller nation-states are necessarily weaker, Nehru sees a federated India as better equipped to thrive on the world stage. "The idea of the national state," Nehru writes, "was giving place to the multinational state or to large federations."[40] Nehru suggests that the model nation will throw off the shackles of exclusionary difference in its preparation for a global political institution that incorporates and subordinates cultural difference to a larger unity. The articulation of organicist nationalism comes across simply as a necessary phase in the march toward a transnational, global state. Yet, with this phase of organicist nationalism comes the distasteful

consequences of irrational, atavistic enthusiasms, which, based upon the homol-
ogy of religion and state in the partition debates, could only further inflame
exclusionary violence. The pre-partition Nehru puts forward a geography within
which the cultural plurality of India finds expression within a state sovereignty,
but that sovereignty itself was to be founded and sustained within the "rational" realms of a planned economy, a modern technologized infrastructure, and
democratic political institutions.

Where Nehru, in his pre-partition writings, uses the geography of India to justify a pluralist nation based on the idea of "variety within unity," others used geography to justify a separatist outlook. In his 1945 pamphlet "Is India Geographically
One?" Kazi Said-ud-din Ahmad, a Muslim geographer at the Aligarh Muslim
University, uses the discourse of geography to contradict Nehru's pluralist argument. Ahmad begins his essay by explicitly connecting questions of geographical
unity and political sovereignty: "Geography and politics may, to some, appear a
strange combination. But while it can be said that no state in the history of the
world has ever been carved out purely on geographical considerations, this science
would certainly help in the creation of more homogeneous groups, political, racial,
cultural, and economic, out of a vast complex."[41] Ahmad makes a conventional
appeal to geography as a science, giving it an epistemological authority from which
political structures may be derived. While granting that India might have a "superficial geographical unity" to a "casual observer," in reality it is more analogous to a
continent than to a sovereign nation. Ahmad goes on to divide India into four geographical units: Western, Northern, Eastern, and the Deccan, or Southern region
of the subcontinent. These regions, according to Ahmad, have not only a geographical unity, but racial and cultural unity as well. In what appears almost as an
afterthought, Ahmad notes that Muslims predominate in the Eastern and Western
regions, while Hindus form a majority in the Northern and Southern regions, thus
mirroring the division of a proposed partition. The final sections of the pamphlet
undertake a comparative analysis to other regions in the world, concluding that in
fact there is no necessary relationship between a region's geographical "unity" and
its expression in the form of a sovereign nation-state. Ahmad's article concludes
that, regarding the formation of sovereign states, "the principal factor has been the
will of the people inhabiting a particular region."[42] Ahmad communicates a two-
sided message here: although he acknowledges that geographical homogeneity is
not necessarily tied to sovereign nationhood, the will of a "people" can be more
effectively executed when they are concentrated as a clear majority in a particular
"region." Although Ahmad's argument avoids this kind of geographical determinism in the letter, it advocates it in spirit. Just as Nehru uses geography to support

an argument for a federalist India, Ahmad likewise uses the same discourse to advance a separatist argument.[43]

The tension between the mutually constituting relationship between India and Pakistan and the idea that each nation goes forth by itself into a global community can be seen in Nehru's famous "tryst with destiny" speech made at the moment of Indian Independence on August 15, 1947. This speech is typically read as a celebratory commemoration of India's entrance onto the global stage as a sovereign state free from the domination of British rule. Nehru imaginatively gathers the citizens of India into one geo-body: he speaks of the achievement of Independence as a moment "when the soul of a nation, long suppressed, finds utterance."[44] Moreover, this new geo-body now enters the global community as a sovereign nation, as Nehru proclaims utopian aspirations not only "for India, but...also for the world."[45] Nehru speaks of a world "that can no longer be split into isolated fragments," yet his very speech commemorates such a splitting: the birth of India also meant the death of regional, local, even familial communities that found themselves sundered by the capricious abstraction of Radcliffe's line. In a version of the speech reprinted in newspapers later that morning, Nehru addresses the new citizens of Pakistan—many of whom did not yet know to which nation they belonged—not as Pakistanis but as exiled Indians: "We think also of our brothers and sisters who have been cut off from us by political boundaries and who unhappily cannot share at present in the freedom that has come. They are of us and will remain of us whatever may happen."[46] The "tryst with destiny" speech displays Nehru's deep ambivalence about territorial nationhood. Although Pakistanis will remain "brothers and sisters" lost on the other side of the boundary, the language of national destiny demands that, in the empty, homogeneous time of nationhood, the fates of India and Pakistan are no longer related, that the drawing of the boundary line has been a clean break, allowing each nation to pursue its destiny as an autonomous agent in the neutral realm of world politics. The idea of a division of sovereign territory formalizes, once and for all, social and cultural divisions that have been complex and contextual. Regardless of the multiple affiliations of inhabitants in the subcontinent in 1947, all were drawn into the dualistic worldview that saw only Islamic Pakistan and Hindu India. Other religious affiliations—Sikhs, Parsees, Christians—had no claim to a collective identity that would be accommodated in either state. Other social distinctions, such as class, caste, and gender, were also subordinated to two overarching, polarizing views. As a poignant scene from Deepa Mehta's 1999 film *Earth* (an adaptation of Bapsi Sidhwa's novel *Cracking India*) demonstrates, the public life of Lahore (now in Pakistan) devolved from a thriving social and religious diversity to angry mobs shouting "Pakistan Zindabad, Hindustan Murdabad!" ("Long live Pakistan! Death to India!") as Nehru's speech plays over the radio. Nehru's claim that the world can no longer be fragmented seems an especially cruel irony, given that such fragmentations were multiplying exponentially as Radcliffe's boundary line metaphorically reproduced itself within communities, families, and even individuals. Even as he appeals to the exiled Indians across the border, there is no mention of the Pakistani state in his speech. The nation's "tryst with destiny," it would seem, does not include the ongoing embrace of India and Pakistan. Yet post-partition history demonstrates that the embrace between the two (now three) nations in the almost sixty years since partition has become, if anything, a stranglehold.

The course of Nehru's writings from his autobiography through the parliamentary speech at Independence shows a reconciliation between a modernist individualism and a political nationalism. Nehru's individual "destiny" as a character in his own self-narrated bildungsroman is alchemized into a national destiny at the moment of Independence. Yet, even as Nehru spatializes India's destiny according to a belief in the historical and geographical intercourse between cultures, he bows to the territorial logic of the nation-state, which both commemorates the birth of the Indian nation and mourns the sundering of its lands in the east and west. Nehru contracts his earlier dream of the "whole" India to the shrunken size of the amputated territory ultimately inscribed on the map.

Boundary Allegory: *The Shadow Lines*

Because it invokes the bildungsroman as a mode for transforming a personal biography into a national autobiography, Nehru's narratives can be read alongside fictional accounts of the partition to assess precisely how partition might be imaginatively rendered in a way that refuses to naturalize the nation-state. At a first glance, the bildungsroman seems to fit hand in glove with narratives of national allegory: Nehru's autobiography (whose title, *Toward Freedom*, suggests just such a personification), G. V. Desani's *All About H. Hatterr* (1948), and Salman Rushdie's *Midnight's Children* (1981) all lend themselves readily to the structure of the bildungsroman-as-national-allegory. But it is important to note that in each of these cases, an internally fragmented protagonist requires that thematic—and thus ideological—contradictions be either repressed (as in Nehru's case) or ironized (as in the case of Desani and Rushdie). Desani's protagonist notes from the outset that "biologically, I am fifty-fifty of the species," having been born from a nationally unspecified "European" father and a similarly vague "Oriental" mother.[47] Rushdie's

Saleem Sinai likewise begins in a split subjective space, claiming he was born "once upon a time" before confessing that he was in fact born precisely at midnight on August 15, 1947, the moment of India's Independence.[48] These ruptured origins suggest the impossibility of beginning one's personal (and national) story from a point of view of achieved wholeness and identity. For Desani and Rushdie, the national allegory will be one in which the allegorical referent is always seen, as it were, through fictional narration. The fact of partition, then, is not confronted directly in these narratives but is rather represented by other literary motifs of fracture, splitting, and division. Such self-conscious narratives of partition therefore contradict Fredric Jameson's pronouncement that "all third-world texts are necessarily... *national allegories.*"[49]

I would like to examine a novel that more overtly presents a different kind of allegory, one that confronts the facts of partition in a more direct, literal way. Amitav Ghosh's 1988 novel, *The Shadow Lines*, does not locate itself from within the perspective of a national culture (be it Indian, Pakistani, or English), but it instead incorporates the very notion of the territorial border into its fictional structure: rather than a national allegory, it is what I will call a boundary allegory. One of the central points of *The Shadow Lines* is that the wish for separate destinies implied through the act of partition is not only illusory but also destructive. Ghosh exposes the tragic, though completely logical, consequence of modern territorial nationalism: that the drawing of borders can become an imprisoning limit to the individual and collective lives of the people enclosed by those borders. The formalism of the line assumes many guises in Ghosh's novel. It is, of course, the boundary line separating India from Pakistan and Bangladesh, but it is also the line that binds these nations together. The line extends through time as well as space, sometimes separating characters from their histories and sometimes binding these individual histories even more tightly. Ghosh's complex attitude toward the lines of his title is reflected in the novel's frequent use of spatial and temporal ellipses: as if in response to the fundamental divisions instituted by partition, Ghosh insists on crossing spatial, temporal, and interpersonal lines throughout the book. The novel is narrated retrospectively by an Indian Bengali man born in the 1950s (who remains nameless throughout), yet this narration enters into the stories and recollections of other characters, often recalling times and places of which the narrator has had no direct experience. The opening pages, which evoke the narrator's childhood fondness for his older cousin Tridib, quickly assume the perspective of Tridib's childhood memories of a trip to London during World War II (before the narrator is even born). Later, the narrator will retell stories of his grandmother, who grew up in pre-partition Dhaka in the early twentieth century.

Finally, in a climactic point near the novel's conclusion, the narrator recounts, and so relives, the experience of Tridib's English fiancée, May Price, who witnessed Tridib's death at the hands of a Dhaka mob. So, even though Ghosh gives us a first-person narrator, this narrator takes up the stories of others with such detail that it seems as if the novel is composed out of several narrative perspectives.

The novel's structure, and the narrator's own storytelling ethic, takes its cue from Tridib's advice to use "imagination with precision," combining the desire to enter into a kind of transpersonal, transcultural understanding with the imperative to remain as faithful as possible to the circumstances of individual experience (*SL* 24). When discussing the possibility of such an epistemological perspective with his cousin Ila, his desire for "precise imagination" is belittled by his more worldly cousin: "Why should we try [to imagine with precision], why not just take the world as it is?" The narrator responds, claiming that the act of imagining is necessary to individual and cultural identity: "If we didn't try ourselves, we would never be free of other people's inventions" (*SL* 31). The exchange indicates the difference between two types of traveling. Ila's version is portrayed as an empty globetrotting cosmopolitanism, which levels all experience into a detached ennui, as her experience of the diverse places in the world is reduced to her knowledge of the finest distinctions and variations in the many airports she continually moves through. By contrast, Tridib's ethic of imaginative transference, which the narrator sees as a more valuable, transformational form of experience, is a "pure, painful, and primitive desire, a longing...that carried one beyond the limits of one's mind to other times and other places" (*SL* 29). Early in the novel, at least, Ila is a tourist who never sees or learns anything of value, while the narrator, whose travel is in his imagination alone, nonetheless moves toward a more profound sort of knowledge. The novel's form, with its continuous jumping across time and space and its refusal to name the narrator, bears out this ethic of imaginative transference.

The novel approaches the question of the 1947 partition indirectly; it is not, like Khushwant Singh's *Train to Pakistan* or Bapsi Sidhwa's *Cracking India*, a partition novel as such. Ghosh pointedly uses a narrator who does not experience partition directly but is subsequently forced, as an Indian Bengali, to live within its inventions. The narrator is given much of his frame of reference for partition from his grandmother, who tells stories of her childhood in pre-partition Bengal. One of the stories the narrator loves to hear again and again concerns his grandmother's childhood house in Dhaka, which (so the story goes) was literally partitioned by her quarrelsome father and uncle, both of whom had a legal claim on the house. The two brothers build a wooden partition through the house that bisects doorways, furniture, and even a commode. Even with the obvious absurdity of the partition wall, the brothers "insist[ed] on their rights with a lawyer-like precision" (*SL* 123). The painful lesson learned by the two brothers comes too late: "They had longed for the house to be divided when the quarrels were at their worst, but once it had actually happened and each family had moved into their own part of it, instead of the peace they had so much looked forward to, they found that a strange, eerie silence had descended on the house. It was never the same again; the life went out of it" (*SL* 123).

The tale of the partitioned house is passed down through the generations with almost mythical embellishments, as the two sisters (both of whom were very young at the time of the partition) begin to invent stories about the odd "upside-down" things that occur on the other side of the wall. They begin meals with dessert and end with soup, they cook with brooms and clean with ladles, and they write with umbrellas and go walking with pencils (*SL* 123–124). After the sisters have moved to India, the story of the partitioned house becomes a kind of narrative currency passed between the two sisters, a way to make sense of their exile. The opposite side of the house, far from being erased from their memories, becomes a founding myth against which they can construct and measure their own identities. Ghosh suggests that the same dynamics occur through the partition of nations: the "upside-down" world of the "other" nation is not cast into absence but is refracted back as an inverted mirror image. Later in the novel, when the grandmother plans to take an airplane trip from Calcutta to Dhaka, she is dispirited to find that she won't be able to identify the border between India and East Pakistan from the airplane: "I mean, where's the difference then? And if there's no difference both sides will be the same; it'll be just like it used to be before, when we used to catch a train in Dhaka and get off in Calcutta the next day without anybody stopping us. What was it all for then—partition and all the killing and everything—if there isn't something in between?" (*SL* 151). The narrator's grandmother cannot believe that the act of partition, something that can separate destinies even within the same family, cannot be visibly read and understood on the landscape. The myth of the partitioned nation builds up such conceptual lines between neighboring nations, that the idea of any continuity between the two, even of the landscape, is almost unthinkable.

This episode prefigures the narrator's later, more personal epiphany about the fictitiousness of partition, leading him not toward a political conclusion about the history of partition but instead to a critical understanding of its form. His realization occurs when, as a graduate student studying in England, he recalls riots that took place in 1964 in Calcutta at the same time that his cousin Tridib was murdered by an angry mob in Dhaka, across the border. Only then, fifteen years after the fact, does he realize that the riots he witnessed in Calcutta and the murder of Tridib in Dhaka were related events. Before this realization, the narrator sees the world through a perspective that stops at the India-Pakistan boundary, as the borderline between the two states sets a limit to his own psychic reality: "I believed in the reality of space; I believed that distance separates, that it is a corporeal substance; I believed in the reality of nations and borders; I believed that across the border there existed another reality" (*SL* 219). The "events" in Calcutta and in Dhaka appeared to the narrator as isolated, wholly contained by the borders of each nation. The narrator pointedly admits that his inability to "connect" the riots in Calcutta with the riots in Dhaka comes not from an objectively mandated silence but from one that has its source at a deeper, more unconscious level—a silence of negation rather than a silence of coercion. "It is not," the narrator remarks, "the silence of an imperfect memory. Nor is it a silence enforced by a ruthless state—nothing like that, no barbed wire, no checkpoints to tell me where its boundaries lie. I know nothing of this silence except that it lies outside the reach of my intelligence, beyond words" (*SL* 218). The narrator realizes that the only relationships recognized between territorial nation-states are "war and friendship." The myth of nationalism permits nothing so ambiguous as simultaneous riots in different nations to be understood within a frame of international relations. The riots of Calcutta and Dhaka, though in response to the same cause (the theft of the Prophet's hair from a mosque in Srinigar, Kashmir), are not allowed to enter into "official" history. The consequence of this silence for the narrator is his inability to make sense of his cousin's death except as a random, inexplicable tragedy. The recognition that Tridib's murder can be placed in some sort of larger political context at least affords him the ability to properly mourn, even if it occurs fifteen years too late.

As a response to the lines that divided the narrator from the circumstances of his cousin's death, and earlier divided the narrator's grandmother from her home in Dhaka, the narrator actively remaps the spaces of the world, drawing lines of connection that counterbalance the isolating lines of partition. Earlier in the novel, when he first goes to London as a graduate student, he was held up to ridicule by Ila and her English fiancé for memorizing the A to Z map of London and excitedly navigating a way through the city even though he had never been there. Yet, later in the novel, when he struggles to understand the events that led to the murder of his cousin, he has a more active, creative engagement with the abstractions of the map. Idly thumbing through an old atlas, he finds a compass and draws a circle with the compass point on Khulna, in Bangladesh, where the initial riots started, and the tip of the pencil on Srinigar, in Kashmir, where the events that precipitated the riots initially took place. As the narrator puts it, "It was an amazing circle," moving counterclockwise from Kashmir, through Pakistan and the Arabian Sea, touching land again at the southern tip of the Indian peninsula, moving out again to the Indian Ocean, across Sumatra, Thailand, Cambodia, Laos, and the southwestern part of China, before returning again to Kashmir (*SL* 231). The narrator is surprised to learn that "Hanoi and Chungking are nearer Khulna than Srinigar, and yet, did the people of Khulna care at all about the fate of the mosques in Vietnam and China...? I doubted it" (*SL* 232). The lesson seems to explain to the narrator both the personal loss of Tridib and the collective fiction of partition: "there had never been a moment in the four-thousand-year-old history of that map, when the places we know as Dhaka and Calcutta were more closely bound to each other than after they had drawn their lines" (*SL* 233). The lines of partition, the narrator learns, bind as well as divide: India and Pakistan, far from separating nations to pursue their own destinies, only ensured that those destinies would always be intertwined.

The Shadow Lines takes up the modernist preoccupation with the reduction of culture into the formal abstractions of space, but its imaginative remappings give it a highly critical, self-conscious inflection. Ghosh's novel exposes the boundary line as a political fiction that has nonetheless been wholly inscribed onto the landscape of fact, not just in India but in Ireland, in Palestine, and in a number of other geopolitical hotspots where border disputes have become a permanent feature of social and cultural, as well as geographical, space. Ironically, Ghosh finds a conceptual escape from the limited epistemology of partition through one of the most vilified perspectives of modernity: the detached Cartesian gaze of post-Enlightenment cartography. This detached geometrical perspective, precisely because it renders space into a homogeneous medium, allows the narrator to translate the divisive line of partition into an encompassing circle that draws dozens of nations, cultures, and languages into its abstract formal embrace. Though the lines of partition can indeed be destructive, Ghosh reminds us that lines themselves are not the villains of history. Boundaries are but one type of line among many; they are not necessarily the margins of the knowable world.

Coda

By way of conclusion, I want to mention a complicated situation that still persists on the India/Bangladesh border. At various points near the boundary line drawn by Radcliffe, there exist parcels of land, called *chitmahals*, which were originally controlled by princely states that delayed joining either India or Pakistan immediately after partition. By the time that these states opted for one or the other nation, some had acquired parcels of land that were across the "wrong" border. The result has been pockets of land that are literally stateless: bits of India stranded in Bangladesh, and vice versa. The people living on the *chitmahals* are not protected by either country, and they cannot legally return to the country they see as their own. Essentially, these tiny territorial fragments keep them imprisoned in what they see as a foreign land. Obviously, this circumstance gives the lie to the supposed precision of boundary drawing. But even more interesting to me is the frequently told story of the boundary that has become a kind of local folktale. Here it is, in the words of Jagdish Babu, who lives in an Indian *chitmahal* surrounded by the nation-state of Bangladesh:

> You see how this border curls and winds? Which person in his sane mind would draw a boundary like that? You know that Radcliffe? What did he know about anything? He was so confused by what he had to do that he decided, forget it, I'll just get drunk! The bastard drank all night, and then in the morning he woke up and picked up his pen, and naturally he couldn't draw a straight line! So he went this way and that—and botched the whole thing up. And of course we have to live with the consequences![50]

While the tale of an inebriated Radcliffe, drunkenly drawing his curling, winding lines on the map of India, might be small compensation for the consequences in which these stateless citizens must live, it shows that the *dis*enchantment and continuing suspicion of boundary lines proceed apace, outside of official political channels, sustained and renewed within the oral cultures of everyday life. At the smallest scales, boundary lines are inevitably exposed as arbitrary, bureaucratic, whimsical, and, above all, fictional creations. The circuitous, twisting lines of boundary too easily give over to the similarly tangled lines of textuality, which betray the boundary line's eternal subjection to the ambiguous and indeterminate process of signification.

Jagdish Babu's story shows that, often, those living within the uneasy, fractious conditions of the national borderland are frequently those best disposed to see it as less an immutable, almost geological reality, and more as an openended text. This study has proposed alternatives to a view of the world based on interlocking nation-states that compose a totalizing map of the globe. Even as the nation-state has been, for many, a guarantor of individual and group rights, the locus of collective feeling, and the portal from the intimately local to the broad sweep of the global, the naturalization of its particular geographical form—as a planar, enclosed, surveilled territory—continues to encourage caution in the face of celebrations of a fully "globalized" world. From Conrad's and Greene's encounters with the continental difference of Africa to attempts by Forster and Geddes to understand the region as an alternative form of community, the world order established by European imperialism was already generating skeptical responses from within its metropolitan centers. Beginning with Joyce and following through to writers from the late-twentieth-century age of decolonization—Rhys, Kincaid, and Ghosh, among others—narratives from the perspective of emergent nation-states display a heightened awareness of ways in which geographical fictions could be rudely forced into fact. The internal colony, the island, and the boundary line, though marginalized in static views of a territorial world order, in fact provide ideal vantage points for the imaginative division and revision of the globe.

Notes

Introduction

1. Anderson, *Imagined Communities*, 5.
2. See Hobsbawm and Ranger, *Invention of Tradition*.
3. This allegorical aesthetic is quite different than the kind of "national allegory" that Fredric Jameson has identified with "third-world" literature. Where Jameson discusses literature that telescopes private, individual destinies projected in the novel with the formation of a public, national culture in newly decolonized states, Manto's rejection of social realism forecloses these possibilities by presenting neither psychologically complex characters nor any kind of shared public sphere. See Jameson, "Third-World Literature."
4. See Kern, *Culture of Time and Space*.
5. Friedman, "Periodizing Modernism," 425.
6. Doyle and Winkiel, "Introduction," 1.
7. Lewis and Wigen, *Myth of Continents*, ix.
8. Colebrook, *Irony* (New Critical Idiom), 3.
9. Manto, "Toba Tek Singh," in *Collected Stories*, 11.
10. Even "imaginary" geographies would fit this definition, as they often presume a global totality, even if that totality is not of our earth. J. R. R. Tolkien's extensive mapping of Middle-earth in the *Hobbit* books is perhaps the most well-known example of this kind of imaginary geography.
11. Moretti, *Atlas of the European Novel*, 5.
12. Bulson, *Novels, Maps, Modernity*, 3.
13. Ibid., 2.
14. In this case, as in many others, *Finnegans Wake* may be the exception that supports the rule.
15. Winkiel and Doyle, "Introduction," 1.
16. Edney, "Reconsidering Enlightenment Geography and Map Making," 175.
17. Mackinder, "On the Scope and Methods of Geography," 141.
18. Ibid.
19. Ibid.
20. See Ó Tuathail, *Critical Geopolitics*, particularly chapters 1 and 4.

21. Mackinder, "On the Scope and Methods of Geography," 143.

22. Ibid.

23. Ibid., 145.

24. Moretti, *Atlas of the European Novel*, 18.

25. These examples are to be distinguished from narratives that append actual maps as either front matter and/or appendices. Metatopographia, as I conceive of it, depends upon the rendering of a visual representation into language (thus making the specific instance of map description one example of the broader rhetorical mode of *ekphrasis*).

26. See Smith, "Contours of a Spatialized Politics," 54–81, and Smith, "Scale Bending and the Fate of the National," 192–212.

27. Mayhew, "Halford Mackinder's 'New' Political Geography," 778.

28. Mackinder, "On the Scope and Methods of Geography," 149.

29. See Jameson, "Modernism and Imperialism," 43–68; Said, *Culture and Imperialism*; Duffy, *Subaltern "Ulysses"*; and Baucom, *Out of Place*.

30. Lefebvre, *Production of Space*, 301.

31. Ibid., author's italics.

32. Ibid., 302.

33. Robbins, *Feeling Global*, 6.

34. Appiah, *Cosmopolitanism*, xvi–xvii.

35. Navari, *Internationalism and the State in the Twentieth Century*, 67. It must be pointed out that what Navari describes as "shared social and political objectives" refers not so much to imagined *inter*national objectives as to *intra*national ones, beginning of course with the objective of sovereignty and self-determination. In other words, whatever the ideological stripe of a particular national ruling class or party, virtually all nations claim to want the *formal* right of autonomy, sovereignty, and self-determination within an arena of international relations.

36. David Ayers, "Roundtable: Modernism and Nation," Modernist Studies Association, 12th Annual Conference, Victoria, BC (November 2010).

37. Sarker, "Afterword," 561.

38. Ibid., 562.

39. Joyce, *Portrait of the Artist as a Young Man*, 9.

40. In a subtle yet surely intentional anticolonial gesture, Joyce's catalog ignores the sovereign state (the United Kingdom) to which the "nation" of Ireland belonged at the time of Stephen's (and Joyce's) school days at Clongowes.

41. Joyce, *Portrait of the Artist as a Young Man*, 9.

42. See Howes, "Goodbye Ireland I'm Going to Gort," 58–77. Howes reads this episode as a resolution between Enlightenment scales of space in Stephen's list and a primary national identification as suggested by Fleming's verse: "Both inscriptions figure the individual climbing the geographical scales from himself to the Irish nation (and beyond) according to the dictates of conventional nationalism" (71). By contrast, I see Stephen (and Joyce) as *unable* to reconcile these versions of spatial identification, which leads to the alternating artistic sensibilities of national identification ("I shall forge in the smithy of my soul the uncreated conscience of my race") and cosmopolitan detachment for the conventional trappings of nationalism (Joyce's scorn for the "rediscovery" of Gaelic, for example).

43. Anderson, *Imagined Communities*, 12.

44. Joyce, *Portrait of the Artist as a Young Man*, 212, 217.

45. Cheah, *Spectral Nationality*, 127.

46. Anderson, *Imagined Communities*, 175.

47. See Mackinder, "On the Scope and Methods of Geography," and Livingstone, *Geographical Tradition*.

48. Brosseau notes that most geographical research on literature "shows a clear preference for the nineteenth-century realist tradition." From the point of view of humanist geography, this literary mode "offers insightful subjective accounts of the experience of place." In other words, both humanist geography and realist fiction look upon space as a stable ground in which various places might be represented, either through the objective rhetoric of social science or the more subjective rhetoric of literary and imaginative representation. The order of space itself is seldom questioned; it functions as an empty container within which people and places exist. See Brosseau, "Geography's Literature," 347.

49. See Shklovsky, "Art as Technique," 15–21.

50. Friel, *Translations*, 52.

Chapter One: Continent

1. Lewis and Wigen, *Myth of Continents,* 30.

2. Livingstone, *Geographical Tradition*, 187.

3. Lewis and Wigen, *Myth of Continents*, 43–44.

4. Mackinder, "Geographical Pivot of History," 422.

5. As the oft-quoted quatrain from Jonathan Swift suggests, "old" maps of Africa were revealed to be more fiction than fact, entertaining as curiosities but bearing no accurate relationship to an existing topography:

> So Geographers in *Afric*-maps,
> With Savage-Pictures fill their Gaps;
> And o'er unhabitable Downs
> Place Elephants for want of Towns.

The map of Africa may have been "full," but as Swift's satire indicates, this plentitude sprang from the fecundity of the cartographer's imagination rather than from the verifiable results of systematic exploration and survey. See Swift, "On Poetry: A Rhapsody," 746.

6. Jacobs, *Story of Geographical Discovery*, 172.

7. Conrad, "Geography and Some Explorers," 10.

8. Lewis and Wigen, *Myth of Continents*, 43.

9. Mackinder, *Britain and the British Seas*, 4, 9.

10. Ibid., 11.

11. Lewis and Wigen, *Myth of Continents*, 44.

12. GoGwilt, *Invention of the West*, 123.

13. Livingstone, *Geographical Tradition*, 221.

14. James Hunt, "On Ethno-Climatology; or the Acclimatization of Man," *Transactions of the Ethnological Society of London* n.s. 2 (1863), 53. Quoted in Livingstone, *Geographical Tradition*, 222.

15. Mackinder, *Britain and the British Seas*, 12.

16. Mackinder, "Geographical Conditions," 467.

17. Achebe, "Image of Africa," 3.

18. Ibid.

19. Ibid.

20. See Edward Said's reading of *Heart of Darkness*, particularly his response to Achebe, in "Two Visions in *Heart of Darkness*," *Culture and Imperialism*, 19–31.

21. Liberia was founded by freed American slaves, as part of a "repatriation" project devised by the American Colonial Society in 1821. This class of former slaves and their descendants eventually formed a political elite in Liberia, declaring its sovereignty in 1847.

22. Thacker, "Journey with Maps," 17.

23. Rhodes, *Primitivism and Modernist Art*, 8.

24. Gikandi, "Picasso, Africa," 457.

25. Geary, *Voyage of King Njoya's Gift*, 16. Njoya's volume was completed in 1931, and it appeared in a French translation as *Histoire et Coutumes des Bamum* in 1952.

26. Ibid., 19.

27. Ibid., 20.

28. Geary, "Art, Politics, and the Transformation of Meaning," 284.

29. Colonial Office, "Letter from Njoya," 5.

30. Njoya's full text reads as follows:

> "LETTER from NJOYA the King of BAMUM
> to
> THE GREAT ALL-POWERFUL KING OF ALL THE ENGLISH.

I, NJOYA, 16th King of Bamum send my humble salutations to the Great King of the English who puts the evil men to flight and the troublesome to prison.

I thank the great English King for sending his strong soldiers to free my country. I have seen the English and I know that they are good and strong people and that all black men follow them. They have delivered me from the hands of the German [*sic*] who are men of darkness, who have no belongings, who are liars, who trouble the people continually.

I have collected all my people and they all wish to belong to the King of the English, and to his sons and the sons of his sons. May he take them into his hand as a father takes his children, may he show them wisdom and help and teach them to be strong even as the English themselves.

I wish to follow the King of England and to be his servant together with my country that my land may be freshened with dew and that the Germans and all unclean things may be driven out. All my people, my old men and my old women my men and my girls [*sic*], the weak and the strong, desire this.

May the God of the English help them in the fight, may the great King remain strong in his town, may his life be long and his descendants numerous.

The German [*sic*] have troubled us and made our hearts cold and foolish. If the evil that they have done could be weighed it would be more than one thousand kilos. I and all my people beg that we may be delivered from their hands.

There is a small thing in my hand which I wish to offer humbly to the English King. It will be nothing in his eyes. It is the chair in which I and my fathers have always sat and which is my strength and power. Also the two large elephant tusks which are on each side of it. There are no other such tusks in the country. The chair and tusks are as nothing to the Great King, but they are all I have.

I, Njoya, and all my headmen and all my people I agree to the English flag which hangs in my town and I give greetings three times and give my land and all that I have to the English. NJOYA. 16th King of Bamum."

31. Ibid., 6.

32. Ibid., 7.

33. Bassett, "Indigenous Mapmaking," 41.

34. Ibid., 43–44.

35. Winichakul, *Siam Mapped*, 55.

36. Ibid., 60–61.

37. Colonial Office, "Letter from Njoya," 1.

38. Ó Tuathail, *Critical Geopolitics*, 15.

39. A recent example of the lingering border conflicts in decolonized Africa is the long-standing dispute between Nigeria and Cameroon over the oil-rich Bakassi Peninsula, which was finally ceded to Cameroon in early 2004. My thanks to Peter Chilson for bringing my attention to this and to many other continued border disputes in contemporary Africa.

Chapter Two: Region

1. For the role of encyclopedism in the history of geography, see Withers, "Encyclopaedism." Withers argues that the practice of ordering geographical knowledge in encyclopedias, dictionaries, and universal grammars has been a structuring feature of post-Enlightenment conceptions of geographical knowledge.

2. Edney, *Mapping an Empire*, 43, author's italics.

3. Lutz, *Cosmopolitan Vistas*, 15.

4. Quoted in Matless, "Uses of Cartographic Literacy," 200.

5. Campbell, "Regionalism and Local Color Fiction."

6. Lutz, *Cosmopolitan Vistas*, 30.

7. Snell, *Regional Novel in Britain and Ireland*, 10. The histories of regional fiction in the American and British literary traditions are not entirely synchronous. Snell goes back to the turn of the eighteenth century, identifying Maria Edgeworth's *Castle Rackrent* (1800) as the first regional novel in Britain, while Campbell more precisely locates the heyday of American regional fiction between the end of the Civil War and the turn of the nineteenth century. Certainly, these differential timelines can be traced to the different histories of urbanization in each nation. Regardless, there seems to be agreement that both British and American traditions saw a heightened interest in and market for regional fiction during the last decades of the nineteenth century.

8. Darby, "Academic Geography in Britain," 15.

9. Vidal de la Blache, *Principles of Human Geography*, 16.

10. See Livingstone, *Geographical Tradition*, 260–290, for a historical perspective on the connection between the French *géographie humaine* and the British regional survey movement.

11. Matless, *Landscapes of Englishness*, 28.

12. Ibid., 129.

13. Ibid.

14. Quoted in ibid., 110.

15. Garrard, *Ecocriticism*, 118.

16. See Carey, *Intellectuals and the Masses*, particularly chapter 3, "The Suburbs and the Clerks."

17. Darby, "Academic Geography in Britain," 15.

18. Fagg, *History of the Regional Survey Movement*, 71.

19. Geddes' concept of the synoptic view calls to mind Bentham's (and Foucault's reading of Bentham's) panopticism. Both involve a surveillance of a surrounding area from a visually removed point. But while Bentham's panopticon is intended specifically as a means of control over an enclosed space, Geddes' notion of the synoptic is intended as a more open-ended, exploratory, epistemological mode. Geddes encourages us to climb down from the tower and connect our "overview" with grounded, street-level, *situated* knowledge.

20. The problem of representing simultaneity, which Geddes broaches here, can be seen as a problem that many modernist novelists, painters, sculptors, and filmmakers attempt to solve as well. I discuss one such solution in the "Wandering Rocks" chapter of Joyce's *Ulysses* in chapter 3.

21. Stalley, *Patrick Geddes*, 26.

22. See Mitchell, "Imperial Landscape," 5–34, and Pratt, *Imperial Eyes*, for an extended discussion of the relationships among landscape, visuality, and imperialism.

23. Because, by the early twentieth century, the camera obscura had become a quaintly obsolete technology, its recovery by Geddes, I would argue, constitutes what Jonathan Crary calls a "counter-deployment" of the technology that denaturalizes its historical associations with epistemological transparency. See Crary, *Techniques of the Observer*.

24. And, conversely, the discourse of urban planning was to be seen as a legitimate "art." Geddes writes, "The survey necessary for the adequate preparation of a Town Planning Scheme involves the collection of detailed information upon the following heads [Geddes appends an outline of topics for such an exhibition]. Such information should be as far as possible expressed in graphic form, i.e. expressed in maps and plans illustrated by drawings, photographs, engravings, etc., with statistical summaries, and with the necessary descriptive text; and is thus suitable for exhibition in town-house, museum, or library; or, when possible, in the city's art galleries" (*CE* 355–356).

25. Matless, "A Modern Stream," 571.

26. Ibid., 572. In its model of recurring spirals within a scheme of progress, Geddes' philosophy sounds less like a Darwinian line of descent than something approximating a Yeatsian gyre.

27. Macdonald, "Sir Patrick Geddes," 432.

28. Geddes and Slater, *Ideas at War*, 246–247.

29. Thacker, *Moving through Modernity*, 59.

30. Ibid.

31. See, for example, Vinroche and Marx, " 'Only Connect,' " 645–650.

32. See Kern, *Culture of Time and Space*, especially chapter 5, "Speed," and chapter 8, "Distance."

33. Trilling, *E. M. Forster*, 118.

34. Holme, *Modern British Domestic Architecture and Decoration*, 9.

35. Muthesius, *The English House*, 7.

36. In "Modernism and Imperialism," Fredric Jameson makes the case that Forster uses figures of unknowable infinitude (the Great North Road being the most telling example) to signify the unrepresentable "elsewhere" of the colonies. That said, Forster does spend a good deal of time discussing, usually in a pejorative way, the effects of the "Imperial" on the structure of British society and culture.

37. Ruth Wilcox as "genius loci" is Jameson's terminology. See "Modernism and Imperialism," 55–56.

38. For a more extended treatment of the architectural modernity of Howards End within the context of Edwardian national culture, see my "Defending the Realm."

39. The London County Council, a body that created the County of London and assumed governance over virtually all boroughs and parishes, was created in 1889. Over the course of the first decade of the twentieth century, a number of metropolitan lines were consolidated and coordinated into what became the London Underground. These events, among others, suggest the emergence of an entity that incorporated city and suburb, a metropolitan sense of London and its environs.

40. Alun Howkins argues that the period of 1880–1914 saw the cultural identification of "rural England" with the specific geography of the nonurbanized "South Country." See "Discovery of Rural England."

41. My reading of the Purbeck Hills passage is similar in spirit to Andrew Thacker's interpretation in his *Moving through Modernity*, although where he considers the view from Purbeck to be "verging on the cartographic," I would emphasize its connections to the regional vision of the "situated eye." The view we see is not one from a "God's-eye view" but one from a high promontory. See Thacker, *Moving through Modernity*, 60–62.

42. See Thacker's incisive reading of the novel's treatment of the "Celtic fringe" in the Oniton Grange episode. *Moving through Modernity*, 59–60.

43. Helgerson, *Forms of Nationhood*, 133.

44. Ibid., 138.

45. Schulten, *Geographical Imagination in America*, 214–215.

46. As a Scot, Geddes was at odds with a hegemonic Englishness within the United Kingdom, though he was not overtly nationalist in his ideological outlook. He was, however, instrumental in the development and implementation of the 1909 Town Planning Act and the subsequent tour of the Cities and Town Planning Exhibition throughout the United Kingdom.

Chapter Three: Internal Colony

1. Huggan, "Decolonizing the Map."

2. Even before the 1802 Act of Union, Ireland was enumerated in geographical and cartographic representations of "Great Britain" as far back as John Speed's 1611 atlas, *Theatre of the Empire of Great Britain*. See Helgerson, *Forms of Nationhood*, 120–122.

3. Hechter, *Internal Colonialism*, 9.

4. Hechter's core-periphery model would disqualify such entities as "African-America," for example, as a case of internal colonialism. In this case, the "periphery," though frequently concentrated within large urban centers, is territorially dispersed throughout the nation-state.

5. Edney, *Mapping an Empire*, 1.

6. Deleuze and Guattari, *A Thousand Plateaus*, 12–13.

7. Corner, "Agency of Mapping," 213, author's italics.

8. Moretti, *Atlas of the European Novel*, 3–4.

9. Quoted in Budgen, *James Joyce and the Making of "Ulysses"*, 69.

10. Some of the books about Joyce and *Ulysses* that read the book in terms of its "real-world" geography include Hutchins, *James Joyce's Dublin*; Pearl, *Dublin in Bloomtime*; Ellmann, *Ulysses on the Liffey*; Hart and Knuth, *Topographical Guide to "Ulysses"*; Delaney, *James Joyce's Odyssey*; and Pierce, *James Joyce's Ireland*. Joycean geographies of Dublin have even expanded into other media, such as the video recording *Walking into Eternity: James Joyce's "Ulysses": A Dublin Guide with Patrick Ryan* (Princeton, NH: Ryan McCarthy Group, 1988).

11. Budgen, *James Joyce and the Making of "Ulysses,"* 124–125.

12. See, especially, Duffy, *Subaltern "Ulysses"*; Cheng, *Joyce, Race, and Empire*; Nolan, *James Joyce and Nationalism*; Attridge and Howes, *Semicolonial Joyce*; and Orr, *Joyce, Imperialism, and Postcolonialism*.

13. For seminal studies of critical cartography, see Harley, "Deconstructing the Map,"; Monmonier, *How to Lie with Maps*; Wood, *Power of Maps*; King, *Mapping Reality*; Black, *Maps and Politics*; and Edney, *Mapping an Empire*.

14. Harley, "Deconstructing the Map," 4.

15. Ibid., 11.

16. Ibid., 12.

17. Edney, *Mapping an Empire*, 2.

18. For a considered treatment of this topic as it relates to Joyce and postcolonial theory, see Howes and Attridge, "Introduction," *Semicolonial Joyce*.

19. J. H. Andrews notes that the Ordnance Survey began selling its six-inch maps to Alexander Thom in 1856. See Andrews, *Paper Landscape*, 228.

20. See Duffy, *Subaltern "Ulysses,"* 12–18.

21. On the connections between the Great Trigonometrical Survey of India and the Ordnance Survey of Ireland, see Edney, *Mapping an Empire*, 247–248.

22. Richards, *Imperial Archive*, 1.

23. Ibid., 42.

24. Edney, *Mapping an Empire*, 50, author's italics.

25. Ibid.

26. "Graticule" refers to the specific grid of longitudinal and latitudinal lines on terrestrial maps onto which topographical details are inscribed. The graticule was an important formal element in projecting a "scientific" cartography.

27. Andrews, *Paper Landscape*, 141.

28. Edney, *Mapping an Empire*, 25.

29. Foucault, *Archaeology of Knowledge*, 127.

30. For a history of the post-Renaissance cartography of Ireland, see Andrews, *Shapes of Ireland*.

31. Quoted in Andrews, *History in the Ordnance Map*, 1.

32. Hamer, "Putting Ireland on the Map," 197.

33. Boland, "That the Science of Cartography Is Limited."

34. Bowen, *The Last September*, 92.

35. Ibid., 92–93.

36. For a significant exception to this and an approach similar in spirit to my own, see Bulson, *Novels, Maps, Modernity*, chapter 3.

37. James Gifford's invaluable *"Ulysses" Annotated* also includes maps that "locate" the main action of each chapter.

38. De Certeau, *Practice of Everyday Life*, 120.

39. Ibid., 121.

40. As Karen Lawrence argues, "Wandering Rocks" (along with "Ithaca") is a representation of a "lateral imagination": "it meticulously strings together facts without establishing any sense of priority among them." See Lawrence, "Style and Narrative," 560.

41. Quoted in Budgen, *James Joyce and the Making of "Ulysses,"* 155.

42. See Gifford, *"Ulysses" Annotated*, 265. There is one such "intrusion" in Episode 1, but what first seem to be intrusions in Episode 2 (10.213–10.214) are in fact close enough to Corny Kelleher and the Constable to be motivated by the contiguous location.

43. Anderson, *Imagined Communities*, 33.

44. Gifford, *"Ulysses" Annotated*, 267.

45. Through the development of aerial structures (such as the Outlook Tower discussed in chapter 2) and the onset of aerial photography around the turn of the century, the city became accessible to a single, subjectified gaze that suggested a coherent, bounded, physical environment. The experience of "seeing" the nation, however, can only be possible through the abstractions of cartography.

46. As Michael Seidel observes of the movements of the chapter, "only the prophetic Elijah leaflet escapes down the Liffey into the bay." See *Epic Geography*, 187.

47. Howes, "Goodbye Ireland," 59.

48. Cosgrove, "Mapping Meaning," 9.

49. On a national map of Britain and Ireland, for example, one sees Dublin and London as fairly distant points, while on a world map, Dublin and London appear to be almost contiguous. If one viewed the latter map, the proximity of the two places would encourage a view of the similarities between the two places as part of the "British Isles" or Northern Europe; if one looked at the former map, the distance between the two would invite considerations of the space (both geographically and culturally) between the two cities.

50. Cosgrove, "Mapping Meaning," 15.

51. The meditation on maps also leads to travels that suggest a more permanent migration than the pleasurable excursions of the tourist. While the tourist always returns home edified by travels but comforted by a return to home, the final three destinations on Bloom's itinerary suggest something more permanent than a brief sojourn with a return ticket. Far from being an armchair tourist who merely plots journeys on a map from the reassuring location of home, Bloom imagines earthly travel as an adumbration of the passage to the ultimate destination "from which no traveller returns."

52. Howes, "Goodbye Ireland," 71.

Chapter Four: Island

1. While this chapter reads both Rhys and Kincaid as "Caribbean" writers, it is worth pointing out the difficulties with this categorization, as the biographies of both Rhys and Kincaid place them both within and at odds with a Caribbean perspective. Rhys was born in Dominica to parents of Welsh and Scottish extraction. She moved to England at the age of sixteen and spent many years of her young adult life in Paris. She lived in England through most of her later years and wrote *Wide Sargasso Sea* while living in the west of England.

Kincaid, as she details in *A Small Place*, was born in Antigua. She emigrated to New York at the age of seventeen to work as an *au pair* and has lived in America since.

2. Mahan, *Influence of Sea Power upon History*, 29.

3. Mackinder, *Britain and the British Seas*, 11.

4. Mackinder, "Geographical Pivot of History." See also O'Tuathaill, *Critical Geopolitics*, especially chapter 3, "Imperial Incitement: Halford Mackinder, the British Empire, and the Writing of Geographical Sight" and GoGwilt, *Fiction of Geopolitics*, especially chapter 1, "The Geopolitical Image: Anarchism, Imperialism, and the Hypothesis of Culture in the Formation of Geopolitics."

5. Selvon, *Lonely Londoners*, 25.

6. While the "boys" in Selvon's novel are unapologetically misogynist, Selvon does offer, through the anecdotes of Tanty and Agnes, an implicit critique of Caribbean masculinity. Tanty, an elderly Jamaican woman, succeeds in persuading a local white shopkeeper to offer credit to West Indian consumers. Agnes, the girlfriend of Lewis, responds to his physical abuse by exercising her rights under British law and prosecuting Lewis for assault. Selvon suggests that in a highly patriarchal, masculinist West Indian culture, women might in fact have reasons to prefer the "rule of law" and protection of rights within the United Kingdom.

7. Selvon, *Lonely Londoners*, 28.

8. For a detailed account of the formation and ultimate dissolution of the West Indian Federation from an institutional and political perspective, see Wallace, *British Caribbean*. For a contemporaneous (if limited) view, see Springer, *Reflections on the Failure of the First West Indian Federation*.

9. Timothy Cresswell notes that this sensibility is a Western one, citing Jonathan Raban's account of Tlingit geographies of water in northwestern America: "Vancouver's journal reports the seemingly nonsensical movements of natives in their canoes in the sea around them. Rather than taking a direct line from point A to point B the natives would take complicated routes that had no apparent logic. To the native canoeists their movements made perfect sense as they read the sea as a set of places associated with particular spirits and particular dangers. While the colonialists looked at the sea and saw blank space, the natives saw place." See Cresswell, *Place: An Introduction*, 9.

10. In *Culture and Imperialism*, Edward Said has written at length about the role of Antigua in Jane Austen's *Persuasion*, which "sublimates the agonies of Caribbean existence to a mere half dozen passing references" to the island (59). Often, British literature referred to islands in the Caribbean with even less specificity.

11. Seeley, *Expansion of England*, 42.

12. See Rosenberg, "Caribbean Models for Modernism," 219–238.

13. One example of such geographical indifference and negligence can be read in the Beach Boys' #1 single from 1988, "Kokomo," which indiscriminately lists places in the Caribbean, associating them with clichéd images of leisure and tourism. "Kokomo," ironically, exists not in the Caribbean but in Indiana. A sampling of the lyrics: "Aruba, Jamaica ooo I wanna take you/To Bermuda, Bahama come on pretty mama/Key Largo, Montego baby why don't we go...Bodies in the sand/Tropical drink melting in your hand/We'll be falling in love/To the rhythm of a steel drum band/Down in Kokomo."

14. Benítez-Rojo, *The Repeating Island*, 2.

15. Kamau Brathwaite captures the sense in which this experiential sovereignty was prevented from utterance, in no small part due to the normative images of Englishness imposed through English-language schooling and English textbooks: "And in terms of what we write, our perceptual models, we are more conscious (in terms of sensibility) of the fall-ing of snow, for instance—the models are all there for the falling of snow—than the force of the hurricanes which take place every year. In other words, we haven't got the syllables, the syllabic intelligence, to describe the hurricane, which is our own experience, whereas we can describe the imported alien experience of the snowfall... This is why there were (are?) Caribbean children who, instead of writing in their 'creole' essays 'the snow was falling on the playing fields of Shropshire'... wrote: *'the snow was falling on the canefields'*: trying to have both cultures at the same time" (Brathwaite, *History of the Voice*, 9, author's italics).

16. Benítez-Rojo, *The Repeating Island*, 3.

17. See Brathwaite, *History of the Voice*.

18. Glissant, *Caribbean Discourse*, 165.

19. Ibid., 223.

20. Emery, *Jean Rhys at "World's End,"* 36.

21. Bongie, *Islands and Exiles*, 18–20.

22. Defoe, *Robinson Crusoe*, 54.

23. "maroon, n.2 and adj.2" and "maroon, v.," *The Oxford English Dictionary*, 3rd ed. *OED Online* (Oxford University Press, 2010), www.oed.com. Accessed December 16, 2010.

24. See, for example, Price, *Maroon Societies*; Campbell, *Maroons of Jamaica*; and Thompson, *Flight to Freedom*.

25. Emery, *Jean Rhys at "World's End,"* 40.

26. The opening section of part III, however, contains the narrative voice of Grace Poole, whom Rochester has hired to be the "keeper" of Antoinette/Bertha. The presentation of the passage is odd: it is largely an italicized reproduction of Grace's narration to another servant, Leah. The last paragraph of this brief section, however, presents Grace's internal monologue, though it does so in the third, rather than the first, person.

27. Helgerson, *Forms of Nationhood*, 120.

28. Raiskin, *Snow on the Cane Fields*, 9.

29. Murdoch, "Rhys's Pieces," 254.

30. Raiskin, *Snow on the Cane Fields*, 151.

31. Baucom, "Charting the 'Black Atlantic'".

32. In fact, the nation-state officially known as "Antigua and Barbuda" contains the aforementioned islands, along with the uninhabited island Redonda. As Kincaid notes, the yoking of these three islands into one nation-state seems odd to the islanders: "Redonda is a barren rock out in the Caribbean Sea—actually closer to the islands of Montserrat and Nevis than to Antigua, but for reasons known only to the English person who did this, Redonda and the islands of Barbuda and Antigua are all lumped together as one country" (51).

33. See Massey, "A Global Sense of Place," in *Space, Place, and Gender*.

34. Baucom, "Charting the 'Black Atlantic,'" 9.

35. Baucom, *Out of Place*, 6.

36. Glissant, *Caribbean Discourse*, 222.

37. Elbow, "Scale and Regional Identity in the Caribbean," 82.

Chapter Five: Boundary

1. Boehmer, *Empire, the National, and the Postcolonial*, 11.

2. Cleary, *Literature, Partition, and the Nation-State*, 3.

3. Quoted in Schaeffer, *Severed States*, 1.

4. Though not concerned with the specifics of the partition, Partha Chatterjee's *Nationalist Thought in the Colonial World* takes up the problem that Western constructions of the nation form the ideological and conceptual framework within which anticolonial nationalisms must take place. His notion of anticolonial nationalisms as a "derivative discourse" suggests the limitations, as well as the transformations, of the vocabulary of nationalism in decolonizing states such as India.

5. Aijaz Ahmad explores the ambiguous role of the partition in national narratives of India. See "'Tryst with Destiny': Free and Divided," in Ahmad, *Lineages of the Present*.

6. Pakistan began its life as a portmanteau word acrostically linking the first letters of several Muslim-dominated regions in the northwest sections of British India: the *P*unjab, the *A*fghan Provinces, *K*ashmir, and *S*ind, with the suffix of Baluchi*stan* tacked onto the end of the word. The name and the idea for a separate Muslim nation of "Pakistan" began not through an indigenous anticolonial nationalist movement but from a group of Punjabi students matriculating at Cambridge University in the 1930s. From its inception, the conception of the nation ran counter to the mythology of "organic" nationalism, which cast the nation in terms of a unified, organically existing homeland existing from time immemorial. Although such organicist narratives were almost always fabricated in some form, the genesis of "Pakistan" made no attempt to cast a myth of origin for the nation. Its existence is cemented not in the materiality of territory but in the semiosis of language. One could even posit that the origin of "Pakistan" as a purely linguistic construction puts into political practice the collage aesthetic of modernism. See Fraser, *Partition in Ireland, India, and Palestine*.

7. The consequences of Radcliffe's line are well known: it precipitated the largest mass migration in history, displacing approximately twelve million people. It also encouraged widespread sectarian violence, murder, rape, and kidnapping. Somewhere between a half million and one and a half million people were killed in the violence that arose from the partition of India and Pakistan. For a detailed look at the process of deciding upon and implementing Radcliffe's line in Bengal, from both a political and cultural view, see Chatterji, "Fashioning of a Frontier."

8. Quoted in Butalia, *Other Side of Silence*, 68.

9. Winichakul, *Siam Mapped*, 17.

10. Ibid.

11. See Schaeffer, *Severed States*, chapter 5; and Ahmad, "Tryst with Destiny."

12. Schaeffer, *Severed States*, 54.

13. Cleary, *Literature, Partition, and the Nation-State*, 22.

14. Holdich, *Political Frontiers and Boundary Making*, 54.

15. Ibid., 169.

16. Fawcett, *Frontiers*, 92.

17. Ibid.

18. Holdich, *Political Frontiers and Boundary Making*, 170.

19. Jones, *Boundary-Making*, 151.

20. Chatterji, "Fashioning of a Frontier," 190.

21. Nehru, *Discovery of India*, 313–314.

22. The canonical status of the "tryst with destiny" speech is suggested by its inclusion in the *Norton Anthology of English Literature*, beginning with the publication of the seventh edition in 2000.

23. Anderson, *Imagined Communities*, 24.

24. Nehru, *Toward Freedom*, 38.

25. Ibid., 44.

26. Ibid.

27. Boehmer, *Empire, the National, and the Postcolonial*, 13.

28. Ibid., 20.

29. Nehru, *Discovery of India*, 8.

30. As men of the educated upper middle-class, Yeats and Nehru both have ties to dominant as well as subaltern cultural identifications. Yet neither can wholly be assimilated into a "British" or "European" cultural identification.

31. William Butler Yeats, "An Irish Airman Foresees His Death," in *Collected Poems of W.B. Yeats*, 135.

32. Matless, "Uses of Cartographic Literacy," 212.

33. Nehru, "Victory over the Air," in *Selected Works, Vol. 2*, 366.

34. Nehru, "The Conquest of the Air," in *Jawaharlal Nehru's Speeches, Vol. I*, 348. The speech was delivered at the South-East Asia Regional Air Navigation Meeting of the International Civil Aviation Organization, New Delhi, November 23, 1948.

35. Kern, *Culture of Time and Space*, 244.

36. Nehru, "Conquest of the Air," 349.

37. See chapter 3.

38. Nehru, *Discovery of India*, 50.

39. Ibid., 51.

40. Ibid., 543.

41. Ahmad, "Is India Geographically One?", 63.

42. Ibid., 70.

43. B. R. Ambedkar, the "untouchable" who became an influential intellectual and eventual author of the Indian constitution, voiced a less common Hindu pro-partition perspective in his 1941 book *Thoughts on Pakistan*. Here, he writes of the increasing nationalist sentiment among Muslims in the subcontinent, also using a rhetoric of cartography to justify the partition:

> It appears to be the dawn of a new vision pointing to a new destiny symbolized by a new name, Pakistan. The Muslims appear to have started a new worship of a new destiny for the first time. But this is really not so. The worship is new because the sun of their new destiny, which was so far hidden in the clouds, has only now made its appearance in full glow.... This destiny spreads itself out in a concrete form over the map of India. No one who just looks at the map can miss it. It lies there as though it is deliberately planned by Providence as a separate National State for Muslims.

(quoted in Hasan, *Inventing Boundaries*, 49–50)

44. Nehru, "Tryst with Destiny," in *Speeches, Vol. I*, 25. Delivered in the Constituent Assembly, New Delhi, August 14, 1947.

45. Ibid., 26.

46. Ibid., 28. There appear to be discrepancies in published versions of Nehru's speech, which is widely anthologized in books and posted on a number of websites. Some versions include the "brothers and sisters" passage, while others do not. In the volume *Jawaharlal Nehru's Speeches*, published by the Ministry of Information and Broadcasting, the "brothers and sisters" passage is omitted from the speech. In the *Selected Works of Jawaharlal Nehru*, published by the Jawaharlal Nehru Memorial Fund, the "tryst with destiny" speech omits the passage, and it appears instead in a reproduction of a newspaper message, titled "The Appointed Day," printed on August 15, 1947.

47. Desani, *All About H. Hatterr*, 31.

48. Rushdie, *Midnight's Children*, 3.

49. Jameson, "Third-World Literature in the Era of Multinational Capitalism," *Social Text* 15 (Autumn 1986), 69, author's italics.

50. Butalia, "The Nowhere People."

Bibliography

Achebe, Chinua. "An Image of Africa." *Research in African Literatures* 9.1 (Spring 1978).

Ahmad, Aijaz. " 'Tryst with Destiny': Free and Divided." In *Lineages of the Present: Ideology and Politics in Contemporary South Asia.* London: Verso, 2000.

Ahmad, Kazi Said-ud-din. "Is India Geographically One?" In *Inventing Boundaries: Gender, Politics, and the Partition of India.* Edited by Mushirul Hasan. Oxford: Oxford University Press, 2000.

Anderson, Benedict. *Imagined Communities: Reflections on the Origin and Spread of Nationalism.* Revised ed. London: Verso, 1991.

Andrews, J. H. *History in the Ordnance Map: An Introduction for Irish Readers.* Dublin: Ordnance Survey, 1974.

———. *A Paper Landscape: The Ordnance Survey in Nineteenth-Century Ireland.* Oxford: Clarendon Press, 1975.

———. *Shapes of Ireland: Maps and Their Makers, 1564–1839.* Dublin: Geography Publications, 1997.

Appiah, Kwame Anthony. *Cosmopolitanism: Ethics in a World of Strangers.* New York: W. W. Norton, 2006.

Attridge, Derek, and Marjorie Howes, eds. *The Semicolonial Joyce.* Cambridge: Cambridge University Press, 2000.

Bassett, Thomas. "Indigenous Mapmaking in Intertropical Africa." In *The History of Cartography, Vol. 2, Book 3: Cartography in the Traditional African, American, Arctic, Australian, and Pacific Societies.* Edited by D. Woodward and G. M. Lewis. Chicago: University of Chicago Press, 1998. 24–50.

Baucom, Ian. "Charting the 'Black Atlantic.'" *Postmodern Culture* 8.1 (September 1997): n.p.

———. *Out of Place: Englishness, Empire, and the Locations of Identity.* Princeton, NJ: Princeton University Press, 1999.

Benítez-Rojo, Antonio. *The Repeating Island: The Caribbean and the Postmodern Perspective.* Translated by James E. Maraniss. Durham, NC: Duke University Press, 1992.

Black, Jeremy. *Maps and Politics.* Chicago: University of Chicago Press, 1997.

Boehmer, Elleke. *Empire, the National, and the Postcolonial, 1890–1920: Resistance in Interaction.* Oxford: Oxford University Press, 2002.

Boggs, S. Whittemore. *International Boundaries: A Study of Boundary Functions and Problems*. Foreword by Isaiah Bowman. New York: Columbia University Press, 1940.

Boland, Eavan. "That the Science of Cartography Is Limited." In *Norton Anthology of English Literature*. Edited by M. H. Abrams, Stephen Greenblatt, et al. 7th ed. Vol. 2. New York: W. W. Norton, 1999.

Bongie, Chris. *Islands and Exiles: The Creole Identities of Post/Colonial Literature*. Stanford, CA: Stanford University Press, 1998.

Bowen, Elizabeth. *The Last September*. 1929. New York: Anchor, 2000.

Brathwaite, Edward Kamau. *The Arrivants: A New World Trilogy*. New York: Oxford University Press, 1988.

———. *History of the Voice: The Development of Nation Language in Anglophone Caribbean Poetry*. London: New Beacon, 1984.

Brosseau, Marc. "Geography's Literature." *Progress in Human Geography* 18.3 (1994): 333–353.

Budgen, Frank. *James Joyce and the Making of "Ulysses" and Other Writings*. 1934. Oxford: Oxford University Press, 1972.

Bulson, Eric. *Novels, Maps, Modernity: The Spatial Imagination, 1850–2000*. New York: Routledge, 2007.

Butalia, Urvashi. "The Nowhere People." *India Seminar: Web Edition* 510 (2002). March 3, 2002. Accessed December 18, 2010. http://www.india-seminar.com/2002/510/510 urvashi butalia.htm.

———. *The Other Side of Silence: Voices from the Partition of India*. Durham, NC: Duke University Press, 2000.

Campbell, Donna M. "Regionalism and Local Color Fiction, 1865–1895." March 21, 2010. Accessed December 1, 2010. http://www.wsu.edu/~campbelld/amlit/lcolor.html.

Campbell, Mavis Christine. *The Maroons of Jamaica, 1655–1796: A History of Resistance, Collaboration and Betrayal*. Granby, MA: Bergin & Garvey, 1988.

Carey, John. *The Intellectuals and the Masses: Pride and Prejudice among the Literary Intelligentsia, 1880–1939*. 1993. Chicago: Academy Chicago, 2005.

Chatterjee, Partha. *Nationalist Thought in the Colonial World—A Derivative Discourse?* London: Zed Books, 1986.

Chatterji, Joya. "The Fashioning of a Frontier: The Radcliffe Line and Bengal's Border Landscape, 1947–1952." *Modern Asian Studies* 33.1 (1999): 185–242.

Cheah, Pheng. *Spectral Nationality: Passages of Freedom from Kant to Literatures of Liberation*. New York: Columbia University Press, 2003.

Cheng, Vincent. *Joyce, Race, and Empire*. Cambridge, Cambridge University Press, 1995.

Cleary, Joe. *Literature, Partition, and the Nation-State: Culture and Conflict in Ireland, Israel, and Palestine*. Cambridge: Cambridge University Press, 2002.

Colebrook, Clare. *Irony* (New Critical Idiom). London: Routledge, 2004.

Colonial Office. "Letter from Njoya, Chief of the Bamum Tribe, to H.M. the King." London: Public Record Office: CO/649/7. 8 pages.

Conrad, Joseph. "Geography and Some Explorers." In *Last Essays*. Garden City, NY: Doubleday, Page, and Co., 1926. 1–21.

———. *Heart of Darkness*. 1902. Edited and with an introduction by Owen Knowles. New York: Penguin, 2007.

Corner, James. "The Agency of Mapping." In Cosgrove, *Mappings*.

Cosgrove, Denis. *Apollo's Eye: A Cartographic Genealogy of the Earth in the Western Imagination*. Baltimore, MD: Johns Hopkins University Press, 2001.

———. "Mapping Meaning." In Cosgrove, *Mappings*.

———, ed. *Mappings*. London: Reaktion, 1999.

Crary, Jonathan. *Techniques of the Observer: On Vision and Modernity in the Nineteenth Century*. Cambridge, MA: MIT Press, 1990.

Cresswell, Timothy. *Place: An Introduction*. Oxford: Blackwell, 2004.

Darby, H. C. "Academic Geography in Britain, 1918–1946." *Transactions of the Institute of British Geographers*, New Series 8.1, "The Institute of British Geographers 1933–1983: A Special Issue to Mark the Fiftieth Anniversary of the Institute" (1983): 14–26.

De Certeau, Michel. *The Practice of Everyday Life*. Translated by Steven Rendall. Berkeley: University of California Press, 1984.

Defoe, Daniel. *Robinson Crusoe*. 1719. With an introduction by J. M. Coetzee. Oxford: Oxford University Press, 1999.

Delaney, Frank. *James Joyce's Odyssey: A Guide to the Dublin of "Ulysses."* New York: Holt Rinehart and Winston, 1982.

Deleuze, Gilles, and Felix Guattari. *A Thousand Plateaus: Capitalism and Schizophrenia*. Translated by Brian Massumi. 1980. Minneapolis: University of Minnesota Press, 1987.

Desani, G. V. *All about H. Hatterr*. 1948. With an introduction by Anthony Burgess. New York: Farrar, Straus, and Giroux, 1970.

Doyle, Laura, and Laura Winkiel. "Introduction: The Global Horizons of Modernism." In *Geomodernisms: Race, Modernism, Modernity*. Edited by Laura Doyle and Laura Winkiel. Bloomington: Indiana University Press, 2005: 1–16.

Driver, Felix. *Geography Militant: Cultures of Exploration and Empire*. Oxford: Blackwell, 2001.

Duffy, Enda. *The Subaltern "Ulysses."* Minneapolis: University of Minnesota Press, 1994.

Edney, Matthew. *Mapping an Empire: The Geographical Construction of British India, 1765–1843*. Chicago: University of Chicago Press, 1997.

———. "Reconsidering Enlightenment Geography and Map Making: Reconnaissance, Mapping, Archive." In *Geography and Enlightenment*. Edited by David N. Livingstone and Charles W. J. Withers. Chicago: University of Chicago Press, 1999: 165–198.

Elbow, Gary S. "Scale and Regional Identity in the Caribbean." In Kaplan and Herb, eds., *Nested Identities*.

Ellmann, Richard. *James Joyce*. Rev.ed.. Oxford: Oxford University Press, (1959) 1982.

Ellmann, Richard. *Ulysses on the Liffey*. New York: Oxford University Press, 1982.

Emery, Mary Lou. *Jean Rhys at "World's End": Novels of Colonial and Sexual Exile*. Austin: University of Texas Press, 1990.

Fagg, C. C. *The History of the Regional Survey Movement*. Canterbury: Regional Survey Section of the Southeastern Union of Scientific Societies, 1928.

Fawcett, C. B. *Frontiers: A Study in Political Geography*. Oxford: Clarendon Press, 1918.

Forster, E. M. *Howards End*. 1910. New York: Vintage, 1989.

Foucault, Michel. *The Archaeology of Knowledge and The Discourse on Language*. New York: Pantheon, 1972.

Frank, Joseph. "Spatial Form in Modern Literature." *The Idea of Spatial Form*. New Brunswick, NJ: Rutgers UP, 1991: 31-66.

Fraser, T. G. *Partition in Ireland, India and Palestine: Theory and Practice*. London: Macmillan, 1984.

Friedman, Susan Stanford. "Periodizing Modernism: Postcolonial Modernities and the Space/Time Borders of Modernist Studies." *Modernism/Modernity* 13.3 (Sept. 2006): 425–443.

Friel, Brian. *Translations*. London: Faber & Faber, 1981.

Garrard, Greg. *Ecocriticism* (New Critical Idiom). London: Routledge, 2004.

Geary, Christraud. "Art, Politics, and the Transformation of Meaning: Bamum Art in the Twentieth Century." In *African Material Culture*. Edited by M. J. Arnoldi et al. Bloomington: Indiana University Press, 1996: 283–307.

———. *The Voyage of King Njoya's Gift: A Beaded Sculpture from the Bamum Kingdom, Cameroon, in the National Museum of African Art*. Washington, DC: Smithsonian Institution, 1994.

Geddes, Patrick. *Cities in Evolution: An Introduction to the Town Planning Movement and to the Study of Civics*. 1915. With an introduction by Percy Johnson-Marshall. New York: Howard Fertig, 1968.

Geddes, Patrick, and Victor Branford. *The Coming Polity: A Study in Reconstruction*. London: Williams and Norgate, 1917.

Geddes, Patrick, and Gilbert Slater. *Ideas at War*. London: Williams and Norgate, 1917.

Ghosh, Amitav. *The Shadow Lines*. Oxford: Oxford University Press, 1988.

Gifford, James. *"Ulysses" Annotated: Notes for James Joyce's "Ulysses."* 2nd ed. Berkeley: University of California Press, 1988.

Gikandi, Simon. *Maps of Englishness: Writing Identity in the Culture of Colonialism*. New York: Columbia University Press, 1996.

———. "Picasso, Africa, and the Schemata of Difference." *Modernism/Modernity* 10.3 (2003): 455–480.

Glissant, Édouard. *Caribbean Discourse: Selected Essays*. 1981. Translated and with an introduction by J. Michael Dash. Charlottesville: University of Virginia Press, 1989.

———. *Poetics of Relation*. 1990. Translated by Betsy Wing. Ann Arbor: University of Michigan Press, 1999.

GoGwilt, Christopher. *The Fiction of Geopolitics: Afterimages of Culture, From Wilkie Collins to Alfred Hitchcock*. Stanford, CA: Stanford University Press, 2000.

———. *The Invention of the West: Joseph Conrad and the Double-Mapping of Europe and Empire*. Stanford, CA: Stanford University Press, 1993.

Greene, Graham. *Journeys without Maps*. 1936. New York: Penguin, 1978.

Hamer, Mary. "Putting Ireland on the Map." *Textual Practice* 3.2 (1989): 184–201.

Harley, J. B. "Deconstructing the Map." *Cartographica* 26.2 (Summer 1989): 1–21.

Hart, Clive, and Leo Knuth. *A Topographical Guide to "Ulysses."* Colchester, UK: Wake Newslitter Press, 1975.

Hasan, Mushirul, ed. *Inventing Boundaries: Gender, Politics, and the Partition of India*. Oxford: Oxford University Press, 2000.

Hechter, Michael. *Internal Colonialism: The Celtic Fringe in British National Development*. 2nd rev. ed. New Brunswick, NJ: Transaction, 1999.

Hegglund, Jon. "Defending the Realm: Domestic Space and Mass Cultural Contamination in *Howards End* and *An Englishman's Home*." *English Literature in Transition 1880–1920* 40.4 (September 1997): 398–423.

Helgerson, Richard. *Forms of Nationhood: The Elizabethan Writing of England*. Chicago: University of Chicago Press, 1992.

Hobsbawm, Eric, and Terence Ranger, eds. *The Invention of Tradition*. Cambridge: Cambridge University Press, 1983.

Holdich, Thomas H. *Political Frontiers and Boundary Making*. London: Macmillan, 1916.

Holme, Charles, ed. *Modern British Domestic Architecture and Decoration*. London: Offices of *The Studio*, 1901.

Howes, Marjorie. "Goodbye Ireland I'm Going to Gort: Geography, Scale, and Narrating the Nation." In Attridge and Howes, *Semicolonial Joyce*.

Howkins, Alun. "The Discovery of Rural England." In *Englishness: Politics and Culture 1880–1920*. Edited by Robert Colls and Phillip Dodd. London: Croon Helm, 1986. 62–88.

Huggan, Graham. "Decolonizing the Map: Postcolonialism, Poststructuralism, and the Cartographic Connection." *ARIEL* 20.4 (October 1989): 115–131.

Hutchins, Patricia. *James Joyce's Dublin*. London: Grey Walls Press, 1950.

Jacobs, Joseph. *The Story of Geographical Discovery*. London: George Newnes, 1899.

Jameson, Fredric. "Modernism and Imperialism." In *Nationalism, Colonialism, and Literature*. Minneapolis: University of Minnesota Press, 1990. 43–68.

———. "Third-World Literature in the Era of Multinational Capitalism." *Social Text* 15 (1986): 65–88.

Jones, Stephen B. *Boundary-Making: A Handbook for Statesmen, Treaty Editors, and Boundary Commissioners*. Foreword by S. Whittemore Boggs. Washington: Carnegie Endowment for International Peace, 1945.

Joyce, James. *A Portrait of the Artist as a Young Man*. 1916. New York: Penguin, 1999.

———. *Ulysses: The Corrected Text*. Edited by Hans Walter Gabler with Wolfhard Steppe and Claus Melchior. 1922. New York: Vintage, 1986.

Jurney, Florence Ramond. "The Island and the Creation of (Hi)Story in the Writings of Michelle Cliff and Jamaica Kincaid." *Anthurium: A Caribbean Studies Journal* 4.1 (Spring 2006): n.p.

Kaplan, David H. "Territorial Identities and Geographic Scale." In Kaplan and Herb, *Nested Identities*.

Kaplan, David H., and Guntram H. Herb, eds. *Nested Identities: Nationalism, Territory, and Scale*. Lanham, MD: Rowman and Littlefield, 1999.

Kern, Stephen. *The Culture of Time and Space, 1880–1918*. Cambridge, MA: Harvard University Press, 1983.

Kincaid, Jamaica. *A Small Place*. New York: Farrar, Straus, and Giroux, 1988.

King, Geoff. *Mapping Reality: An Exploration of Cultural Cartographies*. New York: St. Martins, 1996.

Landau, Paul. "Introduction: An Amazing Distance: Pictures and People in Africa." In *Images and Empires: Visuality in Colonial and Postcolonial Africa*. Edited by Landau and Kaspin. Berkeley: University of California Press, 2002: 1-40.

Lawrence, Karen. "Style and Narrative in the 'Ithaca' Chapter of Joyce's *Ulysses*." *ELH* 47.3 (Autumn 1980): 559–574.

Lechner, Frank J., and John Boli, eds. *The Globalization Reader*. Oxford: Blackwell, 2000.

Lefebvre, Henri. *The Production of Space*. Translated by Donald Nicholson-Smith. 1974. Oxford: Blackwell, 1991.

Lewis, Martin, and Kären Wigen. *The Myth of Continents: A Critique of Metageography*. Berkeley: University of California Press, 1997.

Livingstone, David N. *The Geographical Tradition: Episodes in the History of a Contested Enterprise*. Oxford: Blackwell, 1992.

Lutz, Tom. *Cosmopolitan Vistas: American Regionalism and Literary Value*. Ithaca, NY: Cornell University Press, 2004.

Macdonald, Murdo. "Sir Patrick Geddes: Pilgrimage and Place." In *In Search of Heritage: As Pilgrim or Tourist?* Edited by J. M. Fladmark. Shaftesbury: Donhead, 1998.

Mackinder, Halford. *Britain and the British Seas*. New York: D. Appleton and Company, 1902.

———. "Geographical Conditions Affecting the British Empire: I. The British Islands." *The Geographical Journal* 33.4 (April 1909): 462–476.

———. "The Geographical Pivot of History." *Geographical Journal* 23.4 (1904): 421–444.

———. "On the Scope and Methods of Geography." *Proceedings of the Royal Geographical Society and Monthly Record of Geography* 9.3 (March 1887): 141–174.

Mahan, Alfred Thayer. *The Influence of Sea Power upon History, 1660–1783*. 1890. Boston: Little, Brown, and Co., 1904.

Manto, Saadat Hassan. *Collected Stories*. Translated and with an introduction by Khalid Hassan. New Delhi: Penguin, 2007.

Massey, Doreen. *Space, Place, and Gender*. Minneapolis: University of Minnesota Press, 1994.

Matless, David. *Landscapes of Englishness*. London: Reaktion, 1998.

———. "A Modern Stream: Water, Landscape, Modernism, and Geography." *Environment and Planning D: Society and Space* 10.5 (1992): 569–588.

———. "The Uses of Cartographic Literacy: Mapping, Survey, and Citizenship in Twentieth-Century Britain." In Cosgrove, *Mappings*.

Mayhew, R. "Halford Mackinder's 'New' Political Geography and the Geographical Tradition." *Political Geography* 19 (2000): 771–791.

Mitchell, W. J. T. "Imperial Landscape." In *Landscape and Power*. Edited by W. J. T. Mitchell. Chicago: University of Chicago Press, 1994. 5–34.

Monmonier, Mark. *How to Lie with Maps*. Chicago: University of Chicago Press, 1991.

Moretti, Franco. *Atlas of the European Novel, 1800–1900*. London: Verso, 1998.

Murdoch, H. Adlai. "Rhys's Pieces: Unhomeliness as Arbiter of Caribbean Creolization." *Callaloo* 26.1 (Winter 2003): 252–272.

Muthesius, Hermann. *The English House*. Translated by Janet Seligman. Edited by Dennis Shaw. 1907. New York: Rizzoli, 1979.

Navari, Cornelia. *Internationalism and the State in the Twentieth Century*. London: Routledge, 2000.

Nehru, Jawaharlal. *The Discovery of India*. 1946. Garden City, NY: Anchor, 1960.

———. *Jawaharlal Nehru's Speeches: Vol. 1., Sept. 1946-May 1949*. New Delhi: Ministry of Information and Broadcasting, 1949.

———. *Selected Works, Vol. 2*. Edited by S. Gopal. New Delhi: Orient Longman, 1972.

———. *Selected Works: Second Series, Vol. 3*. Edited by S. Gopal. New Delhi: Jawaharlal Nehru Memorial Fund, 1985.

———. *Toward Freedom: The Autobiography of Jawaharlal Nehru*. New York: John Day, 1941.

Nolan, Emer. *James Joyce and Nationalism*. London: Routledge, 1995.

North, Michael. *Reading 1922: A Return to the Scene of the Modern*. Oxford: Oxford University Press, 1999.

Ó Tuathail, Gearoid. *Critical Geopolitics: The Politics of Writing Global Space*. Minneapolis: University of Minnesota Press, 1996.

Orr, Leonard, ed. *Joyce, Imperialism, and Postcolonialism*. Syracuse, NY: Syracuse University Press, 2008.

Pearl, Cyril. *Dublin in Bloomtime: The City James Joyce Knew*. New York: Viking, 1969.

Pierce, David. *James Joyce's Ireland*. New Haven: Yale University Press, 1992.

Pratt, Mary Louise. *Imperial Eyes: Travel Writing and Transculturation*. London: Routledge, 1992.

Price, Richard, ed. *Maroon Societies: Rebel Slave Communities in the Americas*. Garden City, NY: Anchor, 1973.

Radhakrishnan, R. "Globalization, Desire, and the Politics of Representation." *Comparative Literature* 53.4 (2001): 315–332.

Raiskin, Judith L. *Snow on the Cane Fields: Women's Writing and Creole Subjectivity*. Minneapolis: University of Minnesota Press, 1996.

Rhodes, Colin. *Primitivism and Modernist Art*. London: Thames and Hudson, 1994.

Rhys, Jean. *Wide Sargasso Sea: A Norton Critical Edition*. Edited by Judith L. Raiskin. 1966. New York: Norton, 1999.

Richards, Thomas. *The Imperial Archive: Knowledge and the Fantasy of Empire*. London: Verso, 1993.

Robbins, Bruce. *Feeling Global: Internationalism in Distress*. New York: New York University Press, 1999.

Rosenberg, Leah. "'Caribbean Models for Modernism' in the Work of Claude McKay and Jean Rhys." *Modernism/Modernity* 11.2 (2004): 219–238.

Rushdie, Salman. *Midnight's Children*. 1981. New York: Penguin, 1991.

Said, Edward. *Culture and Imperialism*. New York: Vintage, 1993.

Sarker, Sonita. "Afterword: Modernisms in Our Image...Always, Partially." *Modernism/Modernity* 13.3 (September 2006): 561–566.

Schaeffer, Robert K. *Severed States: Dilemmas of Democracy in a Divided World*. Lanham, MD: Rowman and Littlefield, 1999.

Schulten, Susan. *The Geographical Imagination in America, 1880–1950*. Chicago: University of Chicago Press, 2001.

Seeley, J. R. *The Expansion of England*. Edited and with an introduction by John Gross. 1883. Chicago: University of Chicago Press, 1971.

Seidel, Michael. *Epic Geography: James Joyce's "Ulysses."* Princeton, NJ: Princeton University Press, 1976.

Selvon, Samuel. *The Lonely Londoners*. 1956. New York: Longman, 1985.

Shklovsky, Viktor. "Art as Technique." In *Literary Theory: An Anthology*. Edited by Julie Rivkin and Michael Ryan. Oxford: Blackwell, 1998.

Sidhwa, Bapsi. *Cracking India*. 1991. Minneapolis: Milkweed Editions, 2006.

Singh, Khushwant. *Train to Pakistan*. New York: Grove Press, 1956.

Smith, Neil. *American Empire: Roosevelt's Geographer and the Prelude to Globalization*. Berkeley: University of California Press, 2003.

———. "Contours of a Spatialized Politics: Homeless Vehicles and the Production of Geographical Scale." *Social Text* 33 (1992): 54–81.

———. "Scale Bending and the Fate of the National." In *Scale and Geographic Inquiry: Nature, Society, and Method.* Edited by Eric Sheppard and Robert McMaster. Oxford: Blackwell, 2003: 192-212.

Snell, K. D. M. *The Regional Novel in Britain and Ireland, 1800–1990.* Cambridge: Cambridge University Press, 1998.

Springer, Hugh W. *Reflections on the Failure of the First West Indian Federation.* Cambridge, MA: Harvard Center for International Affairs, 1962.

Stalley, Marshall. *Patrick Geddes: Spokesman for Man and the Environment.* New Brunswick, NJ: Rutgers University Press, 1972.

Swift, Jonathan. "On Poetry: A Rhapsody." In *Collected Poems of Jonathan Swift*, Vol. 2. Edited and with an Introduction by Joseph Horrell. Cambridge, MA: Harvard University Press, 1958.

Thacker, Andrew. "Journey with Maps: Travel Theory, Geography, and the Syntax of Space." In *Cultural Encounters: European Travel Writing in the 1930s.* Edited by Burdett and Duncan. New York: Berghahn, 2002. 11–28.

———. *Moving through Modernity: Space and Geography in Modernism.* Manchester, UK: Manchester University Press, 2003.

Thompson, Alvin O. *Flight to Freedom: African Runaways and Maroons in the Americas.* Kingston: University of West Indies Press, 2006.

Trilling, Lionel. *E. M. Forster.* Norfolk, CT: New Directions, 1943.

Vidal de la Blache, Paul. *Principles of Human Geography.* Translated by Millicent Todd Bingham. London: Constable and Co., 1926.

Vinroche, Mary E., and Gary T. Marx. " 'Only Connect'—E. M. Forster in an Age of Electronic Communication: Computer-Mediated Association and Community Networks." *Sociological Inquiry* 67.1 (1997): 645–650.

Wallace, Elisabeth. *The British Caribbean: From the Decline of Colonialism to the End of Federation.* Toronto: University of Toronto Press, 1977.

Williams, Raymond. *The Country and the City.* Oxford: Oxford University Press, 1973.

Winichakul, Thongchai. *Siam Mapped: A History of the Geo-body of a Nation.* Honolulu: University of Hawaii Press, 1994.

Withers, Charles W. J. "Encyclopaedism, Modernism, and the Classification of Geographical Knowledge." *Transactions of the Institute of British Geographers* 21.1 (1996): 275–298.

Wood, Denis. *The Power of Maps.* New York: Guilford, 1992.

Wrong, Hume. *Government of the West Indies.* Oxford: Clarendon, 1923.

Yeats, William Butler. *The Collected Poems of W. B. Yeats.* 2nd ed. Edited by Richard Finneran. New York: Simon and Schuster, 1996.

Index